COLLECTED VERSE OF RUDYARD KIPLING

Other Books by Rudyard Kipling

Collected Verse

Of
Rudyard Kipling

New York
Doubleday, Page & Company
1907

CONTENTS

CONTENTS

CONTENTS

Service Songs — South African War

CONTENTS

BARRACK ROOM BALLADS. I — INDIAN SERVICE

BARRACK ROOM BALLADS. II — GENERAL

CONTENTS

SERVICE SONGS — SOUTH AFRICAN WAR

THE FIRES

MEN *make them fires on the hearth*
  Each under his roof-tree,
And the Four Winds that rule the earth
  They blow the smokes to me.

Across the high hills and the sea
  And all the changeful skies,
The Four Winds blow the smoke to me
  Till the tears are in my eyes.

Until the tears are in my eyes
  And my heart is wellnigh broke;
For thinking on old memories
  That gather in the smoke.

With every shift of every wind
  The homesick memories come,
From every quarter of mankind
  Where I have made me a home.

Four times a fire against the cold
  And a roof against the rain—
Sorrow fourfold and joy fourfold
  The Four Winds bring again!

How can I answer which is best
  Of all the fires that burn?
I have been too often host or guest
  At every fire in turn.

How can I turn from any fire,
On any man's hearthstone?
I know the wonder and desire
That went to build my own!

How can I doubt man's joy or woe
Where'er his house-fires shine,
Since all that man must undergo
Will visit me at mine?

Oh, you Four Winds that blow so strong
And know that this is true,
Stoop for a little and carry my song
To all the men I knew!

Where there are fires against the cold,
Or roofs against the rain—
With love fourfold and joy fourfold,
Take them my songs again.

COLLECTED VERSE OF RUDYARD KIPLING

DEDICATION FROM "BARRACK ROOM BALLADS"

*BEYOND the path of the outmost sun through utter dark-
    ness hurled —
Further than ever comet flared or vagrant star-dust swirled—
Live such as fought and sailed and ruled and loved and made
    our world.*

*They are purged of pride because they died, they know the
    worth of their bays;
They sit at wine with the Maidens Nine and the Gods of the
    Elder Days —
't is their will to serve or be still as fitteth Our Father's praise.*

*'T is theirs to sweep through the ringing deep where Azrael's
    outposts are,
Or buffet a path through the Pit's red wrath when God goes
    out to war,
Or hang with the reckless Seraphim on the rein of a red-
    maned star.*

*They take their mirth in the joy of the Earth — they dare
    not grieve for her pain —
They know of toil and the end of toil, they know God's Law
    is plain,
So they whistle the Devil to make them sport who know that
    Sin is vain.*

*And ofttimes cometh our wise Lord God, master of every
    trade,
And tells them tales of His daily toil, of Edens newly made;
And they rise to their feet as He passes by, gentlemen un
    afraid.*

*To these who are cleansed of base Desire, Sorrow and Lus
    and Shame —
Gods for they knew the hearts of men, men for they stooper
    to Fame —
Borne on the breath that men call Death, my brother's spiri
    came.*

*He scarce had need to doff his pride or slough the dross o
    Earth —
E'en as he trod that day to God so walked he from his birth,
In simpleness and gentleness and honour and clean mirth.*

*So cup to lip in fellowship they gave him welcome high
And made him place at the banquet board — the Strong Mei
    ranged thereby,
Who had done his work and held his peace and had no fea
    to die.*

*Beyond the loom of the last lone star, through open darknes
    hurled,
Further than rebel comet dared or hiving star-swarm swirled
Sits he with those that praise our God for that they served Hi
    world.*

TO THE TRUE ROMANCE

1893

THY face is far from this our war,
Our call and counter-cry,
* I shall not find Thee quick and kind,*
Nor know Thee till I die.
* Enough for me in dreams to see*
And touch Thy garments' hem:
* Thy feet have trod so near to God*
I may not follow them!

Through wantonness if men profess
They weary of Thy parts,
  E'en let them die at blasphemy
And perish with their arts;
  But we that love, but we that prove
Thine excellence august,
  While we adore, discover more —
Thee perfect, wise, and just.

Since spoken word Man's Spirit stirred
Beyond his belly-need,
  What is is Thine of fair design
In Thought and Craft and Deed;
  Each stroke aright of toil and fight,
That was and that shall be,
  And hope too high wherefore we die,
Has birth and worth in Thee.

Who holds by Thee hath Heaven in fee
To gild his dross thereby,
  And knowledge sure that he endure
A child until he die —

For to make plain that man's disdain
Is but new Beauty's birth —
For to possess in merriness
The joy of all the earth.

As Thou didst teach all lovers speech
And Life all mystery,
So shalt Thou rule by every school
Till life and longing die,
Who wast or yet the Lights were set,
A whisper in the Void,
Who shalt be sung through planets young
When this is clean destroyed.

Beyond the bounds our staring rounds,
Across the pressing dark,
The children wise of outer skies
Look hitherward and mark
A light that shifts, a glare that drifts,
Rekindling thus and thus,
Not all forlorn, for Thou hast borne
Strange tales to them of us.

Time hath no tide but must abide
The servant of Thy will;
Tide hath no time, for to Thy rhyme
The ranging stars stand still —
Regent of spheres that lock our fears
Our hopes invisible,
Oh 't was certes at Thy decrees
We fashioned Heaven and Hell!

Pure Wisdom hath no certain path
That lacks thy morning-eyne,
And captains bold by Thee controlled
Most like to Gods design.

Thou art the Voice to kingly boys
To lift them through the fight,
And Comfortress of Unsuccess,
To give the Dead good-night.

A veil to draw 'twixt God His Law
And Man's infirmity,
A shadow kind to dumb and blind
The shambles where we die;
A rule to trick th' arithmetic,
Too base, of leaguing odds —
The spur of trust, the curb of lust,
Thou handmaid of the Gods!

O Charity, all patiently
Abiding wrack and scaith!
O Faith, that meets ten thousand cheats
Yet drops no jot of faith!
Devil and brute Thou dost transmute
To higher, lordlier show,
Who art in sooth that lovely Truth
The careless angels know!

Thy face is far from this our war,
Our call and counter-cry,
I may not find Thee quick and kind,
Nor know Thee till I die.

Yet may I look with heart unshook
On blow brought home or missed —
Yet may I hear with equal ear
The clarions down the List;
Yet set my lance above mischance
And ride the barriere —
Oh, hit or miss, how little 't is,
My Lady is not there!

SESTINA OF THE TRAMP-ROYAL
1896

SPEAKIN' in general, I 'ave tried 'em all —
The 'appy roads that take you o'er the world.
Speakin' in general, I 'ave found them good
For such as cannot use one bed too long,
But must get 'ence, the same as I 'ave done,
An' go observin' matters till they die.

What do it matter where or 'ow we die,
So long as we 've our 'ealth to watch it all —
The different ways that different things are done,
An' men an' women lovin' in this world;
Takin' our chances as they come along,
An' when they ain't, pretendin' they are good?

In cash or credit — no, it are n't no good;
You 'ave to 'ave the 'abit or you 'd die,
Unless you lived your life but one day long,
Nor did n't prophesy nor fret at all,
But drew your tucker some'ow from the world,
An' never bothered what you might ha' done.

But, Gawd, what things are they I 'ave n't done!
I 've turned my 'and to most, an' turned it good,
In various situations round the world —
For 'im that doth not work must surely die;
But that 's no reason man should labour all
'Is life on one same shift; life 's none so long.

Therefore, from job to job I 've moved along.
Pay could n't 'old me when my time was done,
For something in my 'ead upset me all,
Till I 'ad dropped whatever 't was for good,
An', out at sea, be'eld the dock-lights die,
An' met my mate — the wind that tramps the world!

It 's like a book, I think, this bloomin' world,
Which you can read and care for just so long,
But presently you feel that you will die
Unless you get the page you 're readin' done,
An' turn another — likely not so good;
But what you 're after is to turn 'em all.

Gawd bless this world! Whatever she 'ath done —
Excep' when awful long — I 've found it good.
So write, before I die, " 'E liked it all! "

THE MIRACLES

1894

I SENT a message to my dear —
A thousand leagues and more to Her —
The dumb sea-levels thrilled to hear,
And Lost Atlantis bore to Her!

Behind my message hard I came,
And nigh had found a grave for me;
But that I launched of steel and flame
Did war against the wave for me.

Uprose the deep, in gale on gale,
To bid me change my mind again —
He broke his teeth along my rail,
And, roaring, swung behind again.

I stayed the sun at noon to tell
My way across the waste of it;
I read the storm before it fell
And made the better haste of it.

Afar, I hailed the land at night —
  The towers I built had heard of me —
And, ere my rocket reached its height,
  Had flashed my Love the word of me.

Earth sold her chosen men of strength
  (They lived and strove and died for me)
To drive my road a nation's length,
  And toss the miles aside for me.

I snatched their toil to serve my needs —
  Too slow their fleetest flew for me.
I tired twenty smoking steeds,
  And bade them bait a new for me.

I sent the Lightnings forth to see
  Where hour by hour She waited me.
Among ten million one was She,
  And surely all men hated me!

Dawn ran to meet me at my goal —
  Ah, day no tongue shall tell again! . . .
And little folk of little soul
  Rose up to buy and sell again!

SONG OF THE WISE CHILDREN

1902

WHEN the darkened Fifties dip to the North,
  And frost and the fog divide the air,
And the day is dead at his breaking-forth,
  Sirs, it is bitter beneath the Bear!

Far to Southward they wheel and glance,
   The million molten spears of morn —
The spears of our deliverance
   That shine on the house where we were born.

Flying-fish about our bows,
   Flying sea-fires in our wake:
This is the road to our Father's House,
   Whither we go for our souls' sake!

We have forfeited our birthright,
   We have forsaken all things meet;
We have forgotten the look of light,
   We have forgotten the scent of heat.

They that walk with shaded brows,
   Year by year in a shining land,
They be men of our Father's House,
   They shall receive us and understand.

We shall go back by boltless doors,
   To the life unaltered our childhood knew —
To the naked feet on the cool, dark floors,
   And the high-ceiled rooms that the Trade blows
      through:

To the trumpet-flowers and the moon beyond,
   And the tree-toad's chorus drowning all —
And the lisp of the split banana-frond
   That talked us to sleep when we were small.

The wayside magic, the threshold spells,
   Shall soon undo what the North has done —
Because of the sights and the sounds and the smells
   That ran with our youth in the eye of the sun.

And Earth accepting shall ask no vows,
   Nor the Sea our love, nor our lover the Sky.
When we return to our Father's House
   Only the English shall wonder why!

BUDDHA AT KAMAKURA

1892

" And there is a Japanese idol at Kamakura "

O YE who tread the Narrow Way
By Tophet-flare to Judgment Day,
Be gentle when " the heathen " pray
　To Buddha at Kamakura!

To him the Way, the Law, apart,
Whom Maya held beneath her heart,
Ananda's Lord, the Bodhisat,
　The Buddha of Kamakura.

For though he neither burns nor sees,
Nor hears ye thank your Deities,
Ye have not sinned with such as these,
　His children at Kamakura;

Yet spare us still the Western joke
When joss-sticks turn to scented smoke
The little sins of little folk
　That worship at Kamakura —

The grey-robed, gay-sashed butterflies
That flit beneath the Master's eyes.
He is beyond the Mysteries
　But loves them at Kamakura.

And whoso will, from Pride released,
Contemning neither creed nor priest,
May feel the Soul of all the East
　About him at Kamakura.

Yea, every tale Ananda heard,
Of birth as fish or beast or bird,
While yet in lives the Master stirred,
    The warm wind brings Kamakura.

Till drowsy eyelids seem to see
A-flower 'neath her golden *htee*
The Shwe-Dagon flare easterly
    From Burmah to Kamakura;

And down the loaded air there comes
The thunder of Thibetan drums,
And droned — " *Om mane padme oms* " —
    A world's width from Kamakura.

Yet Brahmans rule Benares still,
Buddh-Gaya's ruins pit the hill,
And beef-fed zealots threaten ill
    To Buddha and Kamakura.

A tourist-show, a legend told,
A rusting bulk of bronze and gold,
So much, and scarce so much, ye hold
    The meaning of Kamakura?

But when the morning prayer is prayed,
Think, ere ye pass to strife and trade,
Is God in human image made
    No nearer than Kamakura?

THE SEA–WIFE

1893

THERE dwells a wife by the Northern Gate,
  And a wealthy wife is she;
She breeds a breed o' rovin' men
  And casts them over sea.

And some are drowned in deep water,
    And some in sight o' shore,
And word goes back to the weary wife
    And ever she sends more.

For since that wife had gate or gear,
    Or hearth or garth or field,
She willed her sons to the white harvest,
    And that is a bitter yield.

She wills her sons to the wet ploughing,
    To ride the horse of tree,
And syne her sons come back again
    Far-spent from out the sea.

The good wife's sons come home again
    With little into their hands,
But the lore of men that ha' dealt with men
    In the new and naked lands;

But the faith of men that have brothered men
    By more than easy breath,
And the eyes o' men that have read with men
    In the open books of Death.

Rich are they, rich in wonders seen,
    But poor in the goods o' men;
So what they ha' got by the skin of their teeth
    They sell for their teeth again.

For whether they lose to the naked life
    Or win to their hearts' desire,
They tell it all to the weary wife
    That nods beside the fire.

Her hearth is wide to every wind
    That makes the white ash spin;
And tide and tide and 'tween the tides
    Her sons go out and in;

(Out with great mirth that do desire
 Hazard of trackless ways,
In with content to wait their watch
 And warm before the blaze) ;

And some return by failing light,
 And some in waking dream,
For she hears the heels of the dripping ghosts
 That ride the rough roof-beam.

Home, they come home from all the ports,
 The living and the dead;
The good wife's sons come home again
 For her blessing on their head!

THE BROKEN MEN

1 9 0 2

FOR things we never mention,
 For Art misunderstood —
For excellent intention
 That did not turn to good;
From ancient tales' renewing,
 From clouds we would not clear —
Beyond the Law's pursuing
 We fled, and settled here.

We took no tearful leaving,
 We bade no long good-byes;
Men talked of crime and thieving,
 Men wrote of fraud and lies.
To save our injured feelings
 'T was time and time to go —
Behind was dock and Dartmoor,
 Ahead lay Callao!

The widow and the orphan
   That pray for ten per cent,
They clapped their trailers on us
   To spy the road we went.
They watched the foreign sailings
   (They scan the shipping still),
And that's your Christian people
   Returning good for ill!

God bless the thoughtful islands
   Where never warrants come;
God bless the just Republics
   That give a man a home,
That ask no foolish questions,
   But set him on his feet;
And save his wife and daughters
   From the workhouse and the street!

On church and square and market
   The noonday silence falls;
You'll hear the drowsy mutter
   Of the fountain in our halls.
Asleep amid the yuccas
   The city takes her ease —
Till twilight brings the land-wind
   To the clicking jalousies.

Day long the diamond weather,
   The high, unaltered blue —
The smell of goats and incense
   And the mule-bells tinkling through.
Day long the warder ocean
   That keeps us from our kin,
And once a month our levee
   When the English mail comes in.

You'll find us up and waiting
   To treat you at the bar;

You 'll find us less exclusive
    Than the average English are.
We 'll meet you with a carriage,
    Too glad to show you round,
But — we do not lunch on steamers,
    For they are English ground.

We sail o' nights to England
    And join our smiling Boards;
Our wives go in with Viscounts
    And our daughters dance with Lords:
But behind our princely doings,
    And behind each coup we make,
We feel there 's Something Waiting,
    And — we meet It when we wake.

Ah God! One sniff of England —
    To greet our flesh and blood —
To hear the hansoms slurring
    Once more through London mud!
Our towns of wasted honour —
    Our streets of lost delight!
How stands the old Lord Warden?
    Are Dover's cliffs still white?

THE SONG OF THE BANJO

1894

Y OU could n't pack a Broadwood half a mile —
    You must n't leave a fiddle in the damp —
You could n't raft an organ up the Nile,
    And play it in an Equatorial swamp.
I travel with the cooking-pots and pails —
    I 'm sandwiched 'tween the coffee and the pork —
And when the dusty column checks and tails,
    You should hear me spur the rearguard to a walk!

With my " *Pilly-willy-winky-winky popp!* "
[Oh, it's any tune that comes into my head!]
So I keep 'em moving forward till they drop;
So I play 'em up to water and to bed.

In the silence of the camp before the fight,
When it's good to make your will and say your prayer,
You can hear my *strumpty-tumpty* overnight,
Explaining ten to one was always fair.
I'm the Prophet of the Utterly Absurd,
Of the Patently Impossible and Vain —
And when the Thing that Could n't has occurred,
Give me time to change my leg and go again.

With my " *Tumpa-tumpa-tumpa-tum-pa tump!* "
In the desert where the dung-fed camp-smoke curled.
There was never voice before us till I led our lonely choru
I — the war-drum of the White Man round the world!

By the bitter road the Younger Son must tread,
Ere he win to hearth and saddle of his own, —
'Mid the riot of the shearers at the shed,
In the silence of the herder's hut alone —
In the twilight, on a bucket upside down,
Hear me babble what the weakest won't confess —
I am Memory and Torment — I am Town!
I am all that ever went with evening dress!

With my " *Tunk-a tunka-tunka-tunka-tunk!* "
[So the lights — the London Lights — grow near an
plain!]
So I rowel 'em afresh towards the Devil and the Flesh,
Till I bring my broken rankers home again.

In desire of many marvels over sea,
Where the new-raised tropic city sweats and roars,
I have sailed with Young Ulysses from the quay
Till the anchor rumbled down on stranger shores.

He is blooded to the open and the sky,
  He is taken in a snare that shall not fail,
He shall hear me singing strongly, till he die,
  Like the shouting of a backstay in a gale.

    With my " *Hya! Heeya! Heeya! Hullah! Haul!* "
      [Oh the green that thunders aft along the deck!]
    Are you sick o' towns and men? You must sign and sail
        again,
        For it 's " Johnny Bowlegs, pack your kit and trek! "

Through the gorge that gives the stars at noon-day clear —
  Up the pass that packs the scud beneath our wheel —
Round the bluff that sinks her thousand fathom sheer —
  Down the valley with our guttering brakes asqueal:
Where the trestle groans and quivers in the snow,
  Where the many-shedded levels loop and twine,
Hear me lead my reckless children from below
  Till we sing the Song of Roland to the pine.

    With my " *Tinka-tinka-tinka-tinka-tink!* "
      [Oh the axe has cleared the mountain, croup and
        crest!]
    And we ride the iron stallions down to drink,
      Through the cañons to the waters of the West!

And the tunes that means so much to you alone —
  Common tunes that make you choke and blow your nose,
Vulgar tunes that bring the laugh that brings the groan —
  I can rip your very heartstrings out with those;
With the feasting, and the folly, and the fun —
  And the lying, and the lusting, and the drink,
And the merry play that drops you, when you 're done,
  To the thoughts that burn like irons if you think.

2

With my " *Plunka-lunka-lunka-lunka-lunk!* "
    Here 's a trifle on account of pleasure past,
Ere the wit that made you win gives you eyes to see you
    sin
    And — the heavier repentance at the last!

Let the organ moan her sorrow to the roof —
    I have told the naked stars the Grief of Man!
Let the trumpets snare the foeman to the proof —
    I have known Defeat, and mocked it as we ran!
My bray ye may not alter nor mistake
    When I stand to jeer the fatted Soul of Things,
But the Song of Lost Endeavour that I make,
    Is it hidden in the twanging of the strings?

    With my " *Ta-ra-rara-rara-ra-ra-rrrp!* "
      [Is it naught to you that hear and pass me by?]
    But the word — the word is mine, when the order move
      the line
      And the lean, locked ranks go roaring down to die!

The grandam of my grandam was the Lyre —
    [O the blue below the little fisher-huts!]
That the Stealer stooping beachward filled with fire,
    Till she bore my iron head and ringing guts!
By the wisdom of the centuries I speak —
    To the tune of yestermorn I set the truth —
I, the joy of life unquestioned — I, the Greek —
    I, the everlasting Wonder Song of Youth!

    With my " *Tinka-tinka-tinka-tinka-tink!* "
      [What d' ye lack, my noble masters?   What d' y
      lack?]
    So I draw the world together link by link:
      Yea, from Delos up to Limerick and back!

THE EXPLORER

1898

"THERE'S no sense in going further — it's the edge of
    cultivation,"
So they said, and I believed it — broke my land and sowed
    my crop —
Built my barns and strung my fences in the little border station
Tucked away below the foothills where the trails run out and
    stop.

Till a voice, as bad as Conscience, rang interminable changes
    On one everlasting Whisper day and night repeated — so:
Something hidden. Go and find it. Go and look behind the
    Ranges —
    "Something lost behind the Ranges. Lost and waiting for
    you. Go!"

So I went, worn out of patience; never told my nearest
    neighbours —
    Stole away with pack and ponies — left 'em drinking in the
    town;
And the faith that moveth mountains didn't seem to help my
    labours
    As I faced the sheer main-ranges, whipping up and leading
    down.

March by march I puzzled through 'em, turning flanks and dodg-
    ing shoulders,
    Hurried on in hope of water, headed back for lack of grass;
Till I camped above the tree-line — drifted snow and naked
    boulders —
    Felt free air astir to windward — knew I'd stumbled on the
    Pass.

'Thought to name it for the finder: but that night the Northe
　　found me —
　　Froze and killed the plains-bred ponies; so I called the cam
　　Despair
　　(It's the Railway Cap to-day, though).　Then my Whispe
　　waked to hound me: —
　　　　"Something lost behind the Ranges.　Over yonder!　Go yo
　　there!"

Then I knew, the while I doubted — knew His Hand was certai
　　o'er me.
　　Still — it might be self-delusion — scores of better men ha
　　died —
　　I could reach the township living, but . . . He knows wha
　　terrors tore me . . .
　　　　But I did n't . . . but I did n't.　I went down the other sid

Till the snow ran out in flowers, and the flowers turned to aloe
　　And the aloes sprung to thickets and a brimming strea
　　ran by;
　　But the thickets dwined to thorn-scrub, and the water draine
　　to shallows,
　　　　And I dropped again on desert — blasted earth, and blastir
　　sky. . . .

I remember lighting fires; I remember sitting by them;
　　I remember seeing faces, hearing voices through the smoke
　　I remember they were fancy — for I threw a stone to try 'em
　　　　"Something lost behind the Ranges" was the only word the
　　spoke.

I remember going crazy.　I remember that I knew it
　　When I heard myself hallooing to the funny folk I saw.
　　Very full of dreams that desert: but my two legs took me throug
　　it . . .
　　　　And I used to watch 'em moving with the toes all black ai
　　raw.

But at last the country altered — White Man's country past
    disputing —
Rolling grass and open timber, with a hint of hills behind —
There I found me food and water, and I lay a week recruiting,
    Got my strength and lost my nightmares. Then I entered
    on my find.

Thence I ran my first rough survey — chose my trees and blazed
    and ringed 'em —
    Week by week I pried and sampled — week by week my
    findings grew.
Saul he went to look for donkeys, and by God he found a
    kingdom !
    But by God, who sent His Whisper, I had struck the worth
    of two !

Up along the hostile mountains, where the hair-poised snow-
    slide shivers —
    Down and through the big fat marshes that the virgin ore-bed
    stains,
Till I heard the mile-wide mutterings of unimagined rivers,
    And beyond the nameless timber saw illimitable plains !

Plotted sites of future cities, traced the easy grades between 'em ;
    Watched unharnessed rapids wasting fifty thousand head an
    hour ;
Counted leagues of water-frontage through the axe-ripe woods
    that screen 'em —
    Saw the plant to feed a people — up and waiting for the
    power !

Well I know who 'll take the credit — all the clever chaps that
    followed —
    Came, a dozen men together — never knew my desert fears ;
Tracked me by the camps I 'd quitted, used the water-holes I 'd
    hollowed.
    They 'll go back and do the talking. *They 'll* be called the
    Pioneers !

They will find my sites of townships — not the cities that I set
    there.
  They will rediscover rivers — not my rivers heard at night.
By my own old marks and bearings they will show me how to
    get there,
56 By the lonely cairns I builded they will guide my feet aright.

Have I named one single river? Have I claimed one single
    acre?
  Have I kept one single nugget — (barring samples)? No
    not I!
Because my price was paid me ten times over by my Maker
  But you wouldn't understand it.   You go up and occupy.

Ores you'll find there; wood and cattle; water-transit sure and
    steady
  (That should keep the railway rates down), coal and iron at
    your doors.
God took care to hide that country till He judged His people
    ready,
64 Then He chose me for His Whisper, and I've found it, and
    it's yours!

Yes, your "Never-never country" — yes, your "edge of
    cultivation"
  And "no sense in going further" — till I crossed the range
    to see.
God forgive me! No, *I* didn't. It's God's present to our
    nation.
  Anybody might have found it but — His Whisper came to
    Me!

THE SEA AND THE HILLS

1902

WHO hath desired the Sea? — the sight of salt water
 unbounded —
The heave and the halt and the hurl and the crash of the
 comber wind-hounded?
The sleek-barrelled swell before storm, grey, foamless, enor-
 mous, and growing —
Stark calm on the lap of the Line or the crazy-eyed hurricane
 blowing —
His Sea in no showing the same — his Sea and the same
 'neath each showing —
 His Sea as she slackens or thrills?
So and no otherwise — so and no otherwise — hillmen desire
 their Hills!

Who hath desired the Sea? — the immense and contemptuous
 surges?
The shudder, the stumble, the swerve, as the star-stabbing
 bowsprit emerges?
The orderly clouds of the Trades, and the ridged, roaring
 sapphire thereunder —
Unheralded cliff-haunting flaws and the headsail's low-
 volleying thunder —
His Sea in no wonder the same — his Sea and the same
 through each wonder:
 His Sea as she rages or stills?
So and no otherwise — so and no otherwise — hillmen desire
 their Hills.

Who hath desired the Sea? Her menaces swift as her
 mercies,
The in-rolling walls of the fog and the silver-winged breeze
 that disperses?

The unstable mined berg going South and the calvings and
    groans that declare it —
White water half-guessed overside and the moon breaking
    timely to bare it ;
His Sea as his fathers have dared — his Sea as his children
    shall dare it —
       His Sea as she serves him or kills?
So and no otherwise — so and no otherwise — hillmen desire
    their Hills.

Who hath desired the Sea?   Her excellent loneliness rather
Than forecourts of kings, and her outermost pits than the
    streets where men gather
Inland, among dust, under trees — inland where the slayer
    may slay him —
Inland, out of reach of her arms, and the bosom whereon he
    must lay him —
His Sea at the first that betrayed — at the last that shall
    never betray him —
       His Sea that his being fulfils?
So and no otherwise — so and no otherwise — hillmen desire
    their Hills.

ANCHOR SONG

1893

HEH! Walk her round. Heave, ah, heave her short
    again!
  Over, snatch her over, there, and hold her on the pawl.
Loose all sail, and brace your yards back and full —
  Ready jib to pay her off and heave short all!

Well, ah, fare you well; we can stay no more with you, my
   love —
   Down, set down your liquor and your girl from off your
      knee;
         For the wind has come to say:
         " You must take me while you may,
         If you 'd go to Mother Carey
         (Walk her down to Mother Carey!),
      Oh, we 're bound to Mother Carey where she feeds her
         chicks at sea! "

Hch! Walk her round. Break, ah break it out o' that!
   Break our starboard-bower out, apeak, awash, and clear!
Port — port she casts, with the harbour-mud beneath her
      foot,
   And that 's the last o' bottom we shall see this year!

Well, ah, fare you well, for we 've got to take her out
   again —
   Take her out in ballast, riding light and cargo-free.
      And it 's time to clear and quit
      When the hawser grips the bitt,
   So we 'll pay you with the foresheet and a promise from
      the sea!

Ieh! Tally on. Aft and walk away with her!
   Handsome to the cathead, now; O tally on the fall!
Stop, seize and fish, and easy on the davit-guy.
   Up, well up the fluke of her, and inboard haul!

Well, ah, fare you well, for the Channel wind 's took hold
   of us,
   Choking down our voices as we snatch the gaskets free.
      And it 's blowing up for night,
      And she 's dropping light on light,
   And she 's snorting and she 's snatching for a breath of
      open sea!

Wheel, full and by; but she'll smell her road alone to-night.
Sick she is and harbour-sick — oh, sick to clear the land!
Roll down to Brest with the old Red Ensign over us —
Carry on and thrash her out with all she'll stand!

Well, ah, fare you well, and it's Ushant slams the door
on us,
Whirling like a windmill through the dirty scud to lee:
Till the last, last flicker goes
From the tumbling water-rows,
And we're off to Mother Carey
(Walk her down to Mother Carey!),
Oh, we're bound for Mother Carey where she feeds her
chicks at sea!

RHYME OF THE THREE SEALERS

1893

A WAY by the lands of the Japanee
Where the paper lanterns glow
And the crews of all the shipping drink
In the house of Blood Street Joe,
At twilight, when the landward breeze
Brings up the harbour noise,
And ebb of Yokohama Bay
Swigs chattering through the buoys,
In Cisco's Dewdrop Dining Rooms
They tell the tale anew
Of a hidden sea and a hidden fight,
When the Baltic *ran from the* Northern Light
And the Stralsund *fought the two.*

Now this is the Law of the Muscovite, that he proves with
shot and steel,
When you come by his isles in the Smoky Sea you must not
take the seal,
Where the grey sea goes nakedly between the weed-hung
shelves,
And the little blue fox he is bred for his skin and the seal they
breed for themselves;
For when the *matkas* [1] seek the shore to drop their pups
aland,
The great man-seal haul out of the sea, aroaring, band by
band.
And when the first September gales have slaked their rutting-
wrath,
The great man-seal haul back to the sea and no man knows
their path.
Then dark they lie and stark they lie — rookery, dune, and
floe,
And the Northern Lights come down o' nights to dance with
the houseless snow;
And God Who clears the grounding berg and steers the
grinding floe,
He hears the cry of the little kit-fox and the wind along the
snow.
But since our women must walk gay and money buys their
gear,
The sealing-boats they filch that way at hazard year by year.
English they be and Japanee that hang on the Brown Bear's
flank,
And some be Scot, but the worst of the lot, and the boldest
thieves, be Yank!

It was the sealer *Northern Light*, to the Smoky Seas she bore.
With a stovepipe stuck from a starboard port and the Rus-
sian flag at her fore.

[1] She-seal.

(*Baltic, Stralsund,* and *Northern Light* — oh! they were birds of a feather —
Slipping away to the Smoky Seas, three seal-thieves together!)
And at last she came to a sandy cove and the *Baltic* lay therein,
But her men were up with the herding seal to drive and club and skin.
There were fifteen hundred skins abeach, cool pelt and proper fur,
When the *Northern Light* drove into the bight and the sea-mist drove with her.
The *Baltic* called her men and weighed — she could not choose but run —
For a stovepipe seen through the closing mist, it shows like a four-inch gun
(And loss it is that is sad as death to lose both trip and ship
And lie for a rotting contraband on Vladivostock slip).
She turned and dived in the sea-smother as a rabbit dives in the whins,
And the *Northern Light* sent up her boats to steal the stolen skins.
They had not brought a load to side or slid their hatches clear,
When they were aware of a sloop-of-war, ghost white and very near.
Her flag she showed, and her guns she showed — three of them, black, abeam,
And a funnel white with the crusted salt, but never a show of steam.

There was no time to man the brakes, they knocked the shackle free,
And the *Northern Light* stood 'out again, goose-winged to open sea.
(For life it is that is worse than death, by .force of Russian law

To work in the mines of mercury that loose the teeth in your
     jaw.)
They had not run a mile from shore — they heard no shots
     behind —
When the skipper smote his hand on his thigh and threw her
     up in the wind:
" Bluffed — raised out on a bluff," said he, " for if my name 's
     Tom Hall,
" You must set a thief to catch a thief — and a thief has
     caught us all!
" By every butt in Oregon and every spar in Maine,
" The hand that spilled the wind from her sail was the hand
     of Reuben Paine!
" He has rigged and trigged her with paint and spar, and,
     faith, he has faked her well —
" But I 'd know the *Stralsund's* deckhouse yet from here to
     the booms o' Hell.
" Oh, once we ha' met at Baltimore, and twice on Boston pier,
" But the sickest day for you, Reuben Paine, was the day
     that you came here —
" The day that you came here, my lad, to scare us from our
     seal
" With your funnel made o' your painted cloth, and your
     guns o' rotten deal!
" Ring and blow for the *Baltic* now, and head her back to the
     bay,
" And we 'll come into the game again — with a double deck
     to play!"

They rang and blew the sealers' call — the poaching cry of
     the sea —
And they raised the *Baltic* out of the mist, and an angry ship
     was she.
And blind they groped through the whirling white and blind
     to the bay again,
Till they heard the creak of the *Stralsund's* boom and the
     clank of her mooring chain.

" But carry him up to the sand-hollows to die as Bering died,
" And make a place for Reuben Paine that knows the fight was
    fair,
"And leave the two that did the wrong to talk it over there !"

Half-steam ahead by guess and lead, for the sun is mostly veiled —
Through fog to fog, by luck and log, sail you as Bering sailed;
And if the light shall lift aright to give your landfall plain,
North and by west, from Zapne Crest you raise the Crosses
    Twain.
Fair marks are they to the inner bay, the reckless poacher knows,
What time the scarred see-catchie lead their sleek seraglios.
Ever they hear the floe-pack clear, and the blast of the old bull-
    whale,
And the deep seal-roar that beats off-shore above the loudest gale.
Ever they wait the winter's hate as the thundering boorga calls,
Where northward look they to St. George, and westward to St.
    Paul's.
Ever they greet the hunted fleet — lone keels off headlands drear —
When the sealing-schooners flit that way at hazard year by year.
Ever in Yokohama port men tell the tale anew
    Of a hidden sea and a hidden fight,
    When the Baltic ran from the Northern Light
And the Stralsund fought the two.

M'ANDREW'S HYMN

1893

LORD, Thou hast made this world below the shadow of a
    dream,
An', taught by time, I tak' it so — exceptin' always Steam.
From coupler-flange to spindle-guide I see Thy Hand, O
    God —

Predestination in the stride o' yon connectin'-rod.
John Calvin might ha' forged the same — enorrmous, certain,
    slow —
Ay, wrought it in the furnace-flame — *my* " Institutio."
I cannot get my sleep to-night; old bones are hard to please;
I 'll stand the middle watch up here — alone wi' God an'
    these
My engines, after ninety days o' race an' rack an' strain
Through all the seas of all Thy world, slam-bangin' home
    again.
Slam-bang too much — they knock a wee — the crosshead-
    gibs are loose,
But thirty thousand mile o' sea has gied them fair excuse. . . .
Fine, clear an' dark — a full-draught breeze, wi' Ushant out
    o' sight,
An' Ferguson relievin' Hay. Old girl, ye 'll walk to-night!
His wife's at Plymouth. . . . Seventy — One — Two —
    Three since he began —
Three turns for Mistress Ferguson . . . and who 's to blame
    the man?
There 's none at any port for me, by drivin' fast or slow,
Since Elsie Campbell went to Thee, Lord, thirty years ago.
(The year the *Sarah Sands* was burned. Oh roads we used
    to tread,
Fra' Maryhill to Pollokshaws — fra' Govan to Parkhead!)
Not but they 're ceevil on the Board. Ye 'll hear Sir Kenneth
    say:
" Good morrn, M'Andrew! Back again? An' how 's your
    bilge to-day? "
Miscallin' technicalities but handin' me my chair
To drink Madeira wi' three Earls — the auld Fleet Engineer
That started as a boiler-whelp — when steam and he were
    low.
I mind the time we used to serve a broken pipe wi' tow!
Ten pound was all the pressure then — Eh! Eh! — a man
    wad drive;
An' here, our workin' gauges give one hunder sixty-five!

We 're creepin' on wi' each new rig — less weight an' larger
  power:
There 'll be the loco-boiler next an' thirty knots an' hour!
Thirty an' more. What I ha' seen since ocean-steam began
Leaves me no doot for the machine: but what about the man?
The man that counts, wi' all his runs, one million mile o' sea:
Four time the span from earth to moon. . . . How far, O
  Lord, from Thee?
That wast beside him night an' day. Ye mind my first
  typhoon?
It scoughed the skipper on his way to jock wi' the saloon.
Three feet were on the stokehold-floor — just slappin' to an'
  fro —
An' cast me on a furnace-door. I have the marks to show.
Marks! I ha' marks o' more than burns — deep in my soul
  an' black,
An' times like this, when things go smooth, my wickudness
  comes back.
The sins o' four an' forty years, all up an' down the seas,
Clack an' repeat like valves half-fed. . . . Forgie 's our
  trespasses!
Nights when I 'd come on deck to mark, wi' envy in my gaze,
The couples kittlin' in the dark between the funnel-stays;
Years when I raked the Ports wi' pride to fill my cup o'
  wrong —
Judge not, O Lord, my steps aside at Gay Street in Hong-
  Kong!
Blot out the wastrel hours of mine in sin when I abode —
Jane Harrigan's an' Number Nine, The Reddick an' Grant
  Road!
An' waur than all — my crownin' sin — rank blasphemy an'
  wild.
I was not four and twenty then — Ye wadna judge a child?
I 'd seen the Tropics first that run — new fruit, new smells,
  new air —
How could I tell — blind-fou wi' sun — the Deil was lurkin'
  there?

By day like playhouse-scenes the shore slid past our sleepy
    eyes;
By night those soft, lasceevious stars leered from those velvet
    skies,
In port (we used no cargo-steam) I'd daunder down the
    streets —
An ijjit grinnin' in a dream — for shells an' parrakeets,
An' walkin'-sticks o' carved bamboo an' blowfish stuffed an'
    dried —
Fillin' my bunk wi' rubbishry the Chief put overside.
Till, off Sambawa Head, Ye mind, I heard a land-breeze ca',
Milk-warm wi' breath o' spice an' bloom: "M'Andrew, come
    awa'!"
Firm, clear an' low — no haste, no hate — the ghostly whis-
    per went,
Just statin' eevidential facts beyon' all argument:
"Your mither's God's a graspin' deil, the shadow o' yoursel',
"Got out o' books by meenisters clean daft on Heaven an'
    Hell.
"They mak' him in the Broomielaw, o' Glasgie cold an' dirt,
"A jealous, pridefu' fetich, lad, that's only strong to hurt,
"Ye'll not go back to Him again an' kiss His red-hot rod,
"But come wi' Us" (Now, who were *They?*) "an' know the
    Leevin' God,
"That does not kipper souls for sport or break a life in
    jest,
"But swells the ripenin' cocoanuts an' ripes the woman's
    breast."
An' there it stopped: cut off: no more; that quiet, certain
    voice —
For me, six months o' twenty-four, to leave or take at choice.
'T was on me like a thunderclap — it racked me through an'
    through —
Temptation past the show o' speech, unnameable an' new —
The Sin against the Holy Ghost? . . . An' under all, our
    screw.
That storm blew by but left behind her anchor-shiftin' swell,

Thou knowest all my heart an' mind, Thou knowest, Lord, I
    fell. —
Third on the *Mary Gloster* then, and first that night in Hell!
Yet was Thy hand beneath my head, about my feet Thy
    care —
Fra' Deli clear to Torres Strait, the trial o' despair,
But when we touched the Barrier Reef Thy answer to my
    prayer!
We dared not run that sea by night but lay an' held our
    fire,
An' I was drowsin' on the hatch — sick — sick wi' doubt
    an' tire:
" *Better the sight of eyes that see than wanderin' o' desire!* "
Ye mind that word? Clear as our gongs — again, an' once
    again,
When rippin' down through coral-trash ran out our moorin'-
    chain;
An' by Thy Grace I had the Light to see my duty plain.
Light on the engine-room — no more — bright as our car-
    bons burn.
I 've lost it since a thousand times, but never past return!

   .   .   .   .

Obsairve. Per annum we 'll have here two thousand souls
    aboard —
Think not I dare to justify myself before the Lord,
But — aaverage fifteen hunder souls safe-borne fra' port to
    port —
I *am* o' service to my kind. Ye wadna blame the thought?
Maybe they steam from Grace to Wrath — to sin by folly
    led, —
It isna mine to judge their path — their lives are on my
    head.
Mine at the last — when all is done it all comes back to me,
The fault that leaves six thousand ton a log upon the sea.
We 'll tak' one stretch — three weeks an' odd by any road
    ye steer —
Fra' Cape Town east to Wellington — ye need an engineer.

Fail there — ye 've time to weld your shaft — ay, eat it, ere
ye 're spoke;
Or make Kerguelen under sail — three jiggers burned wi'
smoke!
An' home again — the Rio run: it 's no child's play to go
Steamin' to bell for fourteen days o' snow an' floe an' blow —
The bergs like kelpies overside that girn an' turn an' shift
Whaur, grindin' like the Mills o' God, goes by the big South
drift.
(Hail, Snow and Ice that praise the Lord: I 've met them at
their work,
An' wished we had anither route or they anither kirk.)
Yon 's strain, hard strain, o' head an' hand, for though Thy
Power brings
All skill to naught, Ye 'll understand a man must think o'
things.
Then, at the last, we 'll get to port an' hoist their baggage
clear —
The passengers, wi' gloves an' canes — an' this is what I 'll
hear:
" Well, thank ye for a pleasant voyage. The tender 's comin'
now."
While I go testin' follower-bolts an' watch the skipper bow.
They 've words for every one but me — shake hands wi' half
the crew,
Except the dour Scots engineer, the man they never knew.
An' yet I like the wark for all we 've dam' few pickin's here —
No pension, an' the most we 'll earn 's four hunder pound a
year.
Better myself abroad? Maybe. *I 'd* sooner starve than
sail
Wi' such as call a snifter-rod *ross*. . . . French for night-
ingale.
Commeesion on my stores? Some do; but I cannot afford
To lie like stewards wi' patty-pans. I 'm older than the
Board.
A bonus on the coal I save? Ou ay, the Scots are close,

But when I grudge the strength Ye gave I 'll grudge their
    food to *those*.
(There 's bricks that I might recommend — an' clink the
    fire-bars cruel.
No! Welsh — Wangarti at the worst — an' damn all patent
    fuel!)
Inventions? Ye must stay in port to mak' a patent pay.
My Deeferential Valve-Gear taught me how that business
    lay,
I blame no chaps wi' clearer head for aught they make or sell
I found that I could not invent an' look to these as well.
So, wrestled wi' Apollyon — Nah! — fretted like a bairn —
But burned the workin'-plans last run wi' all I hoped to earn.
Ye know how hard an Idol dies, an' what that meant to me —
E'en tak' it for a sacrifice acceptable to Thee. . . .
Below there! Oiler! What 's your wark ? Ye find it runnin'
    hard ?
Ye need n't swill the cup wi' oil — this is n't the Cunard!
Ye thought ? Ye are not paid to think. Go, sweat that off
    again!
Tck! Tck! It 's deeficult to sweer nor tak' The Name in
    vain!
Men, ay an' women, call me stern. Wi' these to oversee
Ye 'll note I 've little time to burn on social repartee.
The bairns see what their elders miss; they 'll hunt me to an'
    fro,
Till for the sake of — well, a kiss — I tak' 'em doon below.
That minds me of our Viscount loon — Sir Kenneth's kin —
    the chap
Wi' Russia leather tennis-shoon an' spar-decked yachtin'-cap.
I showed him round last week, o'er all — an' at the last says
    he:
" Mister M'Andrew, don't you think steam spoils romance
    at sea? "
Damned ijjit! I 'd been doon that morn to see what ailed
    the throws,
Manholin', on my back — the cranks three inches off my nose.

Romance! Those first-class passengers they like it very well,
Printed an' bound in little books; but why don't poets tell?
'm sick of all their quirks an' turns — the loves an' doves
    they dream —
Lord, send a man like Robbie Burns to sing the Song o'
    Steam!
To match wi' Scotia's noblest speech yon orchestra sublime
Whaurto — uplifted like the Just — the tail-rods mark the
    time.
The crank-throws give the double-bass, the feed-pump sobs
    an' heaves,
An' now the main eccentrics start their quarrel on the
    sheaves:
Her time, her own appointed time, the rocking link-head
    bides,
Till — hear that note? — the rod's return whings glim-
    merin' through the guides.
They 're all awa! True beat, full power, the clangin' chorus
    goes
Clear to the tunnel where they sit, my purrin' dynamoes.
Interdependence absolute, foreseen, ordained, decreed,
To work, Ye 'll note, at any tilt an' every rate o' speed.
Fra skylight-lift to furnace-bars, backed, bolted, braced an'
    stayed,
An' singin' like the Mornin' Stars for joy that they are
    made;
While, out o' touch o' vanity, the sweatin' thrust-block says:
" Not unto us the praise, or man — not unto us the praise!"
Now, a' together, hear them lift their lesson — theirs an'
    mine:
" Law, Orrder, Duty an' Restraint, Obedience, Discipline!"
Mill, forge an' try-pit taught them that when roarin' they
    arose,
An' whiles I wonder if a soul was gien them wi' the blows.
Oh for a man to weld it then, in one trip-hammer strain,
Till even first-class passengers could tell the meanin' plain!
But no one cares except mysel' that serve an' understand

My seven thousand horse-power here. Eh, Lord! They 'r
    grand — they 're grand!
Uplift am I?   When first in store the new-made beastie
    stood,
Were Ye cast down that breathed the Word declarin' a
    things good?
Not so! O' that warld-liftin' joy no after-fall could vex,
Ye 've left a glimmer still to cheer the Man — the Arrtifex
That holds, in spite o' knock and scale, o' friction, waste ar
    slip,
An' by that light — now, mark my word — we 'll build th
    Perfect Ship:
I 'll never last to judge her lines or take her curve — not
But I ha' lived an' I ha' worked. 'Be thanks to Thee, Mos
    High!
An' I ha' done what I ha' done — judge Thou if ill or well —
Always Thy Grace preventin' me. . . .
                              Losh! Yon 's the " Stand by " bel
Pilot so soon? His flare it is. The mornin'-watch is set.
Well, God be thanked, as I was sayin', I 'm no Pelagian ye
Now I 'll tak' on. . . .
    'Morrn, Ferguson. Man, have ye ever thought
What your good leddy costs in coal? . . . I 'll burn 'e
    down to port.

MULHOLLAND'S CONTRACT

1 8 9 4

THE fear was on the cattle, for the gale was on the sea,
An' the pens broke up on the lower deck an' let the creature
    free —
An' the lights went out on the lower deck, an' no one near bu
    me.

had been singin' to them to keep 'em quiet there,
or the lower deck is the dangerousest, requirin' constant
 care,
n' give to me as the strongest man, though used to drink
 and swear.

see my chance was certain of bein' horned or trod,
or the lower deck was packed with steers thicker 'n peas
 in a pod,
n' more pens broke at every roll — so I made a Contract
 with God.

n' by the terms of the Contract, as I have read the same,
 He got me to port alive I would exalt His Name,
n' praise His Holy Majesty till further orders came.

e saved me from the cattle an' He saved me from the sea,
or they found me 'tween two drownded ones where the roll
 had landed me —
n' a four-inch crack on top of my head, as crazy as could
 be.

ut that were done by a stanchion, an' not by a bullock at all,
n' I lay still for seven weeks convalessing of the fall,
n' readin' the shiny Scripture texts in the Seaman's
 Hospital.

n' I spoke to God of our Contract, an' He says to my prayer:
I never puts on My ministers no more than they can bear.
So back you go to the cattle-boats an' preach My Gospel
 there.

For human life is chancy at any kind of trade,
But most of all, as well you know, when the steers are mad-
 afraid;
So you go back to the cattle-boats an' preach 'em as I 've
 said.

" They must quit drinkin' an' swearin', they must n't knife
    a blow,
" They must quit gamblin' their wages, and you must prea
    it so;
" For now those boats are more like Hell than anything e
    I know."

I did n't want to do it, for I knew what I should get,
An' I wanted to preach Religion, handsome an' out of t
    wet,
But the Word of the Lord were laid on me, an' I done what
    was set.

I have been smit an' bruisèd, as warned would be the case,
An' turned my cheek to the smiter exactly as Scripture says
But following that, I knocked him down an' led him up
    Grace.

An' we have preaching on Sundays whenever the sea is calm
An' I use no knife or pistol an' I never take no harm,
For the Lord abideth back of me to guide my fighting arm.

An' I sign for four-pound-ten a month and save the mon
    clear,
An' I am in charge of the lower deck, an' I never lose a stee
An' I believe in Almighty God an' preach His Gospel her

The skippers say I 'm crazy, but I can prove 'em wrong,
For I am in charge of the lower deck with all that doth
    long —
Which they would not give to a lunatic, and the competit
    so strong!

THE "MARY GLOSTER"

1894

'VE paid for your sickest fancies; I 've humoured your
    crackedest whim —
ick, it 's your daddy, dying; you 've got to listen to him!
ood for a fortnight, am I? The doctor told you? He lied.
shall go under by morning, and —— Put that nurse out-
    side.
Never seen death yet, Dickie? Well, now is your time to learn,
nd you 'll wish you held my record before it comes to your
    turn.
ot counting the Line and the Foundry, the yards and the
    village, too,
've made myself and a million; but I 'm damned if I made
    you.
aster at two-and-twenty, and married at twenty-three —
en thousand men on the pay-roll, and forty freighters at
    sea!
ifty years between 'em, and every year of it fight,
nd now I 'm Sir Anthony Gloster, dying, a baronite:
or I lunched with his Royal 'Ighness — what was it the
    papers had?
Not least of our merchant-princes." Dickie, that 's me, your
    dad!
did n't begin with askings. I took my job and I stuck;
took the chances they would n't, an' now they 're calling
    it luck.
ord, what boats I 've handled — rotten and leaky and old!
an 'em, or — opened the bilge-cock, precisely as I was told.
rub that 'ud bind you crazy, and crews that 'ud turn you
    grey,
nd a big fat lump of insurance to cover the risk on the way.
he others they durs n't do it; they said they valued their
    life

(They 've served me since as skippers). *I* went, and I took n
    wife.
Over the world I drove 'em, married at twenty-three,
And your mother saving the money and making a man of n
I was content to be master, but she said there was better behin
She took the chances I would n't, and I followed your moth
    blind.
She egged me to borrow the money, an' she helped me to clea
    the loan,
When we bought half shares in a cheap 'un and hoisted a fla
    of our own.
Patching and coaling on credit, and living the Lord knew ho
We started the Red Ox freighters — we 've eight-and-thir
    now.
And those were the days of clippers, and the freights we
    clipper-freights,
And we knew we were making our fortune, but she died
    Macassar Straits —
By the Little Paternosters, as you come to the Union Bank -
And we dropped her in fourteen fathom; I pricked it c
    where she sank.
Owners we were, full owners, and the boat was christened f
    her,
And she died in the *Mary Gloster*. My heart, how young v
    were!
So I went on a spree round Java and well-nigh ran her ashor
But your mother came and warned me and I would n't liqu
    no more;
Strict I stuck to my business, afraid to stop or I 'd think,
Saving the money (she warned me), and letting the other m
    drink.
And I met M'Cullough in London (I 'd saved five 'undre
    then),
And 'tween us we started the Foundry — three forges an
    twenty men:
Cheap repairs for the cheap 'uns. It paid, and the busine
    grew,

'or I bought me a steam-lathe patent, and that was a gold
    mine too.
Cheaper to build 'em than buy 'em," *I* said, but M'Cullough
    he shied,
nd we wasted a year in talking before we moved to the Clyde.
.nd the Lines were all beginning, and we all of us started
    fair,
:uilding our engines like houses and staying the boilers
    square.
:ut M'Cullough 'e wanted cabins with marble and maple and
    all,
.nd Brussels an' Utrecht velvet, and baths and a Social Hall,
.nd pipes for closets all over, and cutting the frames too light,
:ut M'Cullough he died in the Sixties, and —— Well, I 'm
    dying to-night. . . .
  knew — *I* knew what was coming, when we bid on the
    Byfleet's keel —
'hey piddled and piffled with iron. I 'd given my orders for
    steel!
teel and the first expansions. It paid, I tell you, it paid,
Vhen we came with our nine-knot freighters and collared the
    long-run trade!
.nd they asked me how I did it, and I gave 'em the Scripture
    text,
  You keep your light so shining a little in front o' the next!"
'hey copied all they could follow, but they could n't copy my
    mind,
.nd I left 'em sweating and stealing a year and a half behind.
'hen came the armour-contracts, but that was M'Cullough's
    side ;
Ie was always best in the Foundry, but better, perhaps, he
    died.
  went through his private papers ; the notes was plainer
    than print ;
.nd I 'm no fool to finish if a man 'll give me a hint.
I remember his widow was angry.) So I saw what the draw-
    ings meant,

And I started the six-inch rollers, and it paid me sixty pe
    cent —
Sixty per cent _with_ failures, and more than twice we could do
And a quarter-million to credit, and I saved it all for you!
I thought — it does n't matter — you seemed to favour you
    ma,
But you 're nearer forty than thirty, and I know the kin
    you are.
Harrer an' Trinity College! I ought to ha' sent you to sea —
But I stood you an education, an' what have you done for me
The things I knew was proper you would n't thank me to give
And the things I knew was rotten you said was the way to
    live.
For you muddled with books and pictures, an' china an
    etchin's an' fans,
And your rooms at college was beastly — more like a whore'
    than a man's —
Till you married that thin-flanked woman, as white and a
    stale as a bone,
An' she gave you your social nonsense; but where 's that ki
    o' your own?
I 've seen your carriages blocking the half o' the Cromwe
    Road,
But never the doctor's brougham to help the missus unload.
(So there is n't even a grandchild, an' the Gloster family '
    done.)
Not like your mother, she is n't. _She_ carried her freight eac
    run.
But they died, the pore little beggars! At sea she had 'e
    — they died.
Only you, an' you stood it. You have n't stood much beside.
Weak, a liar, and idle, and mean as a collier's whelp
Nosing for scraps in the galley. No help — my son was n
    help!
So he gets three 'undred thousand, in trust and the intere
    paid.
I would n't give it you, Dickie — you see, I made it in trad

You 're saved from soiling your fingers, and if you have no
    child,
It all comes back to the business. Gad, won't your wife be
    wild!
'Calls and calls in her carriage, her 'andkerchief up to 'er eye:
" Daddy! dear daddy 's dyin'! " and doing her best to cry.
Grateful? Oh, yes, I 'm grateful, but keep her away from
    here.
Your mother 'ud never ha' stood 'er, and, anyhow, women are
    queer. . . .
There 's women will say I 've married a second time. Not
    quite!
But give pore Aggie a hundred, and tell her your lawyers 'll
    fight.
She was the best o' the boiling — you 'll meet her before it
    ends ;
I 'm in for a row with the mother — I 'll leave you settle my
    friends :
For a man he must go with a woman, which women don't
    understand —
Or the sort that say they can see it they are n't the marrying
    brand.
But I wanted to speak o' your mother that 's Lady Gloster
    still —
I 'm going to up and see her, without its hurting the will.
Here! Take your hand off the bell-pull. Five thousand 's
    waiting for you,
If you 'll only listen a minute, and do as I bid you do.
They 'll try to prove me crazy, and, if you bungle, they can ;
And I 've only you to trust to! (O God, why ain't he a man?)
There 's some waste money on marbles, the same as M'Cullough
    tried —
Marbles and mausoleums — but I call that sinful pride.
There 's some ship bodies for burial — we 've carried 'em,
    soldered and packed ;
Down in their wills they wrote it, and nobody called *them*
    cracked.

But me — I 've too much money, and people might . . . Al
    my fault:
It come o' hoping for grandsons and buying that Wokin
    vault. . . .
I 'm sick o' the 'ole dam' business. I 'm going back where
    came.
Dick, you 're the son o' my body, and you 'll take charge o
    the same!
I want to lie by your mother, ten thousand mile away,
And they 'll want to send me to Woking; and that 's wher
    you 'll earn your pay.
I 've thought it out on the quiet, the same as it ought to b
    done —
Quiet, and decent, and proper — an' here 's your orders, my
    son.
You know the Line? You don't, though. You write to th
    Board, and tell
Your father's death has upset you an' you 're goin' to cruis
    for a spell,
An' you 'd like the *Mary Gloster* — I 've held her ready fo
    this —
They 'll put her in working order and you 'll take her out a
    she is.
Yes, it was money idle when I patched her and put he
    aside
(Thank God, I can pay for my fancies!) — the boat wher
    your mother died,
By the Little Paternosters, as you come to the Union Bank,
We dropped her — I think I told you — and I pricked it of
    where she sank —
['Tiny she looked on the grating — that oily, treacly sea —]
'Hundred and Eighteen East, remember, and South just
    Three.
Easy bearings to carry — Three South — Three to the dot
But I gave M'Andrew a copy in case of dying — or not.
And so you 'll write to M'Andrew, he 's Chief of the Maor
    Line;

They 'll give him leave, if you ask 'em and say it 's business o'
    mine.
I built three boats for the Maoris, an' very well pleased they
    were,
An' I 've known Mac since the Fifties, and Mac knew me —
    and her.
After the first stroke warned me I sent him the money to keep
Against the time you 'd claim it, committin' your dad to the
    deep;
For you are the son o' my body, and Mac was my oldest
    friend,
I 've never asked 'im to dinner, but he 'll see it out to the end.
Stiff-necked Glasgow beggar, I 've heard he 's prayed for my
    soul,
But he could n't lie if you paid him, and he 'd starve before he
    stole!
He 'll take the *Mary* in ballast — you 'll find her a lively
    ship;
And you 'll take Sir Anthony Gloster, that goes on 'is wedding-
    trip,
Lashed in our old deck-cabin with all three port-holes wide,
The kick o' the screw beneath him and the round blue seas out-
    side!
Sir Anthony Gloster's carriage — our 'ouse-flag flyin' free —
Ten thousand men on the pay-rool and forty freighters at
    sea!
He made himself and a million, but this world is a fleetin'
    show,
And he 'll go to the wife of 'is bosom the same as he ought to
    go —
By the heel of the Paternosters — there is n't a chance to
    mistake —
And Mac 'll pay you the money as soon as the bubbles break!
Five thousand for six weeks' cruising, the stanchest freighter
    afloat,
And Mac he 'll give you your bonus the minute I 'm out o' the
    boat!

He 'll take you round to Macassar, and you 'll come back
    alone;
He knows what I want o' the *Mary*. . . . I 'll do what I please
    with my own.
Your mother 'ud call it wasteful, but I 've seven-and-thirty
    more;
I 'll come in my private carriage and bid it wait at the
    door. . . .
For my son 'e was never a credit: 'e muddled with books and
    art,
And 'e lived on Sir Anthony's money and 'e broke Sir An-
    thony's heart.
There is n't even a grandchild, and the Gloster family 's
    done —
The only one you left me, O mother, the only one!
Harrer and Trinity College — me slavin' early an' late —
An' he thinks I 'm dying crazy, and you 're in Macassar
    Strait!
Flesh o' my flesh, my dearie, for ever an' ever amen,
That first stroke come for a warning; I ought to ha' gone to
    you then.
But — cheap repairs for a cheap 'un — the doctors said I 'd
    do:
Mary, why did n't *you* warn me? I 've allus heeded to you,
Excep' — I know — about women; but you are a spirit now
An', wife, they was only women, and I was a man. That 's
    how.
An' a man 'e must go with a woman, as you could not under-
    stand;
But I never talked 'em secrets. I paid 'em out o' hand.
Thank Gawd, I can pay for my fancies! Now what 's five
    thousand to me,
For a berth off the Paternosters in the haven where I would
    be?
I believe in the Resurrection, if I read my Bible plain,
But I wouldn't trust 'em at Wokin'; we 're safer at sea
    again.

For the heart it shall go with the treasure — go down to the
    sea in ships.
I 'm sick of the hired women — I 'll kiss my girl on her lips!
I 'll be content with my fountain, I 'll drink from my own well,
And the wife of my youth shall charm me — an' the rest can
    go to Hell!
(Dickie, *he* will, that 's certain.)   I 'll lie in our standin'-bed,
An' Mac 'll take her in ballast — an' she trims best by the
    head. . . .
Down by the head an' sinkin', her fires are drawn and cold,
And the water 's splashin' hollow on the skin of the empty
    hold —
Churning an' choking and chuckling, quiet and scummy and
    dark —
Full to her lower hatches and risin' steady.   Hark!
That was the after-bulkhead. . . . She 's flooded from stem
    to stern. . . .
Never seen death yet, Dickie? . . . Well, now is your time to
    learn!

THE BALLAD OF "THE BOLIVAR"

1890

SEVEN men from all the world back to Docks again,
Rolling down the Ratcliffe Road drunk and raising Cain:
Give the girls another drink 'fore we sign away —
We that took the " Bolivar " out across the Bay!

We put out from Sunderland loaded down with rails;
  We put back to Sunderland 'cause our cargo shifted;
We put out from Sunderland — met the winter gales —
  Seven days and seven nights to the Start we drifted.

    Racketing her rivets loose, smoke-stack white as snow,
    All the coals adrift adeck, half the rails below,
    Leaking like a lobster-pot, steering like a dray —
    Out we took the *Bolivar,* out across the Bay!

One by one the Lights came up, winked and let us by;
  Mile by mile we waddled on, coal and fo'c'sle short;
Met a blow that laid us down, heard a bulkhead fly;
  Left *The Wolf* behind us with a two-foot list to port.

    Trailing like a wounded duck, working out her soul;
    Clanging like a smithy-shop after every roll;
    Just a funnel and a mast lurching through the spray —
    So we threshed the *Bolivar* out across the Bay!

Felt her hog and felt her sag, betted when she 'd break;
  Wondered every time she raced if she 'd stand the shock;
Heard the seas like drunken men pounding at her strake;
  Hoped the Lord 'ud keep his thumb on the plummer-block.

    Banged against the iron decks, bilges choked with coal;
    Flayed and frozen foot and hand, sick of heart and soul;
    Last we prayed she 'd buck herself into Judgment Day —
    Hi! we cursed the *Bolivar* knocking round the Bay!

O her nose flung up to sky, groaning to be still —
  Up and down and back we went, never time for breath;
Then the money paid at Lloyd's caught her by the heel,
  And the stars ran round and round dancin' at our death!

    Aching for an hour's sleep, dozing off between;
    Heard the rotten rivets draw when she took it green;
    Watched the compass chase its tail like a cat at play —
    That was on the *Bolivar*, south across the Bay.

Once we saw between the squalls, lyin' head to swell —
  Mad with work and weariness, wishin' they was we —
Some damned Liner's lights go by like a grand hotel;
  Cheered her from the *Bolivar* swampin' in the sea.

    Then a greyback cleared us out, then the skipper laughed;
    " Boys, the wheel has gone to Hell — rig the winches aft!
    " Yoke the kicking rudder-head — get her under way! "
    So we steered her, pully-haul, out across the Bay!

Just a pack o' rotten plates puttied up with tar,
In we came, an' time enough, 'cross Bilbao Bar.
Overloaded, undermanned, meant to founder, we
Euchred God Almighty's storm, bluffed the Eternal Sea!

Seven men from all the world back to town again,
Rollin' down the Ratcliffe Road drunk and raising Cain:
Seven men from out of Hell.   Ain't the owners gay,
'Cause we took the " Bolivar " safe across the Bay?

THE BALLAD OF THE "CLAMPHERDOWN"

1892

IT was our war-ship *Clampherdown*
  Would sweep the Channel clean,
Wherefore she kept her hatches close
When the merry Channel chops arose,
  To save the bleached Marine.

She had one bow-gun of a hundred ton,
  And a great stern-gun beside;
They dipped their noses deep in the sea,
They racked their stays and stanchions free
  In the wash of the wind-whipped tide.

It was our war-ship *Clampherdown*
  Fell in with a cruiser light
That carried the dainty Hotchkiss gun
And a pair of heels wherewith to run
  From the grip of a close-fought fight.

She opened fire at seven miles —
  As ye shoot at a bobbing cork —
And once she fired and twice she fired,
Till the bow-gun drooped like a lily tired
  That lolls upon the stalk.

"Captain, the bow-gun melts apace,
    "The deck-beams break below,
"'Twere well to rest for an hour or twain,
"And botch the shattered plates again."
    And he answered, "Make it so."

She opened fire within the mile —
    As you shoot at the flying duck —
And the great stern-gun shot fair and true,
With the heave of the ship, to the stainless blue,
    And the great stern-turret stuck.

"Captain, the turret fills with steam,
    "The feed-pipes burst below —
"You can hear the hiss of the helpless ram,
"You can hear the twisted runners jam."
    And he answered, "Turn and go!"

It was our war-ship *Clampherdown*,
    And grimly did she roll;
Swung round to take the cruiser's fire
As the White Whale faces the Thresher's ire
    When they war by the frozen Pole.

"Captain, the shells are falling fast,
    "And faster still fall we;
"And it is not meet for English stock
"To bide in the heart of an eight-day clock
    "The death they cannot see."

"Lie down, lie down, my bold A.B.,
    "We drift upon her beam;
"We dare not ram, for she can run:
"And dare ye fire another gun,
    "And die in the peeling steam?"

It was our war-ship *Clampherdown*
  That carried an armour-belt;
But fifty feet at stern and bow
Lay bare as the paunch of the purser's sow,
  To the hail of the Nordenfeldt.

"Captain, they lack us through and through;
  "The chilled steel bolts are swift!
"We have emptied the bunkers in open sea,
"Their shrapnel bursts where our coal should be."
  And he answered, "Let her drift."

It was our war-ship *Clampherdown*,
  Swung round upon the tide,
Her two dumb guns glared south and north,
And the blood and the bubbling steam ran forth,
  And she ground the cruiser's side.

"Captain, they cry, the fight is done,
  "They bid you send your sword."
And he answered, "Grapple her stern and bow.
"They have asked for the steel.   They shall have it now;
  "Out cutlasses and board!"

It was our war-ship *Clampherdown*,
  Spewed up four hundred men;
And the scalded stokers yelped delight,
As they rolled in the waist and heard the fight,
  Stamp o'er their steel-walled pen.

They cleared the cruiser end to end
  From conning-tower to hold.
They fought as they fought in Nelson's fleet;
They were stripped to the waist, they were bare to the feet,
  As it was in the days of old.

It was the sinking *Clampherdown*
   Heaved up her battered side —
And carried a million pounds in steel,
To the cod and the corpse-fed conger-eel,
   And the scour of the Channel tide.

It was the crew of the *Clampherdown*
   Stood out to sweep the sea,
On a cruiser won from an ancient foe,
As it was in the days of long ago,
   And as it still shall be!

CRUISERS

1 8 9 9

As our mother the Frigate, bepainted and fine,
Made play for her bully the Ship of the Line;
So we, her bold daughters by iron and fire,
Accost and decoy to our masters' desire.

Now, pray you, consider what toils we endure,
Night-walking wet sea-lanes, a guard and a lure;
Since half of our trade is that same pretty sort
As mettlesome wenches do practise in port.

For this is our office: to spy and make room,
As hiding yet guiding the foe to their doom.
Surrounding, confounding, we bait and betray
And tempt them to battle the seas' width away.

The pot-bellied merchant foreboding no wrong
With headlight and sidelight he lieth along,
Till, lightless and lightfoot and lurking, leap we
To force him discover his business by sea.

And when we have wakened the lust of a foe,
To draw him by flight toward our bullies we go,
Till, 'ware of strange smoke stealing nearer, he flies
Or our bullies close in for to make him good prize.

So, when we have spied on the path of their host,
One flieth to carry that word to the coast;
And, lest by false doubling they turn and go free,
One lieth behind them to follow and see.

Anon we return, being gathered again,
Across the sad valleys all drabbled with rain —
Across the grey ridges all crispèd and curled —
To join the long dance round the curve of the world.

The bitter salt spindrift, the sun-glare likewise,
The moon-track a-tremble, bewilders our eyes,
Where, linking and lifting, our sisters we hail
'Twixt wrench of cross-surges or plunge of head-gale.

As maidens awaiting the bride to come forth
Make play with light jestings and wit of no worth,
So, widdershins circling the bride-bed of death,
Each fleereth her neighbour and signeth and saith: —

"What see ye?   Their signals, or levin afar?
"What hear ye?   God's thunder, or guns of our war?
"What mark ye?   Their smoke, or the cloud-rack outblown?
"What chase ye?   Their lights, or the Daystar low down?"

So, times past all number deceived by false shows,
Deceiving we cumber the road of our foes,
For this is our virtue: to track and betray;
Preparing great battles a sea's width away.

Now peace is at end and our peoples take heart,
For the laws are clean gone that restrained our art;
Up and down the near headlands and against the far wind
We are loosed (O be swift!) to the work of our kind!

THE DESTROYERS

1898

THE strength of twice three thousand horse
That seeks the single goal;
The line that holds the rending course,
The hate that swings the whole:
The stripped hulls, slinking through the gloom,
At gaze and gone again —
The Brides of Death that wait the groom —
The Choosers of the Slain!

Offshore where sea and skyline blend
  In rain, the daylight dies;
The sullen, shouldering swells attend
  Night and our sacrifice.
Adown the stricken capes no flare —
  No mark on spit or bar, —
Girdled and desperate we dare
  The blindfold game of war.

Nearer the up-flung beams that spell
  The council of our foes;
Clearer the barking guns that tell
  Their scattered flank to close.
Sheer to the trap they crowd their way
  From ports for this unbarred.
Quiet, and count our laden prey,
  The convoy and her guard!

On shoal with scarce a foot below,
  Where rock and islet throng,
Hidden and hushed we watch them throw
  Their anxious lights along.

Not here, not here your danger lies —
   (Stare hard, O hooded eyne !)
Save where the dazed rock-pigeons rise
   The lit cliffs give no sign.

Therefore — to break the rest ye seek,
   The Narrow Seas to clear —
Hark to the siren's whimpering shriek —
   The driven death is here !
Look to your van a league away, —
   What midnight terror stays
The bulk that checks against the spray
   Her crackling tops ablaze ?

Hit, and hard hit !   The blow went home,
   The muffled, knocking stroke —
The steam that overruns the foam —
   The foam that thins to smoke —
The smoke that clokes the deep aboil —
   The deep that chokes her throes
Till, streaked with ash and sleeked with oil,
   The lukewarm whirlpools close !

A shadow down the sickened wave
   Long since her slayer fled :
But hear their chartering quick-fires rave
   Astern, abeam, ahead !
Panic that shells the drifting spar —
   Loud waste with none to check —
Mad fear that rakes a scornful star
   Or sweeps a consort's deck !

Now, while their silly smoke hangs thick,
   Now ere their wits they find,
Lay in and lance them to the quick —
   Our gallied whales are blind !

Good luck to those that see the end,
  Good-bye to those that drown —
For each his chance as chance shall send —
  And God for all !   *Shut down!*

The strength of twice three thousand horse
  That serve the one command;
The hand that heaves the headlong force,
  The hate that backs the hand:
The doom-bolt in the darkness freed,
  The mine that splits the main;
The white-hot wake, the 'wildering speed —
  The Choosers of the Slain!

WHITE HORSES

1 8 9 7

*W*HERE run your colts at pasture?
  Where hide your mares to breed?
'Mid bergs about the Ice-cap
  Or wove Sargasso weed;
By chartless reef and channel,
  Or crafty coastwise bars,
But most the ocean-meadows
  All purple to the stars !

Who holds the rein upon you?
  The latest gale let free.
What meat is in your mangers?
  The glut of all the sea.
'Twixt tide and tide's returning
  Great store of newly dead, —
The bones of those that faced us,
  And the hearts of those that fled.

Afar, off-shore and single,
  Some stallion, rearing swift,
Neighs hungry for new fodder,
  And calls us to the drift.
Then down the cloven ridges —
  A million hooves unshod —
Break forth the mad White Horses
  To seek their meat from God!

Girth-deep in hissing water
  Our furious vanguard strains —
Through mist of mighty tramplings
  Roll up the fore-blown manes —
A hundred leagues to leeward,
  Ere yet the deep is stirred,
The groaning rollers carry
  The coming of the herd!

*Whose hand may grip your nostrils —
  Your forelock who may hold?*
E'en they that use the broads with us —
  The riders bred and bold,
That spy upon our matings,
  That rope us where we run —
They know the strong White Horses
  From father unto son.

We breathe about their cradles,
  We race their babes ashore,
We snuff against their thresholds,
  We nuzzle at their door;
By day with stamping squadrons,
  By night in whinnying droves,
Creep up the wise White Horses,
  To call them from their loves.

And come they for your calling?
  No wit of man may save.
They hear the loosed White Horses
  Above their father's grave;
And, kin of those we crippled,
  And, sons of those we slew,
Spur down the wild white riders
  To school the herds anew.

What service have ye paid them,
  Oh jealous steeds and strong?
Save we that throw their weaklings,   .
  Is none dare work them wrong;
While thick around the homestead
  Our snow-backed leaders graze —
A guard behind their plunder,
  And a veil before their ways.

With march and countermarchings —
  With weight of wheeling hosts —
Stray mob or bands embattled —
  We ring the chosen coasts:
And, careless of our clamour
  That bids the stranger fly,
At peace within our pickets
  The wild white riders lie.

        .   .   .   .   .

Trust ye the curdled hollows —
  Trust ye the neighing wind —
Trust ye the moaning groundswell —
  Our herds are close behind!
To bray your foeman's armies —
  To chill and snap his sword —
Trust ye the wild White Horses,
  The Horses of the Lord!

THE DERELICT

1894

"And reports the derelict ' Mary Pollock ' still at sea "

SHIPPING NEWS.

I WAS the staunchest of our fleet
Till the sea rose beneath our feet
Unheralded, in hatred past all measure.
Into his pits he stamped my crew,
Buffeted, blinded, bound and threw,
Bidding me eyeless wait upon his pleasure.

Man made me, and my will
Is to my maker still,
Whom now the currents con, the rollers steer —
Lifting forlorn to spy
Trailed smoke along the sky,
Falling afraid lest any keel come near!

Wrenched as the lips of thirst,
Wried, dried, and split and burst,
Bone-bleached my decks, wind-scoured to the graining;
And jarred at every roll
The gear that was my soul
Answers the anguish of my beams' complaining.

For life that crammed me full,
Gangs of the prying gull
That shriek and scrabble on the riven hatches!
For roar that dumbed the gale,
My hawse-pipes' guttering wail,
Sobbing my heart out through the uncounted watches!

5

Blind in the hot blue ring
Through all my points I swing —
Swing and return to shift the sun anew.
Blind in my well-known sky
I hear the stars go by,
Mocking the prow that cannot hold one true !

White on my wasted path
Wave after wave in wrath
Frets 'gainst his fellow, warring where to send me.
Flung forward, heaved aside,
Witless and dazed I bide
The mercy of the comber that shall end me.

North where the bergs careen,
The spray of seas unseen
Smokes round my head and freezes in the falling;
South where the corals breed,
The footless, floating weed
Folds me and fouls me, strake on strake upcrawling.

I that was clean to run
My race against the sun —
Strength on the deep — am bawd to all disaster;
Whipped forth by night to meet
My sister's careless feet,
And with a kiss betray her to my master !

Man made me, and my will
Is to my maker still —
To him and his, our peoples at their pier:
Lifting in hope to spy
Trailed smoke along the sky,
Falling afraid lest any keel come near !

THE MERCHANTMEN

1893

KING SOLOMON drew merchantmen,
　Because of his desire
For peacocks, apes, and ivory,
　From Tarshish unto Tyre:
With cedars out of Lebanon
　Which Hiram rafted down,
But we be only sailormen
　That use in London town.

Coastwise — cross-seas — round the world and back again —
Where the flaw shall head us or the full Trade suits —
Plain-sail — storm-sail — lay your board and tack again —
And that's the way we'll pay Paddy Doyle for his boots!

We bring no store of ingots,
　Of spice or precious stones,
But that we have we gathered
　With sweat and aching bones:
In flame beneath the tropics,
　In frost upon the floe,
And jeopardy of every wind
　That does between them go.

And some we got by purchase,
　And some we had by trade,
And some we found by courtesy
　Of pike and carronade —
At midnight, 'mid-sea meetings,
　For charity to keep,
And light the rolling homeward-bound
　That rode a foot too deep!

By sport of bitter weather
　We 're walty, strained, and scarred
From the kentledge on the kelson
　To the slings upon the yard.
Six oceans had their will of us
　To carry all away —
Our galley 's in the Baltic,
　And our boom 's in Mossel Bay!

We 've floundered off the Texel,
　Awash with sodden deals,
We 've slipped from Valparaiso
　With the Norther at our heels:
We 've ratched beyond the Crossets
　That tusk the Southern Pole,
And dipped our gunnels under
　To the dread Agulhas roll.

Beyond all outer charting
　We sailed where none have sailed,
And saw the land-lights burning
　On islands none have hailed;
Our hair stood up for wonder,
　But, when the night was done,
There danced the deep to windward
　Blue-empty 'neath the sun!

Strange consorts rode beside us
　And brought us evil luck;
The witch-fire climbed our channels,
　And flared on vane and truck:
Till, through the red tornado,
　That lashed us nigh to blind,
We saw The Dutchman plunging,
　Full canvas, head to wind!

We 've heard the Midnight Leadsman
　That calls the black deep down —

Ay, thrice we 've heard The Swimmer,
   The Thing that may not drown.
On frozen bunt and gasket
   The sleet-cloud drave her hosts,
When, manned by more than signed with us
   We passed the Isle of Ghosts!

And north, amid the hummocks,
   A biscuit-toss below,
We met the silent shallop
   That frighted whalers know;
For, down a cruel ice-lane,
   That opened as he sped,
We saw dead Hendrick Hudson
   Steer, North by West, his dead.

So dealt God's waters with us
   Beneath the roaring skies,
So walked His signs and marvels
   All naked to our eyes:
But we were heading homeward
   With trade to lose or make —
Good Lord, they slipped behind us
   In the tailing of our wake!

Let go, let go the anchors;
   Now shamed at heart are we
To bring so poor a cargo home
   That had for gift the sea!
Let go the great bow-anchors —
   Ah, fools were we and blind —
The worst we stored with utter toil,
   The best we left behind!

Coastwise — cross-seas — round the world and back again,
   Whither flaw shall fail us or the Trades drive down:
Plain-sail — storm-sail — lay your board and tack again —
   And all to bring a cargo up to London Town!

THE SONG OF DIEGO VALDEZ

1902

THE God of Fair Beginnings
   Hath prospered here my hand —
The cargoes of my lading,
   And the keels of my command.
For out of many ventures
   That sailed with hope as high,
My own have made the better trade,
   And Admiral am I!

To me my King's much honour,
   To me my people's love —
To me the pride of Princes
   And power all pride above;
To me the shouting cities,
   To me the mob's refrain: —
" Who knows not noble Valdez,
   " Hath never heard of Spain."

But I remember comrades —
   Old playmates on new seas —
Whenas we traded orpiment
   Among the savages —
A thousand leagues to south'ard
   And thirty years removed —
They knew not noble Valdez,
   But me they knew and loved.

Then they that found good liquor,
   They drank it not alone,
And they that found fair plunder,
   They told us every one,

About our chosen islands
   Or secret shoals between,
When, weary from far voyage,
   We gathered to careen.

There burned our breaming-fagots
   All pale along the shore:
There rose our worn pavilions —
   A sail above an oar:
As flashed each yearning anchor
   Through mellow seas afire,
So swift our careless captains
   Rowed each to his desire.

Where lay our loosened harness?
   Where turned our naked feet?
Whose tavern 'mid the palm-trees?
   What quenchings of what heat?
Oh fountain in the desert!
   Oh cistern in the waste!
Oh bread we ate in secret!
   Oh cup we spilled in haste!

The youth new-taught of longing,
   The widow curbed and wan —
The goodwife proud at season,
   And the maid aware of man;
All souls unslaked, consuming,
   Defrauded in delays,
Desire not more their quittance
   Than I those forfeit days!

I dreamed to wait my pleasure
   Unchanged my spring would bide:
Wherefore, to wait my pleasure,
   I put my spring aside

Till, first in face of Fortune,
    And last in mazed disdain,
I made Diego Valdez
    High Admiral of Spain.

Then walked no wind 'neath Heaven
    Nor surge that did not aid —
I dared extreme occasion,
    Nor ever one betrayed.
They wrought a deeper treason —
    (Led seas that served my needs!)
They sold Diego Valdez
    To bondage of great deeds.

The tempest flung me seaward,
    And pinned and bade me hold
The course I might not alter —
    And men esteemed me bold!
The calms embayed my quarry,
    The fog-wreath sealed his eyes;
The dawn-wind brought my topsails —
    And men esteemed me wise!

Yet 'spite my tyrant triumphs
    Bewildered, dispossessed —
My dream held I before me —
    My vision of my rest;
But, crowned by Fleet and People,
    And bound by King and Pope —
Stands here Diego Valdez
    To rob me of my hope!

No prayer of mine shall move him,
    No word of his set free
The Lord of Sixty Pennants
    And the Steward of the Sea.

His will can loose ten thousand
　To seek their loves again —
But not Diego Valdez,
　High Admiral of Spain.

There walks no wind 'neath Heaven
　Nor wave that shall restore
The old careening riot
　And the clamorous, crowded shore —
The fountain in the desert,
　The cistern in the waste,
The bread we ate in secret,
　The cup we spilled in haste.

Now call I to my Captains —
　For council fly the sign,
Now leap their zealous galleys,
　Twelve-oared, across the brine.
To me the straiter prison,
　To me the heavier chain —
To me Diego Valdez,
　High Admiral of Spain!

THE SECOND VOYAGE

1903

WE 'VE sent our little Cupids all ashore —
　They were frightened, they were tired, they were cold;
Our sails of silk and purple go to store,
　And we 've cut away our mast of beaten gold
　　　　(Foul weather!)
Oh 't is hemp and singing pine for to stand against the brine,
　But Love he is our master as of old!

The sea has shorn our galleries away,
  The salt has soiled our gilding past remede;
Our paint is flaked and blistered by the spray,
  Our sides are half a fathom furred in weed
                (Foul weather!)
And the doves of Venus fled and the petrels came instead,
  But Love he was our master at our need!

'Was Youth would keep no vigil at the bow,
  'Was Pleasure at the helm too drunk to steer —
We 've shipped three able quartermasters now,
  Men call them Custom, Reverence, and Fear
                (Foul weather!)
They are old and scarred and plain, but we 'll run no risk
    again
  From any Port o' Paphos mutineer!

We seek no more the tempest for delight,
  We skirt no more the indraught and the shoal —
We ask no more of any day or night
  Than to come with least adventure to our goal
                (Foul weather!)
What we find we needs must brook, but we do not go to
    look,
  Nor tempt the Lord our God that saved us whole!

Yet, caring so, not overmuch we care
  To brace and trim for every foolish blast,
If the squall be pleased to sweep us unaware,
  He may bellow off to leeward like the last
                (Foul weather!)
We will blame it on the deep (for the watch must have their
    sleep),
  And Love can come and wake us when 't is past.

Oh launch them down with music from the beach,
  Oh warp them out with garlands from the quays —
Most resolute — a damsel unto each —
  New prows that seek the old Hesperides!
              (Foul weather!)
Though we know the voyage is vain, yet we see our path
      again
  In the saffroned bridesails scenting all the seas!
              (Foul weather!)

THE LINER SHE'S A LADY

1894

THE Liner she's a lady, an' she never looks nor 'eeds —
The Man-o'-War's 'er 'usband, an' 'e gives 'er all she needs;
But, oh, the little cargo-boats, that sail the wet seas roun',
They're just the same as you an' me a-plyin' up an' down!

  Plyin' up an' down, Jenny, 'angin' round the Yard,
  All the way by Fratton tram down to Portsmouth 'Ard;
  Anythin' for business, an' we're growin' old —
  Plyin' up an' down, Jenny, waitin' in the cold!

The Liner she's a lady by the paint upon 'er face,
An' if she meets an accident they count it sore disgrace:
The Man-o'-War's 'er 'usband, and 'e's always 'andy by,
But, oh, the little cargo-boats, they've got to load or die!

The Liner she's a lady, and 'er route is cut an' dried;
The Man-o'-War's 'er 'usband, an' 'e always keeps beside;
But, oh, the little cargo-boats that 'ave n't any man,
They've got to do their business first, and make the most they
    can!

The Liner she 's a lady, and if a war should come,
The Man-o'-War 's 'er 'usband, and 'e 'd bid 'er stay at hon
But, oh, the little cargo-boats that fill with every tide!
'E 'd 'ave to up an' fight for them, for they are Englan
     pride.

The Liner she 's a lady, but if she was n't made,
There still would be the cargo-boats for 'ome an' forei
     trade.
The Man-o'-War 's 'er 'usband, but if we was n't 'ere,
'E would n't have to fight at all for 'ome an' friends so de

'Ome an' friends so dear, Jenny, 'angin' round the Yar
All the way by Fratton tram down to Portsmouth 'Ard
Anythin' for business, an' we 're growin' old —
'Ome an' friends so dear, Jenny, waitin' in the cold!

THE FIRST CHANTEY

1896

MINE was the woman to me, darkling I found her:
Haling her dumb from the camp, held her and bound her.
Hot rose her tribe on our track ere I had proved her;
Hearing her laugh in the gloom, greatly I loved her.

Swift through the forest we ran, none stood to guard us,
Few were my people and far; then the flood barred us —
Him we call Son of the Sea, sullen and swollen.
Panting we waited the death, stealer and stolen.

et ere they came to my lance laid for the slaughter,
ightly she leaped to a log lapped in the water;
olding on high and apart skins that arrayed her,
alled she the God of the Wind that He should aid her.

ife had the tree at that word (Praise we the Giver!)
tter-like left he the bank for the full river.
ar fell their axes behind, flashing and ringing,
Vonder was on me and fear — yet she was singing!

ow lay the land we had left. Now the blue bound us,
ven the Floor of the Gods level around us.
Vhisper there was not, nor word, shadow nor showing,
ill the light stirred on the deep, glowing and growing.

hen did He leap to His place flaring from under,
Ie the Compeller, the Sun, bared to our wonder.
ay, not a league from our eyes blinded with gazing,
leared He the Gate of the World, huge and amazing!

his we beheld (and we live) — the Pit of the Burning!
hen the God spoke to the tree for our returning;
ack to the beach of our flight, fearless and slowly,
ack to our slayers went he: but we were holy.   `

Ien that were hot in that hunt, women that followed,
abes that were promised our bones, trembled and wallowed:
ver the necks of the Tribe crouching and fawning —
rophet and priestess we came back from the dawning!

THE LAST CHANTEY

1892

" And there was no more sea "

THUS said the Lord in the Vault above the Cherubim,
Calling to the Angels and the Souls in their degree:
    " Lo! Earth has passed away
    On the smoke of Judgment Day.
That Our word may be established shall We gather up the
    sea? "

Loud sang the souls of the jolly, jolly mariners:
    " Plague upon the hurricane that made us furl and flee!
    But the war is done between us,
    In the deep the Lord hath seen us —
Our bones we 'll leave the barracout', and God may sink
    the sea! "

Then said the soul of Judas that betrayèd Him:
    " Lord, hast Thou forgotten Thy covenant with me?
    How once a year I go
    To cool me on the floe?
And Ye take my day of mercy if Ye take away the sea! "

Then said the soul of the Angel of the Off-shore Wind:
    (He that bits the thunder when the bull-mouthed breakers
        flee):
    " I have watch and ward to keep
    O'er Thy wonders on the deep,
And Ye take mine honour from me if Ye take away the
    sea! "

oud sang the souls of the jolly, jolly mariners:
" Nay, but we were angry, and a hasty folk are we!
   If we worked the ship together
   Till she foundered in foul weather,
 Are we babes that we should clamour for a vengeance on
   the sea? "

'hen said the souls of the slaves that men threw overboard:
" Kennelled in the picaroon a weary band were we;
   But Thy arm was strong to save,
   And it touched us on the wave,
 And we drowsed the long tides idle till Thy Trumpets tore
   the sea."

'hen cried the soul of the stout Apostle Paul to God:
" Once we frapped a ship, and she laboured woundily.
   There were fourteen score of these,
   And they blessed Thee on their knees,
 When they learned Thy Grace and Glory under Malta by
   the sea! "

oud sang the souls of the jolly, jolly mariners,
 Plucking at their harps, and they plucked unhandily:
   " Our thumbs are rough and tarred,
   And the tune is something hard —
 May we lift a Deepsea Chantey such as seamen use at
   sea? "

hen said the souls of the gentlemen-adventurers —
 Fettered wrist to bar all for red iniquity:
   " Ho, we revel in our chains
   O'er the sorrow that was Spain's;
 Heave or sink it, leave or drink it, we were masters of the
   sea! "

Up spake the soul of a grey Gothavn 'speckshioner —
   (He that led the flinching in the fleets of fair Dundee):
      " Oh, the ice-blink white and near,
      And the bowhead breaching clear!
   Will Ye whelm them all for wantonness that wallow in th
      sea? "

Loud sang the souls of the jolly, jolly mariners,
   Crying: " Under Heaven, here is neither lead nor lee!
      Must we sing for evermore
      On the windless, glassy floor?
   Take back your golden fiddles and we 'll beat to open sea!

Then stooped the Lord, and He called the good sea up t
      Him,
   And 'stablished its borders unto all eternity,
      That such as have no pleasure
      For to praise the Lord by measure,
   They may enter into galleons and serve Him on the sea.

Sun, wind, and cloud shall fail not from the face of it,
   Stinging, ringing spindrift, nor the fulmar flying free;
      And the ships shall go abroad
      To the Glory of the Lord
   Who heard the silly sailor-folk and gave them back their
      sea!

THE LONG TRAIL

THERE 'S a whisper down the field where the year has sho
      her yield,
   And the ricks stand grey to the sun,
Singing: " Over then, come over, for the bee has quit th
      clover,
   " And your English summer 's done."

You have heard the beat of the off-shore wind,
And the thresh of the deep-sea rain;
You have heard the song — how long! how long?
Pull out on the trail again!

Ha' done with the Tents of Shem, dear lass,
We 've seen the seasons through,
And it 's time to turn on the old trail, our own trail, the
    out trail,
Pull out, pull out, on the Long Trail — the trail that is
    always new!

It 's North you may run to the rime-ringed sun
    Or South to the blind Horn's hate;
Or East all the way into Mississippi Bay,
    Or West to the Golden Gate;
        Where the blindest bluffs hold good, dear lass,
        And the wildest tales are true,
        And the men bulk big on the old trail, our own trail,
            the out trail,
        And life runs large on the Long Trail — the trail
            that is always new.

The days are sick and cold, and the skies are grey and old,
    And the twice-breathed airs blow damp;
And I 'd sell my tired soul for the bucking beam-sea roll
    Of a black Bilbao tramp;
        With her load-line over her hatch, dear lass,
        And a drunken Dago crew,
        And her nose held down on the old trail, our own trail,
            the out trail
        From Cadiz Bar on the Long Trail — the trail that
            is always new.

There be triple ways to take, of the eagle or the snake,
    Or the way of a man with a maid;
But the sweetest way to me is a ship's upon the sea
    In the heel of the North-East Trade.

6

Can you hear the crash on her bows, dear lass,
And the drum of the racing screw,
As she ships it green on the old trail, our own trail,
    the out trail,
As she lifts and 'scends on the Long Trail — the trail
    that is always new?

See the shaking funnels roar, with the Peter at the fore,
  And the fenders grind and heave,
And the derricks clack and grate, as the tackle hooks the crate,
  And the fall-rope whines through the sheave;
    It 's " Gang-plank up and in," dear lass,
    It 's " Hawsers warp her through ! "
    And it 's " All clear aft " on the old trail, our own
      trail, the out trail,
    We 're backing down on the Long Trail — the trail
      that is always new.

O the mutter overside, when the port-fog holds us tied,
  And the sirens hoot their dread!
When foot by foot we creep o'er the hueless viewless deep
  To the sob of the questing lead!
    It 's down by the Lower Hope, dear lass,
    With the Gunfleet Sands in view,
    Till the Mouse swings green on the old trail, our own
      trail, the out trail,
    And the Gull Light lifts on the Long Trail — the trail
      that is always new.

O the blazing tropic night, when the wake 's a welt of light
  That holds the hot sky tame,
And the steady fore-foot snores through the planet-powdered
  floors
  Where the scared whale flukes in flame!
    Her plates are scarred by the sun, dear lass,
    And her ropes are taunt with the dew,

For we 're booming down on the old trail, our own
    trail, the out trail,
We 're sagging south on the Long Trail — the trail
    that is always new.

Then home, get her home, where the drunken rollers comb,
    And the shouting seas drive by,
And the engines stamp and ring, and the wet bows reel and
    swing,
    And the Southern Cross rides high!
        Yes, the old lost stars wheel back, dear lass,
        That blaze in the velvet blue.
        They 're all old friends on the old trail, our own trail,
            the out trail,
        They 're God's own guides on the Long Trail — the
            trail that is always new.

Fly forward, O my heart, from the Foreland to the Start —
    We 're steaming all too slow,
And it 's twenty thousand mile to our little lazy isle
    Where the trumpet-orchids blow!
        You have heard the call of the off-shore wind
        And the voice of the deep-sea ran;
        You have heard the song. How long — how long?
        Pull out on the trail again!

    The Lord knows what we may find, dear lass,
    And The Deuce knows what we may do —
    But we 're back once more on the old trail, our own trail,
        the out trail,
    We 're down, hull down, on the Long Trail — the trail
        that is always new!

A SONG OF THE ENGLISH

1893

*F*AIR *is our lot — O goodly is our heritage!*
(Humble ye, my people, and be fearful in your mirth!)
   For the Lord our God Most High
   He hath made the deep as dry,
He hath smote for us a pathway to the ends of all the Earth

Yea, though we sinned — and our rulers went from righteous
      ness —
Deep in all dishonour though we stained our garments' hem
   Oh be ye not dismayed,
   Though we stumbled and we strayed,
We were led by evil counsellors — the Lord shall deal with
      them!

Hold ye the Faith — the Faith our Fathers sealèd us;
Whoring not with visions — overwise and overstale.
   Except ye pay the Lord
   Single heart and single sword,
Of your children in their bondage He shall ask them treble
      tale!

Keep ye the Law — be swift in all obedience —
Clear the land of evil, drive the road and bridge the ford
   Make ye sure to each his own
   That he reap where he hath sown;
By the peace among Our peoples let men know we serve the
      Lord!

   .   .   .   .   .   .

Hear now a song — a song of broken interludes —
A song of little cunning; of a singer nothing worth.
   Through the naked words and mean
   May ye see the truth between
As the singer knew and touched it in the ends of all the Earth

THE COASTWISE LIGHTS

OUR brows are bound with spindrift and the weed is on
  our knees;
Our loins are battered 'neath us by the swinging, smoking
  seas.
From reef and rock and skerry — over headland, ness, and
  voe —
The Coastwise Lights of England watch the ships of England
  go!

Through the endless summer evenings, on the lineless, level
  floors;
Through the yelling Channel tempest when the siren hoots
  and roars —
By day the dipping house-flag and by night the rocket's
  trail —
As the sheep that graze behind us so we know them where they
  hail.

We bridge across the dark, and bid the helmsman have a care,
The flash that wheeling inland wakes his sleeping wife to
  prayer;
From our vexed eyries, head to gale, we bind in burning
  chains
The lover from the sea-rim drawn — his love in English
  lanes.

We greet the clippers wing-and-wing that race the Southern
  wool;
We warn the crawling cargo-tanks of Bremen, Leith, and
  Hull;
To each and all our equal lamp at peril of the sea —
The white wall-sided warships or the whalers of Dundee!

Come up, come in from Eastward, from the guardports of th
    Morn!
Beat up, beat in from Southerly, O gipsies of the Horn!
Swift shuttles of an Empire's loom that weave us main t
    main,
The Coastwise Lights of England give you welcome bac
    again!

Go, get you gone up-Channel with the sea-crust on you
    plates;
Go, get you into London with the burden of your freights
Haste, for they talk of Empire there, and say, if any seek,
The Lights of England sent you and by silence shall ye speak

THE SONG OF THE DEAD

*HEAR now the Song of the Dead — in the North by th
    torn berg-edges —
They that look still to the Pole, asleep by their hide-strippe
    sledges.
Song of the Dead in the South — in the sun by their skeleto
    horses,
Where the warrigal whimpers and bays through the dust o
    the sere river-courses.*

*Song of the Dead in the East — in the heat-rotted jungl
    hollows,
Where the dog-ape barks in the kloof — in the brake of th
    buffalo-wallows.
Song of the Dead in the West — in the Barrens, the pas
    that betrayed them,
Where the wolverine tumbles their packs from the camp an
    the grave-mound they made them;
        Hear now the Song of the Dead!*

I

We were dreamers, dreaming greatly, in the man-stifled
town;
We yearned beyond the sky-line where the strange roads go
down.
Came the Whisper, came the Vision, came the Power with the
Need,
Till the Soul that is not man's soul was lent us to lead.
As the deer breaks — as the steer breaks — from the herd
where they graze,
In the faith of little children we went on our ways.
Then the wood failed — then the food failed — then the last
water dried —
In the faith of little children we lay down and died.
On the sand-drift — on the veldt-side — in the fern-scrub we
lay,
That our sons might follow after by the bones on the way.
Follow after — follow after! We have watered the root,
And the bud has come to blossom that ripens for fruit!
Follow after — we are waiting, by the trails that we lost,
For the sounds of many footsteps, for the tread of a host.
Follow after — follow after — for the harvest is sown:
By the bones about the wayside ye shall come to your own!

When Drake went down to the Horn
And England was crowned thereby,
'Twixt seas unsailed and shores unhailed
Our Lodge — our Lodge was born
(And England was crowned thereby!)

Which never shall close again
By day nor yet by night,
While man shall take his life to stake
At risk of shoal or main
(By day nor yet by night)

But standeth even so
As now we witness here,
While men depart, of joyful heart,
Adventure for to know
(*As now bear witness here!*)

II

We have fed our sea for a thousand years
  And she calls us, still unfed,
Though there 's never a wave of all her waves
  But marks our English dead:
We have strawed our best to the weed's unrest,
  To the shark and the sheering gull.
If blood be the price of admiralty,
  Lord God, we ha' paid in full!

There 's never a flood goes shoreward now
  But lifts a keel we manned;
There 's never an ebb goes seaward now
  But drops our dead on the sand —
But slinks our dead on the sands forlore,
  From the Ducies to the Swin.
If blood be the price of admiralty,
If blood be the price of admiralty,
  Lord God, we ha' paid it in!

We must feed our sea for a thousand years,
  For that is our doom and pride,
As it was when they sailed with the *Golden Hind*,
  Or the wreck that struck last tide —
Or the wreck that lies on the spouting reef
  Where the ghastly blue-lights flare.
If blood be the price of admiralty,
If blood be the price of admiralty,
If blood be the price of admiralty,
  Lord God, we ha' bought it fair!

THE DEEP-SEA CABLES

THE wrecks dissolve above us; their dust drops down from
    afar —
Down to the dark, to the utter dark, where the blind white sea-
    snakes are.
There is no sound, no echo of sound, in the deserts of the deep,
Or the great grey level plains of ooze where the shell-burred
    cables creep.

Here in the womb of the world — here on the tie-ribs of earth
    Words, and the words of men, flicker and flutter and beat —
Warning, sorrow, and gain, salutation and mirth —
    For a Power troubles the Still that has neither voice nor
    feet.

They have wakened the timeless Things; they have killed
    their father Time;
    Joining hands in the gloom, a league from the last of the
    sun.
Hush! Men talk to-day o'er the waste of the ultimate slime,
    And a new Word runs between: whispering, "Let us be
    one!"

THE SONG OF THE SONS

ONE from the ends of the earth — gifts at an open door —
Treason has much, but we, Mother, thy sons have more!
From the whine of a dying man, from the snarl of a wolf-pack
    freed,
Turn, and the world is thine. Mother, be proud of thy seed!
Count, are we feeble or few? Hear, is our speech so rude?
Look, are we poor in the land? Judge, are we men of The
    Blood?

Those that have stayed at thy knees, Mother, go call ther
    in —
We that were bred overseas wait and would speak with ou
    kin.
Not in the dark do we fight — haggle and flout and gibe;
Selling our love for a price, loaning our hearts for a bribe.
Gifts have we only to-day — Love without promise or fee —
Hear, for thy children speak, from the uttermost parts of th
    sea!

THE SONG OF THE CITIES

BOMBAY

Royal and Dower-royal, I the Queen
    Fronting thy richest sea with richer hands —
A thousand mills roar through me where I glean
    All races from all lands.

CALCUTTA

Me the Sea-captain loved, the River built,
    Wealth sought and Kings adventured life to hold.
Hail, England! I am Asia — Power on silt,
    Death in my hands, but Gold!

MADRAS

Clive kissed me on the mouth and eyes and brow,
    Wonderful kisses, so that I became
Crowned above Queens — a withered beldame now,
    Brooding on ancient fame.

RANGOON

Hail, Mother! Do they call me rich in trade?
    Little care I, but hear the shorn priest drone,
And watch my silk-clad lovers, man by maid,
    Laugh 'neath my Shwe Dagon.

SINGAPORE

Hail, Mother! East and West must seek my aid
  Ere the spent gear may dare the ports afar.
The second doorway of the wide world's trade
  Is mine to loose or bar.

HONG-KONG

Hail, Mother! Hold me fast; my Praya sleeps
  Under innumerable keels to-day.
Yet guard (and landward), or to-morrow sweeps
  Thy warships down the bay!

HALIFAX

Into the mist my guardian prows put forth,
  Behind the mist my virgin ramparts lie,
The Warden of the Honour of the North,
  Sleepless and veiled am I!

QUEBEC AND MONTREAL

Peace is our portion. Yet a whisper rose,
  Foolish and causeless, half in jest, half hate.
Now wake we and remember mighty blows,
  And, fearing no man, wait!

VICTORIA

From East to West the circling word has passed,
  Till West is East beside our land-locked blue;
From East to West the tested chain holds fast,
  The well-forged link rings true!

CAPETOWN

Hail! Snatched and bartered oft from hand to hand,
  I dream my dream, by rock and heath and pine,
Of Empire to the northward. Ay, one land
  From Lion's Head to Line!

MELBOURNE

Greeting! Nor fear nor favour won us place,
  Got between greed of gold and dread of drouth,
Loud-voiced and reckless as the wild tide-race
  That whips our harbour-mouth!

SYDNEY

Greeting! My birth-stain have I turned to good;
  Forcing strong wills perverse to steadfastness:
The first flush of the tropics in my blood,
  And at my feet Success!

BRISBANE

The northern stirp beneath the southern skies —
  I build a Nation for an Empire's need,
Suffer a little, and my land shall rise,
  Queen over lands indeed!

HOBART

Man's love first found me; man's hate made me Hell;
  For my babes' sake I cleansed those infamies.
Earnest for leave to live and labour well,
  God flung me peace and ease.

AUCKLAND

Last, loneliest, loveliest, exquisite, apart —
  On us, on us the unswerving season smiles,
Who wonder 'mid our fern why men depart
  To seek the Happy Isles!

ENGLAND'S ANSWER

Truly ye come of The Blood; slower to bless than to
    ban;
Little used to lie down at the bidding of any man.
Flesh of the flesh that I bred, bone of the bone that I bare;
Stark as your sons shall be — stern as your fathers were.
Deeper than speech our love, stronger than life our tether,
But we do not fall on the neck nor kiss when we come together.
My arm is nothing weak, my strength is not gone by;
Sons, I have borne many sons, but my dugs are not dry.
Look, I have made ye a place and opened wide the doors,
That ye may talk together, your Barons and Councillors —
Wards of the Outer March, Lords of the Lower Seas,
Ay, talk to your grey mother that bore you on her knees! —
That ye may talk together, brother to brother's face —
Thus for the good of your peoples — thus for the Pride of
    the Race.
Also, we will make promise. So long as The Blood endures,
I shall know that your good is mine: ye shall feel that my
    strength is yours:
In the day of Armageddon, at the last great fight of all,
That Our House stand together and the pillars do not fall.
Draw now the threefold knot firm on the ninefold bands,
And the Law that ye make shall be law after the rule of your
    lands.
This for the waxen Heath, and that for the Wattle-bloom,
This for the Maple-leaf, and that for the southern Broom.
The Law that ye make shall be law and I do not press my will,
Because ye are Sons of The Blood and call me Mother still.
Now must ye speak to your kinsmen and they must speak to
    you,
After the use of the English, in straight-flung words and few.
Go to your work and be strong, halting not in your ways,
Baulking the end half-won for an instant dole of praise.
Stand to your work and be wise — certain of sword and pen,
Who are neither children nor Gods, but men in a world of men!

TO THE CITY OF BOMBAY

1894

THE Cities are full of pride,
  Challenging each to each —
This from her mountain-side,
  That from her burthened beach.

They count their ships full tale —
  Their corn and oil and wine,
Derrick and loom and bale,
  And rampart's gun-flecked line;
City by City they hail:
  " Hast aught to match with mine? "

And the men that breed from them
  They traffic up and down,
But cling to their cities' hem
  As a child to the mother's gown.

When they talk with the stranger bands,
  Dazed and newly alone;
When they walk in the stranger lands,
  By roaring streets unknown;
Blessing her where she stands
  For strength above their own.

(On high to hold her fame
  That stands all fame beyond,
By oath to back the same,
  Most faithful-foolish-fond;
Making her mere-breathed name
  Their bond upon their bond.)

So thank I God my birth
  Fell not in isles aside —
Waste headlands of the earth,
  Or warring tribes untried —
But that she lent me worth
  And gave me right to pride.

Surely in toil or fray
  Under an alien sky,
Comfort it is to say:
  " Of no mean city am I! "

(Neither by service nor fee
  Come I to mine estate —
Mother of Cities to me,
  For I was born in her gate,
Between the palms and the sea,
  Where the world-end steamers wait.)

Now for this debt I owe,
  And for her far-borne cheer
Must I make haste and go
  With tribute to her pier.

And she shall touch and remit
  After the use of kings
(Orderly, ancient, fit)
  My deep-sea plunderings,
And purchase in all lands.
  And this we do for a sign
  Her power is over mine,
And mine I hold at her hands!

OUR LADY OF THE SNOWS
1897

(Canadian Preferential Tariff, 1897)

A NATION spoke to a Nation,
  A Queen sent word to a Throne:
" Daughter am I in my mother's house,
  But mistress in my own.
The gates are mine to open,
  As the gates are mine to close,
And I set my house in order,"
  Said our Lady of the Snows.

" Neither with laughter nor weeping,
  Fear or the child's amaze —
Soberly under the White Man's law
  ·My white men go their ways.
Not for the Gentiles' clamour —
  Insult or threat of blows —
Bow we the knee to Baal,"
  Said our Lady of the Snows.

" My speech is clean and single,
  I talk of common things —
Words of the wharf and the market-place
  And the ware the merchant brings:
Favour to those I favour,
  But a stumbling-block to my foes.
Many there be that hate us,"
  Said our Lady of the Snows.

" I called my chiefs to council
  In the din of a troubled year;
For the sake of a sign ye would not see,
  And a word ye would not hear.

This is our message and answer;
  This is the path we chose:
For we be also a people,"
  Said our Lady of the Snows.

" Carry the word to my sisters —
  To the Queens of the East and the South.
I have proven faith in the Heritage
  By more than the word of the mouth.
They that are wise may follow
  Ere the world's war-trumpet blows,
But I — I am first in the battle,"
  Said our Lady of the Snows.

A Nation spoke to a Nation,
  A Throne sent word to a Throne:
" Daughter am I in my mother's house,
  But mistress in my own.
The gates are mine to open,
  As the gates are mine to close,
And I abide by my Mother's House,"
  Said our Lady of the Snows.

AN AMERICAN

1894

he American spirit speaks:

"IF the Led Striker call it a strike,
  Or the papers call it a war,
They know not much what I am like,
  Nor what he is, my Avatar."

7

Through many roads, by me possessed,
　　He shambles forth in cosmic guise;
He is the Jester and the Jest,
　　And he the Text himself applies.

The Celt is in his heart and hand,
　　The Gaul is in his brain and nerve;
Where, cosmopolitanly planned,
　　He guards the Redskin's dry reserve

His easy unswept hearth he lends
　　From Labrador to Guadeloupe;
Till, elbowed out by sloven friends,
　　He camps, at sufferance, on the stoop.

Calm-eyed he scoffs at sword and crown,
　　Or panic-blinded stabs and slays:
Blatant he bids the world bow down,
　　Or cringing begs a crust of praise;

Or, sombre-drunk, at mine and mart,
　　He dubs his dreary brethren Kings.
His hands are black with blood. His heart
　　Leaps, as a babe's, at little things.

But, through the shift of mood and mood,
　　Mine ancient humour saves him whole —
The cynic devil in his blood
　　That bids him mock his hurrying soul;

That bids him flout the Law he makes,
　　That bids him make the Law he flouts,
Till, dazed by many doubts, he wakes
　　The drumming guns that — have no doubts;

That checks him foolish-hot and fond,
   That chuckles through his deepest ire,
That gilds the slough of his despond
   But dims the goal of his desire;

Inopportune, shrill-accented,
   The acrid Asiatic mirth
That leaves him, careless 'mid his dead,
   The scandal of the elder earth.

How shall he clear himself, how reach
   Your bar or weighed defence prefer?
A brother hedged with alien speech
   And lacking all interpreter.

Which knowledge vexes him a space;
   But while Reproof around him rings,
He turns a keen untroubled face
   Home, to the instant need of things.

Enslaved, illogical, elate,
   He greets th' embarrassed Gods, nor fears
To shake the iron hand of Fate
   Or match with Destiny for beers.

Lo, imperturbable he rules,
   Unkempt, disreputable, vast —
And, in the teeth of all the schools,
   I — I shall save him at the last!

THE YOUNG QUEEN

1 9 0 0

(The Commonwealth of Australia, inaugurated New Year's Day, 1901)

HER hand was still on her sword-hilt, the spur was still on
    her heel,
She had not cast her harness of grey war-dinted steel;
High on her red-splashed charger, beautiful, bold, and
    browned,
Bright-eyed out of the battle, the Young Queen rode to be
    crowned.

She came to the Old Queen's presence, in the Hall of Our
    Thousand Years —
In the Hall of the Five Free Nations that are peers among
    their peers:
Royal she gave the greeting, loyal she bowed the head,
Crying — "Crown me, my Mother!"   And the Old Queen
    stood and said: —

" How can I crown thee further?   I know whose standard
    flies
Where the clean surge takes the Leeuwin or the coral barriers
    rise.
Blood of our foes on thy bridle, and speech of our friends in
    thy mouth —
How can I crown thee further, O Queen of the Sovereign
    South?

" Let the Five Free Nations witness !"   But the Young
    Queen answered swift : —
" It shall be crown of Our crowning to hold Our crown for a
    gift.

n the days when Our folk were feeble thy sword made sure
    Our lands:
Vherefore We come in power to take Our crown at thy
    hands."

\nd the Old Queen raised and kissed her, and the jealous
    circlet prest,
\oped with the pearls of the Northland and red with the gold
    of the West,
,it with her land's own opals, levin-hearted, alive,
\nd the Five-starred Cross above them, for sign of the Na-
    tions Five.

\o it was done in the Presence — in the Hall of Our Thou-
    sand Years,
n the face of the Five Free Nations that have no peer but
    their peers ;
\nd the Young Queen out of the Southland kneeled down at
    the Old Queen's knee,
\nd asked for a mother's blessing on the excellent years
    to be.

\nd the Old Queen stooped in the stillness where the jewelled
    head drooped low : —
Daughter no more but Sister, and doubly Daughter so —
\1other of many princes — and child of the child I bore,
Vhat good thing shall I wish thee that I have not wished
    before?

Shall I give thee delight in dominion — mere pride of thy
    setting forth?
\1ay, we be women together — we know what that lust is
    worth.
\eace in thy utmost borders, and strength on a road untrod?
\hese are dealt or diminished at the secret will of God.

" I have swayed troublous councils, I am wise in terrible
        things;
Father and son and grandson, I have known the hearts of the
        Kings.
Shall I give thee my sleepless wisdom, or the gift all wisdom
        above?
Ay, we be women together — I give thee thy people's love

" Tempered, august, abiding, reluctant of prayers or vows,
Eager in face of peril as thine for thy mother's house.
God requite thee, my Sister, through the excellent years to be
And make thy people to love thee as thou hast loved me! "

THE FLOWERS

1895

" *To our private taste, there is always something a little
exotic, almost artificial, in songs which, under an English
aspect and dress, are yet so manifestly the product of other
skies. They affect us like translations; the very fauna and
flora are alien, remote; the dog's-tooth violet is but an ill
substitute for the rathe primrose, nor can we ever believe
that the wood-robin sings as sweetly in April as the English
thrush.*"   THE ATHENÆUM.

Buy my English posies!
  Kent and Surrey may —
Violets of the Undercliff
  Wet with Channel spray;
Cowslips from a Devon combe —
  Midland furze afire —
Buy my English posies
  And I 'll sell your heart's desire!

Buy my English posies!
  You that scorn the May,
Won't you greet a friend from home
  Half the world away?
 - Green against the draggled drift,
  Faint and frail and first —
Buy my Northern blood-root
  And I'll know where you were nursed:
Robin down the logging-road whistles, "Come to me!"
Spring has found the maple-grove, the sap is running free;
All the winds of Canada call the ploughing-rain.
Take the flower and turn the hour, and kiss your love again!

Buy my English posies!
  Here's to match your need —
Buy a tuft of royal heath,
  Buy a bunch of weed
White as sand of Muisenberg
  Spun before the gale —
Buy my heath and lilies
  And I'll tell you whence you hail!
Under hot Constantia broad the vineyards lie —
Throned and thorned the aching berg props the speckless
    sky —
Slow below the Wynberg firs trails the tilted wain —
Take the flower and turn the hour, and kiss your love again!

Buy my English posies!
  You that will not turn —
Buy my hot-wood clematis,
  Buy a frond o' fern
Gathered where the Erskine leaps
  Down the road to Lorne —
Buy my Christmas creeper
  And I'll say where you were born!

West away from Melbourne dust holidays begin —
They that mock at Paradise woo at Cora Lynn —
Through the great South Otway gums sings the great South
    Main —
Take the flower and turn the hour, and kiss your love again!

      Buy my English posies!
        Here 's your choice unsold!
      Buy a blood-red myrtle-bloom,
        Buy the kowhai's gold
      Flung for gift on Taupo's face,
        Sign that spring is come —
      Buy my clinging myrtle
        And I 'll give you back your home!
Broom behind the windy town; pollen o' the pine —
Bell-bird in the leafy deep where the *ratas* twine —
Fern above the saddle-bow, flax upon the plain —
Take the flower and turn the hour, and kiss your love again!

      Buy my English posies!
        Ye that have your own
      Buy them for a brother's sake
        Overseas, alone!
      Weed ye trample underfoot
        Floods his heart abrim —
      Bird ye never heeded,
        Oh, she calls his dead to him!
Far and far our homes are set round the Seven Seas;
Woe for us if we forget, we who hold by these!
Unto each his mother-beach, bloom and bird and land —
Masters of the Seven Seas, oh, love and understand!

THE NATIVE-BORN

1894

W E 'VE drunk to the Queen — God bless her! —
  We 've drunk to our mothers' land;
We 've drunk to our English brother,
  (But he does not understand);
We 've drunk to the wide creation,
  And the Cross swings low for the morn,
Last toast, and of Obligation,
  A health to the Native-born!

They change their skies above them,
  But not their hearts that roam!
We learned from our wistful mothers
  To call old England " home ";
We read of the English sky-lark,
  Of the spring in the English lanes,
But we screamed with the painted lories
  As we rode on the dusty plains!

They passed with their old-world legends —
  Their tales of wrong and dearth —
Our fathers held by purchase,
  But we by the right of birth;
Our heart 's where they rocked our cradle,
  Our love where we spent our toil,
And our faith and our hope and our honour
  We pledge to our native soil!

I charge you charge your glasses —
  I charge you drink with me
To the men of the Four New Nations,
  And the Islands of the Sea —

To the last least lump of coral
   That none may stand outside,
And our own good pride shall teach us
   To praise our comrade's pride!

To the hush of the breathless morning
   On the thin, tin, crackling roofs,
To the haze of the burned back-ranges
   And the dust of the shoeless hoofs —
To the risk of a death by drowning,
   To the risk of a death by drouth —
To the men of a million acres,
   To the Sons of the Golden South!

To the Sons of the Golden South (Stand up!),
   And the life we live and know,
Let a fellow sing o' the little things he cares about,
If a fellow fights for the little things he cares about
   With the weight of a single blow!

To the smoke of a hundred coasters,
   To the sheep on a thousand hills,
To the sun that never blisters,
   To the rain that never chills —
To the land of the waiting springtime,
   To our five-meal, meat-fed men,
To the tall, deep-bosomed women,
   And the children nine and ten!

And the children nine and ten (Stand up!),
   And the life we live and know,
Let a fellow sing o' the little things he cares about,
If a fellow fights for the little things he cares about
   With the weight of a two-fold blow!

To the far-flung fenceless prairie
    Where the quick cloud-shadows trail,
To our neighbour's barn in the offing
    And the line of the new-cut rail;
To the plough in her league-long furrow
    With the grey Lake gulls behind —
To the weight of a half-year's winter
    And the warm wet western wind!

To the home of the floods and thunder,
    To her pale dry healing blue —
To the lift of the great Cape combers,
    And the smell of the baked Karroo.
To the growl of the sluicing stamp-head —
    To the reef and the water-gold,
To the last and the largest Empire,
    To the map that is half unrolled!

To our dear dark foster-mothers,
    To the heathen songs they sung —
To the heathen speech we babbled
    Ere we came to the white man's tongue.
To the cool of our deep verandas —
    To the blaze of our jewelled main,
To the night, to the palms in the moonlight,
    And the fire-fly in the cane!

To the hearth of Our People's People —
    To her well-ploughed windy sea,
To the hush of our dread high-altar
    Where The Abbey makes us We.
To the grist of the slow-ground ages,
    To the gain that is yours and mine —
To the Bank of the Open Credit,
    To the Power-house of the Line!

We 've drunk to the Queen — God bless her ! —
  We 've drunk to our mothers' land ;
We 've drunk to our English brother
  (And we hope he 'll understand).
We 've drunk as much as we 're able,
  And the Cross swings low for the morn ;
Last toast — and your foot on the table ! —
  A health to the Native-born !

A health to the Native-born (Stand up!),
  We 're six white men arow,
All bound to sing o' the little things we care about,
All bound to fight for the little things we care about
  With the weight of a six-fold blow!
By the might of our cable-tow (Take hands!),
  From the Orkneys to the Horn,
All round the world (and a little loop to pull it by),
All round the world (and a little strap to buckle it),
  A health to the Native-born!

THE LOST LEGION

1895

THERE'S a Legion that never was 'listed,
  That carries no colours or crest.
But, split in a thousand detachments,
  Is breaking the road for the rest.
Our fathers they left us their blessing —
  They taught us, and groomed us, and crammed ;
But we 've shaken the Clubs and the Messes
    To go and find out and be damned
                (Dear boys !),
    To go and get shot and be damned.

So some of us chivy the slaver,
  And some of us cherish the black,
And some of us hunt on the Oil Coast,
  And some on the Wallaby track:
And some of us drift to Sarawak,
  And some of us drift up The Fly,
And some share our tucker with tigers,
  And some with the gentle Masai,
                    (Dear boys!),
  Take tea with the giddy Masai.

We've painted The Islands vermilion,
  We've pearled on half-shares in the Bay,
We've shouted on seven-ounce nuggets,
  We've starved on a Seedeeboy's pay;
We've laughed at the world as we found it, —
  Its women and cities and men —
From Sayyid Burgash in a tantrum
  To the smoke-reddened eyes of Loben,
                    (Dear boys!),
  We've a little account with Loben.

The ends o' the Earth were our portion,
  The ocean at large was our share.
There was never a skirmish to windward
  But the Leaderless Legion was there:
Yes, somehow and somewhere and always
  We were first when the trouble began,
From a lottery-row in Manila,
  To an I.D.B. race on the Pan
                    (Dear boys!),
  With the Mounted Police on the Pan.

We preach in advance of the Army,
  We skirmish ahead of the Church,
With never a gunboat to help us
  When we're scuppered and left in the lurch.

But we know as the cartridges finish,
     And we 're filed on our last little shelves,
That the Legion that never was 'listed
     Will send us as good as ourselves
                              (Good men!),
     Five hundred as good as ourselves!

Then a health (we must drink it in whispers),
     To our wholly unauthorised horde —
To the line of our dusty foreloopers,
     The Gentlemen Rovers abroad —
Yes, a health to ourselves ere we scatter,
     For the steamer won't wait for the train,
And the Legion that never was 'listed
     Goes back into quarters again
                         'Regards!
     Goes back under canvas again.
                         Hurrah!
     The swag and the billy again.
                         Here 's how!
     The trail and the packhorse again.
                         Salue!
     The trek and the lager again!

PHARAOH AND THE SERGEANT

1897

"*. . . Consider that the meritorious services of the Sergeai
Instructors attached to the Egyptian Army have been i
adequately acknowledged. . . . To the excellence of their wo
is mainly due the great improvement that has taken place
the soldiers of H.H. the Khedive.*"

EXTRACT FROM LETTER.

SAID England unto Pharaoh, " I must make a man of you,
    That will stand upon his feet and play the game;
That will Maxim his oppressor as a Christian ought to do,"
    And she sent old Pharaoh Sergeant Whatisname.
        It was not a Duke nor Earl, nor yet a *Viscount* —
        It was not a big brass General that came;
        But a man in khaki kit who could handle men a bit,
        With his bedding labelled Sergeant Whatisname.

Said England unto Pharaoh, " Though at present singing
        small,
    You shall hum a proper tune before it ends,"
And she introduced old Pharaoh to the Sergeant once for all,
    And left 'em in the desert making friends.
        It was not a Crystal Palace nor Cathedral;
        It was not a public-house of common fame;
        But a piece of red-hot sand, with a palm on either hand,
        And a little hut for Sergeant Whatisname.

Said England unto Pharaoh, " You 've had miracles before,
    When Aaron struck your rivers into blood;
But if you watch the Sergeant he can show you something
        more,
    He 's a charm for making riflemen from mud."
        It was neither Hindustani, French, nor Coptics;
        It was odds and ends and leavings of the same,
        Translated by a stick (which is really half the trick),
        And Pharaoh harked to Sergeant Whatisname.

There were years that no one talked of; there were times of
        horrid doubt —
    There was faith and hope and whacking and despair —
While the Sergeant gave the Cautions and he combed old
        Pharaoh out,
    And England did n't seem to know nor care.

That is England's awful way o' doing business —
   She would serve her God or Gordon just the same —
For she thinks her Empire still is the Strand and Ho
   born Hill,
   And she did n't think of Sergeant Whatisname.)

Said England to the Sergeant, " You can let my people go!
   (England used 'em cheap and nasty from the start),
And they entered 'em in battle on a most astonished foe —
   But the Sergeant he had hardened Pharaoh's heart.
   Which was broke, along of all the plagues of Egypt,
      Three thousand years before the Sergeant came —
   And he mended it again in a little more than ten,
      Till Pharaoh fought like Sergeant Whatisname!

It was wicked bad campaigning (cheap and nasty from th
   first),
   There was heat and dust and coolie-work and sun,
There were vipers, flies, and sandstorms, there was choler
   and thirst,
   But Pharaoh done the best he ever done.
   Down the desert, down the railway, down the river,
      Like Israelites from bondage so he came,
   'Tween the clouds o' dust and fire to the land of his desir
      And his Moses, it was Sergeant Whatisname!

We are eating dirt in handfuls for to save our daily bread,
   Which we have to buy from those that hate us most,
And we must not raise the money where the Sergeant raise
   the dead,
   And it 's wrong and bad and dangerous to boast.
   But he did it on the cheap and on the quiet,
      And he 's not allowed to forward any claim —
   Though he drilled a black man white, though he made
      mummy fight,
      He will still continue Sergeant Whatisname —
   Private, Corporal, Colour-Sergeant, and Instructor —
      But the everlasting miracle 's the same!

KITCHENER'S SCHOOL

1898

*Being a translation of the song that was made by a Moham-
medan schoolmaster of Bengal Infantry (some time on service
at Suakim) when he heard that Kitchener was taking money
from the English to build a Madrissa for Hubshees — or a
college for the Sudanese, 1898.*

OH Hubshee, carry your shoes in your hand and bow your
    head on your breast!
This is the message of Kitchener who did not break you in jest.
It was permitted to him to fulfil the long-appointed years;
Reaching the end ordained of old over your dead Emirs.

He stamped only before your walls, and the Tomb ye knew
    was dust:
He gathered up under his armpits all the swords of your
    trust:
He set a guard on your granaries, securing the weak from
    the strong:
He said: — " Go work the waterwheels that were abolished so
    long."

He said: — " Go safely, being abased. I have accomplished
    my vow."
That was the mercy of Kitchener. Cometh his madness now!
He does not desire as ye desire, nor devise as ye devise:
He is preparing a second host — an army to make you wise.

Not at the mouth of his clean-lipped guns shall ye learn his
    name again,
But letter by letter, from Kaf to Kaf, at the mouth of his
    chosen men.

8

He has gone back to his own city, not seeking presents or
    bribcs,
But openly asking the English for money to buy you Hakims
    and scribes.

Knowing that ye are forfeit by battle and have no right to
    live,
He begs for money to bring you learning — and all the Eng-
    lish give.
It is their treasure — it is their pleasure — thus are their
    hearts inclined:
For Allah created the English mad — the maddest of all
    mankind!

They do not consider the Meaning of Things; they consult not
    creed nor clan.
Behold, they clap the slave on the back, and behold, he ariseth
    a man!
They terribly carpet the earth with dead, and before their
    cannon cool,
They walk unarmed by twos and threes to call the living to
    school.

How is this reason (which is their reason) to judge a scholar's
    worth,
By casting a ball at three straight sticks and defending the
    same with a fourth?
But this they do (which is doubtless a spell) and other matters
    more strange,
Until, by the operation of years, the hearts of their scholars
    change:

Till these make come and go great boats or engines upon the
    rail
(But always the English watch near by to prop them when
    they fail);

Till these make laws of their own choice and Judges of their
   own blood;
And all the mad English obey the Judges and say that the
   Law is good.

Certainly they were mad from of old: but I think one new
   thing,
That the magic whereby they work their magic — wherefrom
   their fortunes spring —
May be that they show all peoples their magic and ask no
   price in return.
Wherefore, since ye are bond to that magic, O Hubshee, make
   haste and learn!

Certainly also is Kitchener mad.   But one sure thing I
   know —
If he who broke you be minded to teach you, to his Madrissa
   go!
Go, and carry your shoes in your hand and bow your head
   on your breast,
For he who did not slay you in sport, he will not teach you
   in jest.

BRIDGE-GUARD IN THE KARROO

1901

" and will supply details to guard the Blood River Bridge."
District Orders — Lines of Communication.   South African War.

SUDDEN the desert changes,
   The raw glare softens and clings,
Till the aching Oudtshoorn ranges
   Stand up like the thrones of kings —

Ramparts of slaughter and peril —
  Blazing, amazing, aglow —
'Twixt the sky-line's belting beryl
  And the wine-dark flats below.

Royal the pageant closes,
  Lit by the last of the sun —
Opal and ash-of-roses,
  Cinnamon, umber, and dun.

The twilight swallows the thicket,
  The starlight reveals the ridge;
The whistle shrills to the picket —
  We are changing guard on the bridge.

(Few, forgotten and lonely,
  Where the empty metals shine —
No, not combatants — only
  Details guarding the line.)

We slip through the broken panel
  Of fence by the ganger's shed;
We drop to the waterless channel
  And the lean track overhead;

We stumble on refuse of rations,
  The beef and the biscuit-tins;
We take our appointed stations,
  And the endless night begins.

We hear the Hottentot herders
  As the sheep click past to the fold —
And the click of the restless girders
  As the steel contracts in the cold —

Voices of jackals calling
  And, loud in the hush between,
A morsel of dry earth falling
  From the flanks of the scarred ravine.

And the solemn firmament marches,
  And the hosts of heaven rise
Framed through the iron arches —
  Banded and barred by the ties,

Till we feel the far track humming,
  And we see her headlight plain,
And we gather and wait her coming —
  The wonderful north-bound train.

(Few, forgotten and lonely,
  Where the white car-windows shine —
No, not combatants — only
  Details guarding the line.)

Quick, ere the gift escape us!
  Out of the darkness we reach
For a handful of week-old papers
  And a mouthful of human speech.

And the monstrous heaven rejoices,
  And the earth allows again,
Meetings, greetings, and voices
  Of women talking with men.

So we return to our places,
  As out on the bridge she rolls;
And the darkness covers our faces,
  And the darkness re-enters our souls.

More than a little lonely
  Where the lessening tail-lights shine.
No — not combatants — only
  Details guarding the line!

SOUTH AFRICA
1903

LIVED a woman wonderful,
  (May the Lord amend her!)
Neither simple, kind, nor true,
But her Pagan beauty drew
Christian gentlemen a few
  Hotly to attend her.

Christian gentlemen a few
  From Berwick unto Dover;
For she was South Africa,
And she was South Africa,
She was Our South Africa,
  Africa all over!

Half her land was dead with drouth,
  Half was red with battle;
She was fenced with fire and sword
Plague on pestilence outpoured,
Locusts on the greening sward
  And murrain on the cattle!

True, ah true, and overtrue;
  That is why we love her!
For she is South Africa,
And she is South Africa,
She is Our South Africa,
  Africa all over!

Bitter hard her lovers toiled,
  Scandalous their payment, —
Food forgot on trains derailed;
Cattle-dung where fuel failed;
Water where the mules had staled;
  And sackcloth for their raiment!

So she filled their mouths with dust
    And their bones with fever;
Greeted them with cruel lies;
Treated them despiteful-wise;
Meted them calamities
    Till they vowed to leave her!

They took ship and they took sail,
    Raging, from her borders, —
In a little, none the less,
They forgat their sore duresse,
They forgave her waywardness
    And returned for orders!

They esteemed her favour more
    Than a Throne's foundation.
For the glory of her face
Bade farewell to breed and race —
Yea, and made their burial-place
    Altar of a Nation!

Wherefore, being bought by blood,
    And by blood restorèd
To the arms that nearly lost,
She, because of all she cost,
Stands, a very woman, most
    Perfect and adorèd!

On your feet, and let them know
    This is why we love her!
For she is South Africa,
She is Our South Africa,
Is Our Own South Africa,
    Africa all over!

THE BURIAL

1902

(C. J. Rhodes, buried in the Matoppos, April 10, 1902)

WHEN that great Kings return to clay,
  Or Emperors in their pride,
Grief of a day shall fill a day,
  Because its creature died.
But we — we reckon not with those
  Whom the mere Fates ordain,
This Power that wrought on us and goes
  Back to the Power again.

Dreamer devout, by vision led
  Beyond our guess or reach,
The travail of his spirit bred
  Cities in place of speech.
So huge the all-mastering thought that drove —
  So brief the term allowed —
Nations, not words, he linked to prove
  His faith before the crowd.

It is his will that he look forth
  Across the world he won —
The granite of the ancient North —
  Great spaces washed with sun.
There shall he patient take his seat
  (As when the Death he dared),
And there await a people's feet
  In the paths that he prepared.

There, till the vision he foresaw
  Splendid and whole arise,
And unimagined Empires draw
  To council 'neath his skies,

The immense and brooding Spirit still
  Shall quicken and control.
Living he was the land, and dead,
  His soul shall be her soul!

THE SETTLER

1903

(Peace, May, 1902)

HERE, where my fresh-turned furrows run,
  And the deep soil glistens red,
I will repair the wrong that was done
  To the living and the dead.
Here, where the senseless bullet fell,
  And the barren shrapnel burst,
I will plant a tree, I will dig a well,
  Against the heat and the thirst.

Here, in a large and a sunlit land,
  Where no wrong bites to the bone,
I will lay my hand in my neighbour's hand,
  And together we will atone
For the set folly and the red breach
  And the black waste of it all,
Giving and taking counsel each
  Over the cattle-kraal.

Here will we join against our foes —
  The hailstroke and the storm,
And the red and rustling cloud that blows
  The locust's mile-deep swarm;
Frost and murrain and floods let loose
  Shall launch us side by side
In the holy wars that have no truce
  'Twixt seed and harvest tide.

Earth, where we rode to slay or be slain,
　　Our love shall redeem unto life;
We will gather and lead to her lips again
　　The waters of ancient strife,
From the far and fiercely guarded streams
　　And the pools where we lay in wait,
Till the corn cover our evil dreams
　　And the young corn our hate.

And when we bring old fights to mind,
　　We will not remember the sin —
If there be blood on his head of my kind,
　　Or blood on my head of his kin —
For the ungrazed upland, the untilled lea
　　Cry, and the fields forlorn:
" The dead must bury their dead, but ye —
　　Ye serve an host unborn."

Bless then, our God, the new-yoked plough .
　　And the good beasts that draw,
And the bread we eat in the sweat of our brow
　　According to Thy Law.
After us cometh a multitude —
　　Prosper the work of our hands,
That we may feed with our land's food
　　The folk of all our lands!

Here, in the waves and the troughs of the plains,
　　Where the healing stillness lies,
And the vast, benignant sky restrains
　　And the long days make wise —
Bless to our use the rain and the sun
　　And the blind seed in its bed,
That we may repair the wrong that was done
　　To the living and the dead!

SUSSEX

1902

GOD gave all men all earth to love,
  But since our hearts are small,
Ordained for each one spot should prove
  Beloved over all;
That, as He watched Creation's birth,
  So we, in godlike mood,
May of our love create our earth
  And see that it is good.

So one shall Baltic pines content,
  As one some Surrey glade,
Or one the palm-grove's droned lament
  Before Levuka's Trade.
Each to his choice, and I rejoice
  The lot has fallen to me
In a fair ground — in a fair ground —
  Yea, Sussex by the sea!

No tender-hearted garden crowns,
  No bosomed woods adorn
Our blunt, bow-headed, whale-backed Downs,
  But gnarled and writhen thorn —
Bare slopes where chasing shadows skim,
  And through the gaps revealed
Belt upon belt, the wooded, dim
  Blue goodness of the Weald.

Clean of officious fence or hedge,
  Half-wild and wholly tame,
The wise turf cloaks the white cliff edge
  As when the Romans came.

What sign of those that fought and died
    At shift of sword and sword?
The barrow and the camp abide,
    The sunlight and the sward.

Here leaps ashore the full Sou'west
    All heavy-winged with brine,
Here lies above the folded crest
    The Channel's leaden line;
And here the sea-fogs lap and cling,
    And here, each warning each,
The sheep-bells and the ship-bells ring
    Along the hidden beach.

We have no waters to delight
    Our broad and brookless vales —
Only the dewpond on the height
    Unfed, that never fails,
Whereby no tattered herbage tells
    Which way the season flies —
Only our close-bit thyme that smells
    Like dawn in Paradise.

Here through the strong and shadeless days
    The tinkling silence thrills;
Or little, lost, Down churches praise
    The Lord who made the hills:
But here the Old Gods guard their round,
    And, in her secret heart,
The heathen kingdom Wilfrid found
    Dreams, as she dwells, apart.

Though all the rest were all my share,
    With equal soul I 'd see
Her nine-and-thirty sisters fair,
    Yet none more fair than she.

Choose ye your need from Thames to Tweed,
  And I will choose instead
Such lands as lie 'twixt Rake and Rye,
  Black Down and Beachy Head.

I will go out against the sun
  Where the rolled scarp retires,
And the Long Man of Wilmington
  Looks naked toward the shires;
And east till doubling Rother crawls
  To find the fickle tide,
By dry and sea-forgotten walls,
  Our ports of stranded pride.

I will go north about the shaws
  And the deep ghylls that breed
Huge oaks and old, the which we hold
  No more than Sussex weed;
Or south where windy Piddinghoe's
  Begilded dolphin veers
And red beside wide-bankèd Ouse
  Lie down our Sussex steers.

So to the land our hearts we give
  Till the sure magic strike,
And Memory, Use, and Love make live
  Us and our fields alike —
That deeper than our speech and thought,
  Beyond our reason's sway,
Clay of the pit whence we were wrought
  Yearns to its fellow-clay.

God gives all men all earth to love,
  But since man's heart is small,
Ordains for each one spot shall prove
  Beloved over all.

Each to his choice, and I rejoice
The lot has fallen to me
In a fair ground — in a fair ground —
Yea, Sussex by the sea!   .

DIRGE OF DEAD SISTERS

1902

(For the nurses who died in the South African war)

WHO recalls the twilight and the ranged tents in order
　(Violet peaks uplifted through the crystal evening air?
And the clink of iron teacups and the piteous, noble laughter
　And the faces of the Sisters with the dust upon their hair?

(Now and not hereafter, while the breath is in our nostrils,
　Now and not hereafter, ere the meaner years go by —
Let us now remember many honourable women,
　Such as bade us turn again when we were like to die.)

Who recalls the morning and the thunder through the foot
　hills
　(Tufts of fleecy shrapnel strung along the empty plains?
And the sun-scarred Red-Cross coaches creeping guarded to
　the culvert,
　And the faces of the Sisters looking gravely from the trains

(When the days were torment and the nights were clouded
　terror,
　When the Powers of Darkness had dominion on our soul —
When we fled consuming through the Seven Hells of fever,
　These put out their hands to us and healed and made us
　whole.)

Who recalls the midnight by the bridge's wrecked abutment
  (Autumn rain that rattled like a Maxim on the tin?)
And the lightning-dazzled levels and the streaming, straining
    wagons,
  And the faces of the Sisters as they bore the wounded in?

Till the pain was merciful and stunned us into silence —
  When each nerve cried out on God that made the misused
    clay;
When the Body triumphed and the last poor shame de-
    parted —
  These abode our agonies and wiped the sweat away.)

Who recalls the noontide and the funerals through the market
  (Blanket-hidden bodies, flagless, followed by the flies?)
And the footsore firing-party, and the dust and stench and
    staleness,
  And the faces of the Sisters and the glory in their eyes?

Bold behind the battle, in the open camp all-hallowed,
  Patient, wise, and mirthful in the ringed and reeking town,
These endured unresting till they rested from their labours —
  Little wasted bodies, ah, so light to lower down!)

Yet their graves are scattered and their names are clean for-
    gotten,
  Earth shall not remember, but the Waiting Angel knows
Them that died at Uitvlugt when the plague was on the city—
  Her that fell at Simon's Town in service on our foes.

Therefore we they ransomed, while the breath is in our
    nostrils,
  Now and not hereafter, ere the meaner years go by,
Raise with love and worship many honourable women,
  Those that gave their lives for us when we were like to die!

THE ENGLISH FLAG

1891

Above the portico a flag-staff bearing the Union Jac
remained fluttering in the flames for some time, but ultimate
when it fell the crowds rent the air with shouts, and seem
to see significance in the incident.

DAILY PAPERS.

WINDS of the World, give answer! They are whir
    pering to and fro —
And what should they know of England who only Englar
    know? —
The poor little street-bred people that vapour and fume ar
    brag,
They are lifting their heads in the stillness to yelp at t.
    English Flag!

Must we borrow a clout from the Boer — to plaster anew wi
    dirt?
An Irish liar's bandage, or an English coward's shirt?
We may not speak of England; her Flag 's to sell or shar
What is the Flag of England? Winds of the World, declar

The North Wind blew: — " From Bergen my steel-shod va
    guards go;
" I chase your lazy whalers home from the Disko floe;
" By the great North Lights above me I work the will of Go
" And the liner splits on the ice-field or the Dogger fills wi
    cod.

" I barred my gates with iron, I shuttered my doors wi
    flame,
" Because to force my ramparts your nutshell navies cam
" I took the sun from their presence, I cut them down wi
    my blast,
" And they died, but the Flag of England blew free ere t
    spirit passed.

The lean white bear hath seen it in the long, long Arctic
    night,
The musk-ox knows the standard that flouts the Northern
    Light:
What is the Flag of England? Ye have but my bergs to
    dare,
Ye have but my drifts to conquer. Go forth, for it is there!"

The South Wind sighed: — " From the Virgins my mid-sea
    course was ta'en
Over a thousand islands lost in an idle main,
Where the sea-egg flames on the coral and the long-backed
    breakers croon
Their endless ocean legends to the lazy, locked lagoon.

Strayed amid lonely islets, mazed amid outer keys,
I waked the palms to laughter — I tossed the scud in the
    breeze —
Never was isle so little, never was sea so lone,
But over the scud and the palm-trees an English flag was
    flown.

I have wrenched it free from the halliards to hang for a
    wisp on the Horn;
I have chased it north to the Lizard — ribboned and rolled
    and torn;
I have spread its fold o'er the dying, adrift in a hopeless
    sea;
I have hurled it swift on the slaver, and seen the slave set
    free.

My basking sunfish know it, and wheeling albatross,
Where the lone wave fills with fire beneath the Southern
    Cross.
What is the Flag of England? Ye have but my reefs to
    dare,
Ye have but my seas to furrow. Go forth, for it is there!"

The East Wind roared: — " From the Kuriles, the Bitter
    Seas, I come,
" And me men call the Home-Wind, for I bring the English
    home.
" Look — look well to your shipping!   By the breath of my
    mad typhoon
" I swept your close-packed Praya and beached your best at
    Kowloon!

" The reeling junks behind me and the racing seas before,
" I raped your richest roadstead — I plundered Singapore!
" I set my hand on the Hoogli; as a hooded snake she rose,
" And I flung your stoutest steamers to roost with the
    startled crows.

" Never the lotos closes, never the wild-fowl wake,
" But a soul goes out on the East Wind that died for Eng-
    land's sake —
" Man or woman or suckling, mother or bride or maid —
" Because on the bones of the English the English Flag is
    stayed.

" The desert-dust hath dimmed it, the flying wild-ass knows,
" The scared white leopard winds it across the taintless
    snows.
" What is the Flag of England?   Ye have but my sun to dare,
" Ye have but my sands to travel.   Go forth, for it is there!"

The West Wind called: — " In squadrons the thoughtless
    galleons fly
" That bear the wheat and cattle lest street-bred people die.
" They make my might their porter, they make my house their
    path,
" Till I loose my neck from their rudder and whelm them all
    in my wrath.

I draw the gliding fog-bank as a snake is drawn from the
 hole,
They bellow one to the other, the frighted ship-bells toll,
For day is a drifting terror till I raise the shroud with my
 breath,
And they see strange bows above them and the two go
 locked to death.

But whether in calm or wrack-wreath, whether by dark or
 day,
I heave them whole to the conger or rip their plates away,
First of the scattered legions, under a shrieking sky,
Dipping between the rollers, the English Flag goes by.

The dead dumb fog hath wrapped it — the frozen dews
 have kissed —
The naked stars have seen it, a fellow-star in the mist.
What is the Flag of England? Ye have but my breath to
 dare,
Ye have but my waves to conquer. Go forth, for it is
 there!"

WHEN EARTH'S LAST PICTURE IS PAINTED

1892

WHEN Earth's last picture is painted and the tubes are
 twisted and dried,
When the oldest colours have faded, and the youngest critic
 has died,
We shall rest, and, faith, we shall need it — lie down for an
 æon or two,
'ill the Master of All Good Workmen shall put us to work
 anew.

And those that were good shall be happy: they shall sit in
    golden chair;
They shall splash at a ten-league canvas with brushes o
    comets' hair;
They shall find real saints to draw from — Magdalene, Pete
    and Paul;
They shall work for an age at a sitting and never be tired a
    all!

And only the Master shall praise us, and only the Maste
    shall blame;
And no one shall work for money, and no one shall work fo
    fame,
But each for the joy of the working, and each, in his separat
    star,
Shall draw the Thing as he sees It for the God of Things a
    They are!

"CLEARED"

1890

(In memory of the Parnell Commission)

HELP for a patriot distressed, a spotless spirit hurt,
Help for an honourable clan sore trampled in the dirt!
From Queenstown Bay to Donegal, Oh listen to my song,
The honourable gentlemen have suffered grievous wrong.

Their noble names were mentioned — Oh the burning blac
    disgrace! —
By a brutal Saxon paper in an Irish shooting-case;
They sat upon it for a year, then steeled their heart to brav
    it,
And " coruscating innocence " the learned Judges gave it.

Bear witness, Heaven, of that grim crime beneath the surgeon's knife,
The honourable gentlemen deplored the loss of life!
Bear witness of those chanting choirs that burk and shirk and snigger,
No man laid hand upon the knife or finger to the trigger!

Cleared in the face of all mankind beneath the winking skies,
Like phœnixes from Phœnix Park (and what lay there) they rise!
Go shout it to the emerald seas — give word to Erin now,
Her honourable gentlemen are cleared — and this is how: —

They only paid the Moonlighter his cattle-hocking price,
They only helped the murderer with counsel's best advice,
But — sure it keeps their honour white — the learned Court believes
They never give a piece of plate to murderers and thieves.

They never told the ramping crowd to card a woman's hide,
They never marked a man for death — what fault of theirs he died? —
They only said " intimidate," and talked and went away —
By God, the boys that did the work were braver men than they!

Their sin it was that fed the fire — small blame to them that heard —
The boys get drunk on rhetoric, and madden at a word —
They knew whom they were talking at, if they were Irish too,
The gentlemen that lied in Court, they knew, and well they knew.

They only took the Judas-gold from Fenians out of jail,
They only fawned for dollars on the blood-dyed Clan-na-Gael.
If black is black or white is white, in black and white it 's down,
They 're only traitors to the Queen and rebels to the Crown.

" Cleared," honourable gentlemen! Be thankful it's no
    more: —
The widow's curse is on your house, the dead are at your
    door.
On you the shame of open shame, on you from North to
    South
The hand of every honest man flat-heeled across your mouth.

" Less black than we were painted" ? — Faith, no word of
    black was said;
The lightest touch was human blood, and that, you know
    runs red.
It 's sticking to your fist to-day for all your sneer and scoff
And by the Judge's well-weighed word you cannot wipe it off.

Hold up those hands of innocence — go, scare your sheep
    together,
The blundering, tripping tups that bleat behind the old bell-
    wether;
And if they snuff the taint and break to find another pen,
Tell them it 's tar that glistens so, and daub them yours
    again!

" The charge is old " ? — As old as Cain — as fresh as
    yesterday;
Old as the Ten Commandments — have ye talked those laws
    away?
If words are words, or death is death, or powder sends the
    ball,
You spoke the words that sped the shot — the curse be on
    you all.

" Our friends believe "? Of course they do — as sheltered
    women may;
But have they seen the shrieking soul ripped from the quiver-
    ing clay?

They! — If their own front door is shut, they 'll swear the
    whole world 's warm;
What do they know of dread of death or hanging fear of
    harm?

The secret half a county keeps, the whisper in the lane,
The shriek that tells the shot went home behind the broken
    pane,
The dry blood crisping in the sun that scares the honest bees,
And shows the boys have heard your talk — what do they
    know of these?

But you — you know — ay, ten times more; the secrets of
    the dead,
Black terror on the country-side by word and whisper bred,
The mangled stallion's scream at night, the tail-cropped
    heifer's low.
Who set the whisper going first? You know, and well you
    know!

My soul! I 'd sooner lie in jail for murder plain and straight,
Pure crime I 'd done with my own hand for money, lust, or
    hate,
Than take a seat in Parliament by fellow-felons cheered,
While one of those " not provens " proved me cleared as you
    are cleared.

Cleared — you that " lost " the League accounts — go,
    guard our honour still,
Go, help to make our country's laws that broke God's law
    at will —
One hand stuck out behind the back, to signal " strike
    again ";
The other on your dress-shirt-front to show your heart is
    clane.

If black is black or white is white, in black and white it 's
    down,
You 're only traitors to the Queen and rebels to the Crown.
If print is print or words are words, the learned Court
    perpends : —
We are not ruled by murderers, but only — by their friends.

THE BALLAD OF EAST AND WEST

1889

OH, East is East, and West is West, and never the twain
    shall meet,
Till Earth and Sky stand presently at God's great Judgment
    Seat;
But there is neither East nor West, Border, nor Breed, nor
    Birth,
When two strong men stand face to face, tho' they come from
    the ends of the earth!

Kamal is out with twenty men to raise the Borderside,
And he has lifted the Colonel's mare that is the Colonel's pride:
He has lifted her out of the stable-door between the dawn and
    the day,
And turned the calkins upon her feet, and ridden her far away.
Then up and spoke the Colonel's son that led a troop of the
    Guides :
" Is there never a man of all my men can say where Kamal
    hides? "
Then up and spoke Mohammed Khan, the son of the
    Ressaldar :
" If ye know the track of the morning-mist, ye know where
    his pickets are.

"At dusk he harries the Abazai — at dawn he is into
Bonair,

"But he must go by Fort Bukloh to his own place to fare,

"So if ye gallop to Fort Bukloh as fast as a bird can fly,

"By the favour of God ye may cut him off ere he win to the
Tongue of Jagai.

"But if he be past the Tongue of Jagai, right swiftly turn
ye then,

"For the length and the breadth of that grisly plain is sown
with Kamal's men.

"There is rock to the left, and rock to the right, and low lean
thorn between,

"And ye may hear a breech-bolt snick where never a man is
seen."

The Colonel's son has taken a horse, and a raw rough dun
was he,

With the mouth of a bell and the heart of Hell and the head
of a gallows-tree.

The Colonel's son to the Fort has won, they bid him stay to
eat —

Who rides at the tail of a Border thief, he sits not long at his
meat.

He 's up and away from Fort Bukloh as fast as he can fly,

Till he was aware of his father's mare in the gut of the
Tongue of Jagai,

Till he was aware of his father's mare with Kamal upon her
back,

And when he could spy the white of her eye, he made the pistol
crack.

He has fired once, he has fired twice, but the whistling ball
went wide.

"Ye shoot like a soldier," Kamal said. "Show now if ye
can ride."

It 's up and over the Tongue of Jagai, as blown dust-devils
go,

The dun he fled like a stag of ten, but the mare like a barren
doe.

The dun he leaned against the bit and slugged his head above,
But the red mare played with the snaffle-bars, as a maiden
    plays with a glove.
There was rock to the left and rock to the right, and low lean
    thorn between,
And thrice he heard a breech-bolt snick tho' never a man was
    seen.
They have ridden the low moon out of the sky, their hoofs
    drum up the dawn,
The dun he went like a wounded bull, but the mare like a new-
    roused fawn.
The dun he fell at a water-course — in a woeful heap fell he,
And Kamal has turned the red mare back, and pulled the rider
    free.
He has knocked the pistol out of his hand — small room was
    there to strive,
" 'T was only by favour of mine," quoth he, " ye rode so long
    alive:
" There was not a rock for twenty mile, there was not a clump
    of tree,
" But covered a man of my own men with his rifle cocked on his
    knee.
" If I had raised my bridle-hand, as I have held it low,
" The little jackals that flee so fast were feasting all in a
    row:
" If I had bowed my head on my breast, as I have held it
    high,
" The kite that whistles above us now were gorged till she
    could not fly."
Lightly answered the Colonel's son: " Do good to bird and
    beast,
" But count who come for the broken meats before thou makest
    a feast.
" If there should follow a thousand swords to carry my bones
    away,
" Belike the price of a jackal's meal were more than a thief
    could pay.

" They will feed their horse on the standing crop, their men
    on the garnered grain,
" The thatch of the byres will serve their fires when all the
    cattle are slain.
" But if thou thinkest the price be fair, — thy brethren wait
    to sup,
" The hound is kin to the jackal-spawn, — howl, dog, and
    call them up!
" And if thou thinkest the price be high, in steer and gear and
    stack, '
" Give me my father's mare again, and I 'll fight my own way
    back!"
Kamal has gripped him by the hand and set him upon his
    feet.
" No talk shall be of dogs," said he, " when wolf and grey
    wolf meet.
" May I eat dirt if thou hast hurt of me in deed or breath;
" What dam of lances brought thee forth to jest at the dawn
    with Death?"
Lightly answered the Colonel's son: " I hold by the blood of
    my clan:
" Take up the mare for my father's gift — by God, she has
    carried a man!"
The red mare ran to the Colonel's son, and nuzzled against
    his breast;
" We be two strong men," said Kamal then, " but she loveth
    the younger best.
" So she shall go with a lifter's dower, my turquoise-studded
    rein,
" My broidered saddle and saddle-cloth, and silver stirrups
    twain."
The Colonel's son a pistol drew, and held it muzzle-end,
" Ye have taken the one from a foe," said he; " will ye take
    the mate from a friend?"
" A gift for a gift," said Kamal straight; " a limb for the
    risk of a limb.
" Thy father has sent his son to me, I 'll send my son to him!"

With that he whistled his only son, that dropped from a mountain-crest —

He trod the ling like a buck in spring, and he looked like a lance in rest.

" Now here is thy master," Kamal said, " who leads a troop of the Guides,

" And thou must ride at his left side as shield on shoulder rides.

" Till Death or I cut lose the tie, at camp and board and bed,

" Thy life is his — thy fate it is to guard him with thy head.

" So, thou must eat the White Queen's meat, and all her foes are thine,

" And thou must harry thy father's hold for the peace of the Border-line,

" And thou must make a trooper tough and hack thy way to power —

" Belike they will raise thee to Ressaldar when I am hanged in Peshawur."

They have looked each other between the eyes, and there they found no fault,

They have taken the Oath of the Brother-in-Blood on leavened bread and salt :

They have taken the Oath of the Brother-in-Blood on fire and fresh-cut sod,

On the hilt and the haft of the Khyber knife, and the Wondrous Names of God.

The Colonel's son he rides the mare and Kamal's boy the dun,

And two have come back to Fort Bukloh where there went forth but one.

And when they drew to the Quarter-Guard, full twenty swords flew clear —

There was not a man but carried his feud with the blood of the mountaineer.

" Ha' done ! ha' done ! " said the Colonel's son. " Put up the steel at your sides !

" Last night ye had struck at a Border thief — to-night 't is a man of the Guides ! "

Oh, East is East, and West is West, and never the twain shall
  meet,
Till Earth and Sky stand presently at God's great Judgment
  Seat;
But there is neither East nor West, Border, nor Breed, nor
  Birth,
When two strong men stand face to face, tho' they come from
  the ends of the earth!

THE LAST SUTTEE

1 8 8 9

Not many years ago a King died in one of the Rajpoot
States.   His wives, disregarding the orders of the English
against Suttee, would have broken. out of the palace and
burned themselves with the corpse had not the gates been
barred.   But one of them, disguised as the King's favourite
dancing-girl, passed through the line of guards and reached
the pyre.   There, her courage failing, she prayed her cousin,
a baron of the court, to kill her.   This he did, not knowing
who she was.

UDAI CHAND lay sick to death
  In his hold by Gungra hill.
All night we heard the death-gongs ring
For the soul of the dying Rajpoot King,
All night beat up from the women's wing
  A cry that we could not still.

All night the barons came and went,
  The Lords of the Outer Guard:
All night the cressets glimmered pale
On Ulwar sabre and Tonk jezail,
Mewar headstall and Marwar mail,
  That clinked in the palace yard.

In the Golden Room on the palace roof
   All night he fought for air:
And there were sobbings behind the screen,
Rustle and whisper of women unseen,
And the hungry eyes of the Boondi Queen
   On the death she might not share.

He passed at dawn — the death-fire leaped
   From ridge to river-head,
From the Malwa plains to the Abu scars:
And wail upon wail went up to the stars
Behind the grim zenana-bars,
   When they knew that the King was dead.

The dumb priest knelt to tie his mouth
   And robe him for the pyre.
The Boondi Queen beneath us cried:
" See, now, that we die as our mothers died
" In the bridal-bed by our master's side!
   " Out, women! — to the fire! "

We drove the great gates home apace:
   White hands were on the sill:
But ere the rush of the unseen feet
Had reached the turn to the open street,
The bars shot down, the guard-drum beat —
   We held the dovecot still.

A face looked down in the gathering day,
   And laughing spoke from the wall:
" Ohé, they mourn here: let me by —
" Azizun, the Lucknow nautch-girl, I!
" When the house is rotten, the rats must fly,
   " And I seek another thrall.

"For I ruled the King as ne'er did Queen, —
  "To-night the Queens rule me!
"Guard them safely, but let me go,
"Or ever they pay the debt they owe
"In scourge and torture!"   She leaped below,
  And the grim guard watched her flee.

They knew that the King had spent his soul
  On a North-bred dancing-girl:
That he prayed to a flat-nosed Lucknow god,
And kissed the ground where her feet had trod,
And doomed to death at her drunken nod,
  And swore by her lightest curl.

We bore the King to his fathers' place,
  Where the tombs of the Sun-born stand:
Where the grey apes swing, and the peacocks preen
On fretted pillar and jewelled screen,
And the wild boar couch in the house of the Queen
  On the drift of the desert sand.

The herald read his titles forth,
  We set the logs aglow:
"Friend of the English, free from fear,
"Baron of Luni to Jeysulmeer,
"Lord of the Desert of Bikaneer,
  "King of the Jungle, — go!"

All night the red flame stabbed the sky
  With wavering wind-tossed spears:
And out of a shattered temple crept
A woman who veiled her head and wept,
And called on the King — but the great King slept,
  And turned not for her tears.

One watched, a bow-shot from the blaze,
　　The silent streets between,
Who had stood by the King in sport and fray,
To blade in ambush or boar at bay,
And he was a baron old and grey,
　　And kin to the Boondi Queen.

Small thought had he to mark the strife —
　　Cold fear with hot desire —
When thrice she leaped from the leaping flame,
And thrice she beat her breast for shame,
And thrice like a wounded dove she came
　　And moaned about the fire.

He said: " O shameless, put aside
　　" The veil upon thy brow!
" Who held the King and all his land
" To the wanton will of a harlot's hand!
" Will the white ash rise from the blistered brand?
　　" Stoop down, and call him now! "

Then she: " By the faith of my tarnished soul,
　　" All things I did not well,
" I had hoped to clear ere the fire died,
" And lay me down by my master's side
" To rule in Heaven his only bride,
　　" While the others howl in Hell.

" But I have felt the fire's breath,
　　" And hard it is to die!
" Yet if I may pray a Rajpoot lord
" To sully the steel of a Thakur's sword
" With base-born blood of a trade abhorred," —
　　And the Thakur answered, " Ay."

He drew and struck: the straight blade drank
  The life beneath the breast.
" I had looked for the Queen to face the flame,
" But the harlot dies for the Rajpoot dame —
" Sister of mine, pass, free from shame.
  "Pass with thy King to rest! "

The black log crashed above the white:
  The little flames and lean,
Red as slaughter and blue as steel,
That whistled and fluttered from head to heel,
Leaped up anew, for they found their meal
  On the heart of — the Boondi Queen!

GENERAL JOUBERT

1 9 0 0

(*Died March* 27, 1900).

WITH those that bred, with those that loosed the strife,
  He had no part whose hands were clear of gain;
But subtle, strong, and stubborn, gave his life
  To a lost cause, and knew the gift was vain.

Later shall rise a people, sane and great,
  Forged in strong fires, by equal war made one;
Telling old battles over without hate —
  Not least his name shall pass from sire to son.

He may not meet the onsweep of our van
  In the doomed city when we close the score;
Yet o'er his grave — his grave that holds a man —
  Our deep-tongued guns shall answer his once more!

10

THE BALLAD OF THE KING'S MERCY

1889

A BDHUR RAHMAN, the Durani Chief, of him is the
story told.
His mercy fills the Khyber hills — his grace is manifold.
He has taken toll of the North and the South — his
glory reacheth far,
And they tell the tale of his charity from Balkh to
Kandahar.

Before the old Peshawur Gate, where Kurd and Kaffir meet,
The Governor of Kabul dealt the Justice of the Street,
And that was strait as running noose and swift as plunging
knife,
Tho' he who held the longer purse might hold the longer life.
There was a hound of Hindustan had struck a Euzufzai,
Wherefore they spat upon his face and led him out to die.
It chanced the King went forth that hour when throat was
bared to knife;
The Kaffir grovelled under-hoof and clamoured for his life.

Then said the King: "Have hope, O friend! Yea, Death
disgraced is hard;
"Much honour shall be thine;" and called the Captain of the
Guard,
Yar Khan, a bastard of the Blood, so city-babble saith,
And he was honoured of the King — the which is salt to
Death;
And he was son of Daoud Shah, the Reiver of the Plains,
And blood of old Durani Lords ran fire in his veins;
And 't was to tame an Afghan pride nor Hell nor Heaven
could bind,
The King would make him butcher to a yelping cur of Hind.

' Strike!" said the King. "King's blood art thou — his
   death shall be his pride!"
Then louder, that the crowd might catch: "Fear not — his
   arms are tied!"
Yar Khan~ drew clear the Khyber knife, and struck, and
   sheathed again.
" O man, thy will is done," quoth he; "A King this dog hath
   slain."

> *Abdhur Rahman, the Durani Chief, to the North and the*
>   *South is sold.*
> *The North and the South shall open their mouth to a*
>   *Ghilzai flag unrolled,*
> *When the big guns speak to the Khyber peak, and his*
>   *dog-Heratis fly:*
> *Ye have heard the song — How long ?   How long ?*
>   *Wolves of the Abazai!*

That night before the watch was set, when all the streets were
   clear,
The Governor of Kabul spoke: "My King, hast thou no
   fear?
" Thou knowest — thou hast heard," — his speech died at his
   master's face.
And grimly said the Afghan King: "I rule the Afghan race.
" My path is mine — see thou to thine — to-night upon thy
   bed
" Think who there be in Kabul now that clamour for thy
   head."

That night when all the gates were shut to City and to
   throne,
Within a little garden-house the King lay down alone.
Before the sinking of the moon, which is the Night of Night,
Yar Khan came softly to the King to make his honour white.
The children of the town had mocked beneath his horse's hoofs,
The harlots of the town had hailed him "butcher!" from their
   roofs.

But as he groped against the wall, two hands upon him fell,
The King behind his shoulder spake: " Dead man, thou dos
not well!
" 'T is ill to jest with Kings by day and seek a boon by night
" And that thou bearest in thy hand is all too sharp to write.
" But three days hence, if God be good, and if thy strengtl
remain,
" Thou shalt demand one boon of me and bless me in thy pain
" For I am merciful to all, and most of all to thee.
" My butcher of the shambles, rest — no knife hast thou fo
me!"

Abdhur Rahman, the Durani Chief, holds hard by the Soutl
and the North;
But the Ghilzai knows, ere the melting snows, when th
swollen banks break forth,
When the red-coats crawl to the sungar wall, and his Usbeg
lances fail:
Ye have heard the song—How long? How long? Wolve
of the Zuka Kheyl!

They stoned him in the rubbish-field when dawn was in the sky
According to the written word, " See that he do not die."
They stoned him till the stones were piled above him on th
plain,
And those the labouring limbs displaced they tumbled bacl
again.

One watched beside the dreary mound that veiled the battere(
thing,
And him the King with laughter called the Herald of the King

It was upon the second night, the night of Ramazan,
The watcher leaning earthward heard the message of Yai
Khan.
From shattered breast through shrivelled lips broke forth th
rattling breath,
" Creature of God, deliver me from agony of Death."

They sought the King among his girls, and risked their lives
    thereby:
" Protector of the Pitiful, give orders that he die! "

" Bid him endure until the day," a lagging answer came;
" The night is short, and he can pray and learn to bless my
    name."
Before the dawn three times he spoke, and on the day once
    more:
" Creature of God, deliver me, and bless the King therefor! "

They shot him at the morning prayer, to ease him of his pain,
And when he heard the matchlocks clink, he blessed the King
    again.

Which thing the singers made a song for all the world to sing,
So that the Outer Seas may know the mercy of the King.

Abdhur Rahman, the Durani Chief, of him is the story told,
He has opened his mouth to the North and the South, they
    have stuffed his mouth with gold.
Ye know the truth of his tender ruth — and sweet his
    favours are:
Ye have heard the song—How long? How long? from
    Balkh to Kandahar.

THE BALLAD OF THE KING'S JEST
1890

WHEN spring-time flushes the desert grass,
Our kafilas wind through the Khyber Pass.
Lean are the camels but fat the frails,
Light are the purses but heavy the bales,
As the snowbound trade of the North comes down
To the market-square of Peshawur town.

In a turquoise twilight, crisp and chill,
A kafila camped at the foot of the hill.
Then blue smoke-haze of the cooking rose,
And tent-peg answered to hammer-nose;
And the picketed ponies, shag and wild,
Strained at their ropes as the feed was piled;
And the bubbling camels beside the load
Sprawled for a furlong adown the road;
And the Persian pussy-cats, brought for sale,
Spat at the dogs from the camel-bale;
And the tribesmen bellowed to hasten the food;
And the camp-fires twinkled by Fort Jumrood;
And there fled on the wings of the gathering dusk
A savour of camels and carpets and musk,
A murmur of voices, a reek of smoke,
To tell us the trade of the Khyber woke.

The lid of the flesh-pot chattered high,
The knives were whetted and — then came I
To Mahbub Ali the muleteer,
Patching his bridles and counting his gear,
Crammed with the gossip of half a year.
But Mahbub Ali the kindly said,
" Better is speech when the belly is fed."
So we plunged the hand to the mid-wrist deep
In a cinnamon stew of the fat-tailed sheep,
And he who never hath tasted the food,
By Allah! he knoweth not bad from good.

We cleansed our beards of the mutton-grease,
We lay on the mats and were filled with peace,
And the talk slid north, and the talk slid south,
With the sliding puffs from the hookah-mouth.

Four things greater than all things are, —
Women and Horses and Power and War.
We spake of them all, but the last the most,
For I sought a word of a Russian post,

Of a shifty promise, an unsheathed sword
And a grey-coat guard on the Helmund ford,
Then Mahbub Ali lowered his eyes
In the fashion of one who is weaving liés.
Quoth he: " Of the Russians who can say?
" When the night is gathering all is grey.
" But we look that the gloom of the night shall die
" In the morning flush of a blood-red sky.
" Friend of my heart, is it meet or wise
" To warn a King of his enemies?
" We know what Heaven or Hell may bring,
" But no man knoweth the mind of the King.
" That unsought counsel is cursed of God
" Attesteth the story of Wali Dad.

" His sire was leaky of tongue and pen,
" His dam was a clucking Khuttuck hen;
" And the colt bred close to the vice of each,
" For he carried the curse of an unstanched speech.
" Therewith madness — so that he sought
" The favour of kings at the Kabul court;
" And travelled, in hope of honour, far
" To the line where the grey-coat squadrons are.
" There have I journeyed too — but I
" Saw naught, said naught, and — did not die!
" *He* hearked to rumour, and snatched at a breath
" Of ' this one knoweth ' and ' that one saith,' —
" Legends that ran from mouth to mouth
" Of a grey-coat coming, and sack of the South.
" These have I also heard — they pass
" With each new spring and the winter grass.

" Hot-foot southward, forgotten of God,
" Back to the city ran Wali Dad,
" Even to Kabul — in full durbar
" The King held talk with his Chief in War.
" Into the press of the crowd he broke,
" And what he had heard of the coming spoke.

" Then Gholam Hyder, the Red Chief, smiled,
" As a mother might on a babbling child;
" But those who would laugh restrained their breath,
" When the face of the King showed dark as death.
" Evil it is in full durbar
" To cry to a ruler of gathering war!
" Slowly he led to a peach-tree small,
" That grew by a cleft of the city wall.
" And he said to the boy: ' They shall praise thy zeal
" ' So long as the red spurt follows the steel.
" ' And the Russ is upon us even now?
" ' Great is thy prudence — await them, thou.
" ' Watch from the tree. Thou art young and strong.
" ' Surely thy vigil is not for long.
" ' The Russ is upon us, thy clamour ran?
" ' Surely an hour shall bring their van.
" ' Wait and watch. When the host is near,
" ' Shout aloud that my men may hear.'

" Friend of my heart, is it meet or wise
" To warn a King of his enemies?
" A guard was set that he might not flee —
" A score of bayonets ringed the tree.
" The peach-bloom fell in showers of snow,
" When he shook at his death as he looked below.
" By the power of God, who alone is great,
" Till the seventh day he fought with his fate.
" Then madness took him, and men declare
" He mowed in the branches as ape and bear,
" And last as a sloth, ere his body failed,
" And he hung like a bat in the forks, and wailed,
" And sleep the cord of his hands untied,
" And he fell, and was caught on the points and died.

" Heart of my heart, is it meet or wise
" To warn a King of his enemies?
" We know what Heaven or Hell may bring,
" But no man knoweth the mind of the King.

" Of the grey-coat coming who can say?
" When the night is gathering all is grey.
" Two things greater than all things are,
" The first is Love, and the second War.
" And since we know not how War may prove,
" Heart of my heart, let us talk of Love! "

WITH SCINDIA TO DELHI

1890

*More than a hundred years ago, in a great battle fought
near Delhi, an Indian Prince rode fifty miles after the day
was lost with a beggar-girl, who had loved him and followed
him in all his camps, on his saddle-bow. He lost the girl
when almost within sight of safety. A Mahratta trooper
tells the story: —*

THE wreath of banquet overnight lay withered on the neck,
  Our hands and scarves were saffron-dyed for signal of
    despair,
When we went forth to Paniput to battle with the *Mlech*, —
  Ere we came back from Paniput and left a kingdom there.

Thrice thirty thousand men were we to force the Jumna
    fords —
  The hawk-winged horse of Damajee, mailed squadrons of
    the Bhao,
Stark levies of the southern hills, the Deccan's sharpest
    swords,
  And he! the harlot's traitor son! the goatherd Mulhar
    Rao!

Thrice thirty thousand men were we before the mists had
 cleared,
  The low white mists of morning heard the war-conch scream
   and bray;
We called upon Bhowani and we gripped them by the beard,
  We rolled upon them like a flood and washed their ranks
   away.

The children of the hills of Khost before our lances ran,
  We drove the black Rohillas back as cattle to the pen;
'T was then we needed Mulhar Rao to end what we began,
  A thousand men had saved the charge; he fled the field
   with ten!

There was no room to clear a sword — no power to strike a
 blow,
  For foot to foot, ay, breast to breast, the battle held us
   fast —
Save where the naked hill-men ran, and stabbing from below
  Brought down the horse and rider and we trampled them
   and passed.

To left the roar of musketry rang like a falling flood —
  To right the sunshine rippled red from redder lance and
   blade —
Above the dark *Upsaras* [1] flew, beneath us plashed the blood,
  And, bellying black against the dust, the Bhagwa Jhanda
   swayed.

I saw it fall in smoke and fire, the Banner of the Bhao;
  I heard a voice across the press of one who called in vain : —
" Ho! Anand Rao Nimbalkhur, ride! Get aid of Mulhar
   Rao!
  " Go shame his squadrons into fight — the Bhao — the
   Bhao is slain!"

[1] The Choosers of the Slain.

Thereat, as when a sand-bar breaks in clotted spume and
    spray —
When rain of later autumn sweeps the Jumna water-head,
Before their charge from flank to flank our riven ranks gave
    way;
    But of the waters of that flood the Jumna fords ran red.

 held by Scindia, my lord, as close as man might hold;
    A Soobah of the Deccan asks no aid to guard his life;
But Holkar's Horse were flying, and our chiefest chiefs were
    cold,
    And like a flame among us leapt the long lean Northern
    knife.

 held by Scindia — my lance from butt to tuft was dyed,
    The froth of battle bossed the shield and roped the bridle-
    chain —
What time beneath our horses' feet a maiden rose and cried,
    And clung to Scindia, and I turned a sword-cut from the
    twain.

He set a spell upon the maid in woodlands long ago,
    A hunter by the Tapti banks, she gave him water there:
He turned her heart to water, and she followed to her woe.
    What need had he of Lalun who had twenty maids as fair?)

Now in that hour strength left my lord; he wrenched his mare
    aside;
    He bound the girl behind him and we slashed and struggled
    free.
Across the reeling wreck of strife we rode as shadows ride
    From Paniput to Delhi town, but not alone were we.

T'was Lutuf-Ullah Populzai laid horse upon our track,
    A swine-fed reiver of the North that lusted for the maid;
 might have barred his path awhile, but Scindia called me
    back,
    And I — O woe for Scindia! — I listened and obeyed.

League after league the formless scrub took shape and glided
    by —
    League after league the white road swirled behind the white
      mare's feet —
League after league, when leagues were done, we heard the
    Populzai,
    Where sure as Time and swift as Death the tireless footfall
      beat.

Noon's eye beheld that shame of flight, the shadows fell, we
    fled
    Where steadfast as the wheeling kite he followed in our
      train;
The black wolf warred where we had warred, the jackal
    mocked our dead,
    And terror born of twilight-tide made mad the labouring
      brain.

I gasped: — "A kingdom waits my lord; her love is but her
    own.
    "A day shall mar, a day shall cure for her — but what for
      thee?
"Cut loose the girl: he follows fast. Cut loose and ride
    alone!"
    Then Scindia 'twixt his blistered lips: — "My Queens'
      Queen shall she be!

"Of all who ate my bread last night 't was she alone that came
    "To seek her love between the spears and find her crown
      therein!
"One shame is mine to-day, what need the weight of double
    shame?
    "If once we reach the Delhi gate, though all be lost, I win!"

We rode — the white mare failed — her trot a staggering
    stumble grew, —
    The cooking-smoke of even rose and weltered and hung low
And still we heard the Populzai and still we strained anew,
    And Delhi town was very near, but nearer was the foe.

Yea, Delhi town was very near when Lalun whispered: —
    " Slay!
    " Lord of my life, the mare sinks fast — stab deep and let
       me die! "
But Scindia would not, and the maid tore free and flung
       away,
    And turning as she fell we heard the clattering Populzai.

Then Scindia checked the gasping mare that rocked and
       groaned for breath,
    And wheeled to charge and plunged the knife a hands-
       breadth in her side —
The hunter and the hunted know how that last pause is
       death —
    The blood had chilled about her heart, she reared and fell
       and died.

Our Gods were kind. Before he heard the maiden's piteous
       scream
    A log upon the Delhi road, beneath the mare he lay —
Lost mistress and lost battle passed before him like a dream;
    The darkness closed about his eyes. I bore my King away.

THE DOVE OF DACCA

1892

THE freed dove flew to the Rajah's tower —
    Fled from the slaughter of Moslem kings —
And the thorns have covered the city of Gaur.
    Dove — dove — oh, homing dove!
Little white traitor, with woe on thy wings!

The Rajah of Dacca rode under the wall;
  He set in his bosom a dove of flight —
" If she return, be sure that I fall."
  Dove — dove — oh, homing dove!
Pressed to his heart in the thick of the fight.

" Fire the palace, the fort, and the keep —
  Leave to the foeman no spoil at all.
In the flame of the palace lie down and sleep
  If the dove, if the dove — if the homing dove
Come and alone to the palace wall."

The Kings of the North they were scattered abroad —
  The Rajah of Dacca he slew them all.
Hot from slaughter he stooped at the ford,
  And the dove — the dove — oh, the homing dove!
She thought of her cote on the palace wall.

She opened her wings and she flew away —
  Fluttered away beyond recall;
She came to the palace at break of day.
  Dove — dove — oh, homing dove!
Flying so fast for a kingdom's fall.

The Queens of Dacca they slept in flame —
  Slept in the flame of the palace old —
To save their honour from Moslem shame.
  And the dove — the dove — oh, the homing dove!
She cooed to her young where the smoke-cloud rolled.

The Rajah of Dacca rode far and fleet,
  Followed as fast as a horse could fly,
He came and the palace was black at his feet;
  And the dove — the dove — the homing dove,
Circled alone in the stainless sky.

So the dove flew to the Rajah's tower —
    Fled from the slaughter of Moslem kings;
So the thorns covered the city of Gaur,
    And Dacca was lost for a white dove's wings.
Dove — dove — oh, homing dove,
    Dacca is lost from the Roll of the Kings!

THE BALLAD OF BOH DA THONE

1888

(*Burma War*, 1883-85)

This is the ballad of Boh Da Thone,
Erst a Pretender to Theebaw's throne,
Who harried the district of Alalone:
How he met with his fate and the V. P. P.[1]
At the hand of Harendra Mukerji, ·
·   *Senior Gomashta, G. B. T.*[2]

BOH DA THONE was a warrior bold:
His sword and his Snider were bossed with gold,

And the Peacock Banner his henchmen bore
Was stiff with bullion, but stiffer with gore.

He shot at the strong and he slashed at the weak
From the Salween scrub to the Chindwin teak:

He crucified noble, he sacrificed mean,
He filled old ladies with kerosene:

While over the water the papers cried,
"The patriot fights for his countryside!"

[1] Value Payable Post = C. O. D. delivery.
[2] Head Clerk Government Bullock Train.

But little they cared for the Native Press,
The worn white soldiers in khaki dress,

Who tramped through the jungle and camped in the byre,
Who died in the swamp and were tombed in the mire,

Who gave up their lives, at the Queen's Command,
For the Pride of their Race and the Peace of the Land.

Now, first of the foemen of Boh Da Thone
Was Captain O'Neil of the " Black Tyrone,"

And his was a Company, seventy strong,
Who hustled that dissolute Chief along.

There were lads from Galway and Louth and Meath
Who went to their death with a joke in their teeth,

And worshipped with fluency, fervour, and zeal
The mud on the boot-heels of " Crook " O'Neil.

But ever a blight on their labours lay,
And ever their quarry would vanish away,

Till the sun-dried boys of the Black Tyrone
Took a brotherly interest in Boh Da Thone:

And, sooth, if pursuit in possession ends,
The Boh and his trackers were best of friends.

The word of a scout — a march by night —
A rush through the mist — a scattering fight —

A volley from cover — a corpse in the clearing —
The glimpse of a loin-cloth and heavy jade earring —

The flare of a village — the tally of slain —
And . . . the Boh was abroad on the raid again!

They cursed their luck, as the Irish will,
They gave him credit for cunning and skill,

They buried their dead, they bolted their beef,
And started anew on the track of the thief

Till, in place of the " Kalends of Greece," men said,
" When Crook and his darlings come back with the head."

They had hunted the Boh from the hills to the plain —
He doubled and broke for the hills again:

They had crippled his power for rapine and raid,
They had routed him out of his pet stockade,

And at last, they came, when the Daystar tired,
To a camp deserted — a village fired.

A black cross blistered the Morning-gold,
And the body upon it was stark and cold.

The wind of the dawn went merrily past,
The high grass bowed her plumes to the blast.

And out of the grass, on a sudden, broke
A spirtle of fire, a whorl of smoke —

And Captain O'Neil of the Black Tyrone
Was blessed with a slug in the ulnar-bone —
The gift of his enemy Boh Da Thone.

(Now a slug that is hammered from telegraph-wire
Is a thorn in the flesh and a rankling fire.)

· · · · · · ·

The shot-wound festered — as shot-wounds may
In a steaming barrack at Mandalay.

11

The left arm throbbed, and the Captain swore,
" I 'd like to be after the Boh once more! "

The fever held him — the Captain said,
" I 'd give a hundred to look at his head! "

The Hospital punkahs creaked and whirred,
But Babu Harendra (Gomashta) heard.

He thought of the cane-brake, green and dank,
That girdled his home by the Dacca tank.

He thought of his wife and his High School son,
He thought — but abandoned the thought — of a gun.

His sleep was broken by visions dread
Of a shining Boh with a silver head.

He kept his counsel and went his way,
And swindled the cartmen of half their pay.

.   .   .   .

And the months went on, as the worst must do
And the Boh returned to the raid anew.

But the Captain had quitted the long-drawn strife,
And in far Simoorie had taken a wife.

And she was a damsel of delicate mould,
With hair like the sunshine and heart of gold,

And little she knew the arms that embraced
Had cloven a man from the brow to the waist:

And little she knew that the loving lips
Had ordered a quivering life's eclipse,

And the eye that lit at her lightest breath
Had glared unawed in the Gates of Death.

For these be matters a man would hide,
As a general rule, from an innocent Bride.)

And little the Captain thought of the past,
And, of all men, Babu Harendra last.

   .   .   .   .   .

But slow, in the sludge of the Kathun road,
The Government Bullock Train toted its load.

Speckless and spotless and shining with *ghee*,[1]
In the rearmost cart sat the Babu-jee.

And ever a phantom before him fled
Of a scowling Boh with a silver head.

Then the lead-cart stuck, though the coolies slaved,
And the cartmen flogged and the escort raved;

And out of the jungle, with yells and squeals,
Pranced Boh Da Thone, and his gang at his heels!

Then belching blunderbuss answered back
The Snider's snarl and the carbine's crack,

And the blithe revolver began to sing
To the blade that twanged on the locking-ring,

And the brown flesh blued where the bay'net kissed,
As the steel shot back with a wrench and a twist,

And the great white bullocks with onyx eyes
Watched the souls of the dead arise,

And over the smoke of the fusillade
The Peacock Banner staggered and swayed.

[1] Butter.

The Babu shook at the horrible sight,
And girded his ponderous loins for flight,

But Fate had ordained that the Boh should start
On a lone-hand raid of the rearmost cart,

And out of that cart, with a bellow of woe,
The Babu fell — flat on the top of the Boh!

For years had Harendra served the State,
To the growth of his purse and the girth of his *pêt*.[1]

There were twenty stone, as the tally-man knows,
On the broad of the chest of this best of Bohs.

And twenty stone from a height discharged
Are bad for a Boh with a spleen enlarged.

Oh, short was the struggle — severe was the shock —
He dropped like a bullock — he lay like a block;

And the Babu above him, convulsed with fear,
Heard the labouring life-breath hissed out in his ear.

And thus in a fashion undignified
The princely pest of the Chindwin died.
    .   .   .   .

Turn now to Simoorie, where, all at his ease,
The Captain is petting the Bride on his knees,

Where the *whit* of the bullet, the wounded man's scream
Are mixed as the mist of some devilish dream —

Forgotten, forgotten the sweat of the shambles
Where the hill-daisy blooms and the grey monkey gambols,

---

[1] Stomach.

'rom the sword-belt set free and released from the steel,
'he Peace of the Lord is on Captain O'Neil!

Jp the hill to Simoorie — most patient of drudges —
'he bags on his shoulder, the mail-runner trudges.

For Captain O'Neil, *Sahib*. One hundred and ten
Rupees to collect on delivery."

Then

Their breakfast was stopped while the screw-jack and
     hammer
'ore waxcloth, split teak-wood, and chipped out the
   dammer;)

'pen-eyed, open-mouthed, on the napery's snow,
Vith a crash and a thud, rolled — the Head of the Boh!

.nd gummed to the scalp was a letter which ran: —

" IN FIELDING FORCE SERVICE.
" Encampment,
" 10th Jan.

Dear Sir, — I have honour to send, *as you said*,
For final approval (see under) Boh's Head;

Was took by myself in most bloody affair.
By High Education brought pressure to bear.

Now violate Liberty, time being bad,
To mail V. P. P. (rupees hundred) Please add

Whatever Your Honour can pass. Price of Blood
Much cheap at one hundred, and children want food;

" So trusting Your Honour will somewhat retain
" True love and affection for Govt. Bullock Train,

" And show awful kindness to satisfy me,

　　　" I am,
　　　　" Graceful Master,
　　　　　　" Your
　　　　　　　" H. MUKERJI."

.　　.　　.　　.　　.　　.　　.

As the rabbit is drawn to the rattlesnake's power,
As the smoker's eye fills at the opium hour,

As a horse reaches up to the manger above,
As the waiting ear yearns for the whisper of love,

From the arms of the Bride, iron-visaged and slow,
The Captain bent down to the Head of the Boh.

And e'en as he looked on the Thing where It lay
'Twixt the winking new spoons and the napkins' array,

The freed mind fled back to the long-ago days —
The hand-to-hand scuffle — the smoke and the blaze —

The forced march at night and the quick rush at dawn —
The banjo at twilight, the burial ere morn —

The stench of the marshes — the raw, piercing smell
When the overhand stabbing-cut silenced the yell —

The oaths of his Irish that surged when they stood
Where the black crosses hung o'er the Kuttamow flood.

As a derelict ship drifts away with the tide
The Captain went out on the Past from his Bride,

Back, back, through the springs to the chill of the year,
When he hunted the Boh from Maloon to Tsaleer.

As the shape of a corpse dimmers up through deep water,
In his eye lit the passionless passion of slaughter,

And men who had fought with O'Neil for the life
Had gazed on his face with less dread than his wife.

For she who had held him so long could not hold him —
Though a four-month Eternity should have controlled him —

But watched the twin Terror — the head turned to head —
The scowling, scarred Black, and the flushed savage Red —

The spirit that changed from her knowing and flew to
Some grim hidden Past she had never a clue to.

But It knew as It grinned, for he touched it unfearing,
And muttered aloud, "So you kept that jade earring!"

Then nodded, and kindly, as friend nods to friend,
"Old man, you fought well, but you lost in the end."

.   .   .   .

The visions departed, and Shame followed Passion: —
"He took what I said in this horrible fashion?

"*I 'll* write to Harendra!" With language unsainted
The Captain came back to the Bride . . . who had fainted.

.   .   .   .

And this is a fiction? No. Go to Simoorie
And look at their baby, a twelve-month old Houri,

A pert little, Irish-eyed Kathleen Mavournin —
She 's always about on the Mall of a mornin' —

And you 'll see, if her right shoulder-strap is displaced,
This: *Gules* upon *argent*, a Boh's Head, *erased!*

THE SACRIFICE OF ER–HEB

1887

*E*R-HEB *beyond the Hills of Ao-Safai*
Bears witness to the truth, and Ao-Safai
Hath told the men of Gorukh. Thence the tale
Comes westward o'er the peaks to India.

The story of Bisesa, Armod's child, —
A maiden plighted to the Chief in War,
The Man of Sixty Spears, who held the Pass
That leads to Thibet, but to-day is gone
To seek his comfort of the God called Budh
The Silent — showing how the Sickness ceased
Because of her who died to save the tribe.

Taman is One and greater than us all,
Taman is One and greater than all Gods:
Taman is Two in One and rides the sky,
Curved like a stallion's croup, from dusk to dawn,
And drums upon it with his heels, whereby
Is bred the neighing thunder in the hills.

This is Taman, the God of all Er-Heb,
Who was before all Gods, and made all Gods,
And presently will break the Gods he made,
And step upon the Earth to govern men
Who give him milk-dry ewes and cheat his Priests,
Or leave his shrine unlighted — as Er-Heb
Left it unlighted and forgot Taman,
When all the Valley followed after Kysh
And Yabosh, little Gods but very wise,
And from the sky Taman beheld their sin.

He sent the Sickness out upon the hills
The Red Horse Sickness with the iron hooves,
To turn the Valley to Taman again.

And the Red Horse snuffed thrice into the wind,
The naked wind that had no fear of him;
And the Red Horse stamped thrice upon the snow,
The naked snow that had no fear of him;
And the Red Horse went out across the rocks,
The ringing rocks that had no fear of him;
And downward, where the lean birch meets the snow,
And downward, where the grey pine meets the birch,
And downward, where the dwarf oak meets the pine,
Till at his feet our cup-like pastures lay.

That night, the slow mists of the evening dropped,
Dropped as a cloth upon a dead man's face,
And weltered in the valley, bluish-white
Like water very silent — spread abroad,
Like water very silent, from the Shrine
Unlighted of Taman to where the stream
Is dammed to fill our cattle-troughs — sent up
White waves that rocked and heaved and then were still,
Till all the Valley glittered like a marsh,
Beneath the moonlight, filled with sluggish mist
Knee-deep, so that men waded as they walked.

That night, the Red Horse grazed above the Dam,
Beyond the cattle-troughs. Men heard him feed,
And those that heard him sickened where they lay.

Thus came the sickness to Er-Heb, and slew
Ten men, strong men, and of the women four;
And the Red Horse went hillward with the dawn,
But near the cattle-troughs his hoof-prints lay.

That night, the slow mists of the evening dropped,
Dropped as a cloth upon the dead, but rose
A little higher, to a young girl's height;
Till all the valley glittered like a lake,
Beneath the moonlight, filled with sluggish mist.

That night, the Red Horse grazed beyond the Dam
A stone's-throw from the troughs. Men heard him feed,
And those that heard him sickened where they lay.
Thus came the sickness to Er-Heb, and slew
Of men a score, and of the women eight,
And of the children two.

                          Because the road
To Gorukh was a road of enemies,
And Ao-Safai was blocked with early snow,
We could not flee from out the Valley. Death
Smote at us in a slaughter-pen, and Kysh
Was mute as Yabosh, though the goats were slain;
And the Red Horse grazed nightly by the stream,
And later, outward, towards the Unlighted Shrine,
And those that heard him sickened where they lay.

Then said Bisesa to the Priests at dusk,
When the white mist rose up breast-high, and choked
The voices in the houses of the dead: —
" Yabosh and Kysh avail not. If the Horse
" Reach the Unlighted Shrine we surely die.
" Ye have forgotten of all Gods the chief,
" Taman ! " Here rolled the thunder through the Hill.
And Yabosh shook upon his pedestal.
" Ye have forgotten of all Gods the chief
" Too long." And all were dumb save one, who cried
On Yabosh with the Sapphire 'twixt His knees,
But found no answer in the smoky roof,
And, being smitten of the sickness, died
Before the altar of the Sapphire Shrine.

Then said Bisesa: — " I am near to Death,
" And have the Wisdom of the Grave for gift
" To bear me on the path my feet must tread.
" If there be wealth on earth, then I am rich,
" For Armod is the first of all Er-Heb ;

"If there be beauty on the earth," — her eyes
Dropped for a moment to the temple floor, —
"Ye know that I am fair. If there be Love,
"Ye know that love is mine." The Chief in War,
The Man of Sixty Spears, broke from the press,
And would have clasped her, but the Priests withstood,
Saying: — "She has a message from Taman."
Then said Bisesa: — "By my wealth and love
"And beauty, I am chosen of the God
"Taman." Here rolled the thunder through the Hills
And Kysh fell forward on the Mound of Skulls.

In darkness, and before our Priests, the maid
Between the altars cast her bracelets down,
Therewith the heavy earrings Armod made,
When he was young, out of the water-gold
Of Gorukh — threw the breast-plate thick with jade
Upon the turquoise anklets — put aside
The bands of silver on her brow and neck;
And as the trinkets tinkled on the stones,
The thunder of Taman lowed like a bull.

Then said Bisesa, stretching out her hands,
As one in darkness fearing Devils: — "Help!
"O Priests, I am a woman very weak.
"And who am I to know the will of Gods?
"Taman hath called me — whither shall I go?"
The Chief in War, the Man of Sixty Spears,
Howled in his torment, fettered by the Priests,
But dared not come to her to drag her forth,
And dared not lift his spear against the Priests,
Then all men wept.

There was a Priest of Kysh
Bent with a hundred winters, hairless, blind,
And taloned as the great Snow-Eagle is.
His seat was nearest to the altar-fires,

And he was counted dumb among the Priests.
But, whether Kysh decreed, or from Taman
The impotent tongue found utterance we know
As little as the bats beneath the eaves.
He cried so that they heard who stood without: —
" To the Unlighted Shrine ! " and crept aside
Into the shadow of his fallen God
And whimpered, and Bisesa went her way.

That night, the slow mists of the evening dropped,
Dropped as a cloth upon the dead, and rose
Above the roofs, and by the Unlighted Shrine
Lay as the slimy water of the troughs
When murrain thins the cattle of Er-Heb:
And through the mist men heard the Red Horse feed.

In Armod's house they burned Bisesa's dower,
And killed her black bull Tor, and broke her wheel,
And loosed her hair, as for the marriage-feast,
With cries more loud than mourning for the dead.

Across the fields, from Armod's dwelling-place,
We heard Bisesa weeping where she passed
To seek the Unlighted Shrine; the Red Horse neighed
And followed her, and on the river-mint
His hooves struck dead and heavy in our ears.

Out of the mists of evening, as the star
Of Ao-Safai climbs through the black snow-blur
To show the Pass is clear, Bisesa stepped
Upon the great grey slope of mortised stone,
The Causeway of Taman.   The Red Horse neighed
Behind her to the Unlighted Shrine — then fled
North to the Mountain where his stable lies.

They know who dared the anger of Taman,
And watched that night above the clinging mists,
Far up the hill, Bisesa's passing in.

She set her hand upon the carven door,
Fouled by a myriad bats, and black with time,
Whereon is graved the Glory of Taman
In letters older than the Ao-Safai;
And twice she turned aside and twice she wept,
Cast down upon the threshold, clamouring
For him she loved — the Man of Sixty Spears,
And for her father, — and the black bull Tor,
Hers and her pride. Yea, twice she turned away
Before the awful darkness of the door,
And the great horror of the Wall of Man ·
Where Man is made the plaything of Taman,
An Eyeless Face that waits above and laughs.

But the third time she cried and put her palms
Against the hewn stone leaves, and prayed Taman
To spare Er-Heb and take her life for price.

They know who watched, the doors were rent apart
And closed upon Bisesa, and the rain
Broke like a flood across the Valley, washed
The mist away; but louder than the rain
The thunder of Taman filled men with fear.

Some say that from the Unlighted Shrine she cried
For succour, very pitifully, thrice,
And others that she sang and had no fear.
And some that there was neither song nor cry,
But only thunder and the lashing rain.

Howbeit, in the morning men rose up,
Perplexed with horror, crowding to the Shrine.
And when Er-Heb was gathered at the doors
The Priests made lamentation and passed in
To a strange Temple and a God they feared
But knew not.

            From the crevices the grass
Had thrust the altar-slabs apart, the walls
Were grey with stains unclean, the roof-beams swelled
With many-coloured growth of rottenness,
And lichen veiled the Image of Taman
In leprosy. The Basin of the Blood
Above the altar held the morning sun:
A winking ruby on its heart: below
Face hid in hands, the maid Bisesa lay.

Er-Heb beyond the Hills of Ao-Safai
Bears witness to the truth, and Ao-Safai
Hath told the men of Gorukh. Thence the tale
Comes westward o'er the peaks to India.

THE LAMENT OF THE BORDER CATTLE THIEF

1888

O WOE is me for the merry life
    I led beyond the Bar,
And a treble woe for my winsome wife
    That weeps at Shalimar.

They have taken away my long jezail,
    My shield and sabre fine,
And heaved me into the Central Jail
    For lifting of the kine.

The steer may low within the byre,
    The Jut may tend his grain,
But there 'll be neither loot nor fire
    Till I come back again.

And God have mercy on the Jut
  When once my fetters fall,
And Heaven defend the farmer's hut
  When I am loosed from thrall.

It 's woe to bend the stubborn back
  Above the grinching quern,
It 's woe to hear the leg-bar clack
  And jingle when I turn!

But for the sorrow and the shame,
  The brand on me and mine,
I 'll pay you back in leaping flame
  And loss of the butchered kine.

For every cow I spared before —
  In charity set free —
If I may reach my hold once more
  I 'll reive an honest three.

For every time I raised the lowe
  That scared the dusty plain,
By sword and cord, by torch and tow
  I 'll light the land with twain!

Ride hard, ride hard to Abazai,
  Young Sahib with the yellow hair —
Lie close, lie close as khuttucks lie,
  Fat herds below Bonair!

The one I 'll shoot at twilight-tide,
  At dawn I 'll drive the other;
The black shall mourn for hoof and hide,
  The white man for his brother.

'T is war, red war, I 'll give you then,
  War till my sinews fail;
For the wrong you have done to a chief of men,
  And a thief of the Zukka Kheyl.

And if I fall to your hand afresh
I give you leave for the sin,
That you cram my throat with the foul pig's flesh,
And swing me in the skin!

THE FEET OF THE YOUNG MEN

1897

Now the Four-way Lodge is opened, now the Huntin
Winds are loose —
Now the Smokes of Spring go up to clear the brain;
Now the Young Men's hearts are troubled for the whisper
the Trues,
Now the Red Gods make their medicine again!
Who hath seen the beaver busied?   Who hath watched tl
black-tail mating?
Who hath lain alone to hear the wild-goose cry?
Who hath worked the chosen water where the ouananiche
waiting,
Or the sea-trout's jumping-crazy for the fly?

He must go — go — go away from here!
On the other side the world he's overdue.
'Send your road is clear before you when the old Sprin
fret comes o'er you,
And the Red Gods call for you!

So for one the wet sail arching through the rainbow roun
the bow,
And for one the creak of snow-shoes on the crust;
And for one the lakeside lilies where the bull-moose waits tl
cow,
And for one the mule-train coughing in the dust.

Vho hath smelt wood-smoke at twilight? Who hath heard the
birch-log burning?
Who is quick to read the noises of the night?
.et him follow with the others, for the Young Men's feet are
turning
To the camps of proved desire and known delight!

    Let him go — go, etc.

I

)o you know the blackened timber — do you know that racing
stream
With the raw, right-angled log-jam at the end;
.nd the bar of sun-warmed shingle where a man may bask
and dream
To the click of shod canoe-poles round the bend?
t is there that we are going with our rods and reels and traces,
To a silent, smoky Indian that we know —
'o a couch of new-pulled hemlock, with the starlight on our
faces,
For the Red Gods call us out and we must go!

    They must go — go, etc.

II

)o you know the shallow Baltic where the seas are steep and
short,
Where the bluff, lee-boarded fishing-luggers ride?
)o you know the joy of threshing leagues to leeward of your
port
On a coast you 've lost the chart of overside?
t is there that I am going, with an extra hand to bale her —
Just one able 'long-shore loafer that I know.
Ie can take his chance of drowning, while I sail and sail and
sail her,
For the Red Gods call me out and I must go!

    He must go — go, etc.

12

III

Do you know the pile-built village where the sago-dealers
  trade —
  Do you know the reek of fish and wet bamboo?
Do you know the steaming stillness of the orchid-scented glade
  When the blazoned, bird-winged butterflies flap through?
It is there that I am going with my camphor, net, and boxes
  To a gentle, yellow pirate that I know —
To my little wailing lemurs, to my palms and flying-foxes,
  For the Red Gods call me out and I must go!

  He must go — go, etc.

IV

Do you know the world's white roof-tree — do you know that
  windy rift
  Where the baffling mountain-eddies chop and change?
Do you know the long day's patience, belly-down on frozen
  drift,
  While the head of heads is feeding out of range?
It is there that I am going, where the boulders and the snow
  lie,
  With a trusty, nimble tracker that I know.
I have sworn an oath, to keep it on the Horns of Ovis Poli,
  And the Red Gods call me out and I must go!

  He must go — go, etc.

Now the Four-way Lodge is opened — now the Smokes of
  Council rise —
  Pleasant smokes, ere yet 'twixt trail and trail they choose —
Now the girths and ropes are tested: now they pack their last
  supplies:
  Now our Young Men go to dance before the Trues!
Who shall meet them at those altars — who shall light them
  to that shrine?
  Velvet-footed, who shall guide them to their goal?

Unto each the voice and vision: unto each his spoor and
    sign —
Lonely mountain in the Northland, misty sweat-bath 'neath
    the Line —
    And to each a man that knows his naked soul!
White or yellow, black or copper, he is waiting, as a lover,
    Smoke of funnel, dust of hooves, or beat of train —
Where the high grass hides the horseman or the glaring flats
    discover —
Where the steamer hails the landing, or the surf-boat brings
    the rover —
Where the rails run out in sand-drift . . . Quick! ah, heave
    the camp-kit over!
    For the Red Gods make their medicine again!

    And we go — go — go away from here!
      On the other side the world we're overdue!
    'Send the road is clear before you when the old Spring-
      fret comes o'er you,
      And the Red Gods call for you!

THE TRUCE OF THE BEAR

1898

YEARLY, with tent and rifle, our careless white men go
By the pass called Muttianee, to shoot in the vale below.
Yearly by Muttianee he follows our white men in —
Matun, the old blind beggar, bandaged from brow to chin.

Eyeless, noseless, and lipless — toothless, broken of speech,
Seeking a dole at the doorway he mumbles his tale to each;
Over and over the story, ending as he began:
' Make ye no truce with Adam-zad — the Bear that walks like
    a man!

" There was a flint in my musket — pricked and primed wa
    the pan,
When I went hunting Adam-zad — the Bear that stands lik
    a man.
I looked my last on the timber, I looked my last on the snow
When I went hunting Adam-zad fifty summers ago!

" I knew his times and his seasons, as he knew mine, that fe
By night in the ripened maizefield and robbed my house o
    bread;
I knew his strength and cunning, as he knew mine, that crep
At dawn to the crowded goat-pens and plundered while I slept

" Up from his stony playground — down from his well-digge
    lair —
Out on the naked ridges ran Adam-zad the Bear;
Groaning, grunting, and roaring, heavy with stolen meals
Two long marches to northward, and I was at his heels!

" Two full marches to northward, at the fall of the secon
    night,
I came on mine enemy Adam-zad all panting from his flight.
There was a charge in the musket — pricked and primed wa
    the pan —
My finger crooked on the trigger — when he reared up lik
    a man.

" Horrible, hairy, human, with paws like hands in prayer,
Making his supplication rose Adam-zad the Bear!
I looked at the swaying shoulders, at the paunch's swag an
    swing,
And my heart was touched with pity for the monstrous, plead
    ing thing.

" Touched with pity and wonder, I did not fire then . . .
I have looked no more on women — I have walked no mor
    with men.

Nearer he tottered and nearer, with paws like hands that
     pray —
From brow to jaw that steel-shod paw, it ripped my face
     away!

" Sudden, silent, and savage, searing as flame the blow —
Faceless I fell before his feet, fifty summers ago.
I heard him grunt and chuckle — I heard him pass to his den,
He left me blind to the darkened years and the little mercy of
     men.

" Now ye go down in the morning with guns of the newer
     style,
That load (I have felt) in the middle and range (I have heard)
     a mile?
Luck to the white man's rifle, that shoots so fast and true,
But — pay, and I lift my bandage and show what the Bear
     can do!"

(Flesh like slag in the furnace, knobbed and withered and
     grey —
Matun, the old blind beggar, he gives good worth for his
     pay.)
" Rouse him at noon in the bushes, follow and press him
     hard —
Not for his ragings and roarings flinch ye from Adam-zad.

' But (pay, and I put back the bandage) this is the time to
     fear,
When he stands up like a tired man, tottering near and near;
When he stands up as pleading, in wavering, man-brute guise,
When he veils the hate and cunning of the little, swinish eyes;

' When he shows as seeking quarter, with paws like hands in
     prayer,
That is the time of peril — the time of the Truce of the Bear!"

Eyeless, noseless, and lipless, asking a dole at the door,
Matun, the old blind beggar, he tells it o'er and o'er;
Fumbling and feeling the rifles, warming his hands at the
    flame,
Hearing our careless white men talk of the morrow's game;

Over and over the story, ending as he began: —
" *There is no truce with Adam-zad, the Bear that looks like a*
    man! "

THE PEACE OF DIVES

1903

THE Word came down to Dives in Torment where he lay:
" Our World is full of wickedness, My Children maim and
    slay,
    " And the Saint and Seer and Prophet
    " Can make no better of it
" Than to sanctify and prophesy and pray.

" Rise up, rise up, thou Dives, and take again thy gold,
" And thy women and thy housen as they were to thee of old.
    " It may be grace hath found thee
    " In the furnace where We bound thee,
" And that thou shalt bring the peace My Son foretold."

Then merrily rose Dives and leaped from out his fire,
And walked abroad with diligence to do the Lord's desire;
    And anon the battles ceased,
    And the captives were released,
And Earth had rest from Goshen to Gadire.

The Word came down to Satan that raged and roared alone,
'Mid the shouting of the peoples by the cannon overthrown
  (But the Prophets, Saints, and Seers
  Set each other by the ears,
For each would claim the marvel as his own):

" Rise up, rise up, thou Satan, upon the Earth to go,
" And prove the Peace of Dives if it be good or no:
  " For all that he hath planned
  " We deliver to thy hand,
" As thy skill shall serve, to break it or bring low."

Then mightily rose Satan, and about the Earth he hied,
And breathed on Kings in idleness and Princes drunk with
    pride;
  But for all the wrong he breathed
  There was never sword unsheathed,
And the fires he lighted flickered out and died.

Then terribly rose Satan, and he darkened Earth afar,
Till he came on cunning Dives where the money-changers are;
  And he saw men pledge their gear
  For the gold that buys the spear,
And the helmet and the habergeon of war.

Yea to Dives came the Persian and the Syrian and the
    Mede —
And their hearts were nothing altered, nor their cunning nor
    their greed —
  And they pledged their flocks and farms
  For the King-compelling arms,
And Dives lent according to their need.

Then Satan said to Dives:— " Return again with me,
" Who hast broken His Commandment in the day He set thee
    free,

" Who grindest for thy greed,
" Man's belly-pinch and need;
" And the blood of Man to filthy usury!"

Then softly answered Dives where the money-changers sit: —
" My refuge is Our Master, O My Master in the Pit;
    " But behold all Earth is laid
    " In the Peace which I have made,
" And behold I wait on thee to trouble it!"

Then angrily turned Satan, and about the Seas he fled,
To shake the new-sown peoples with insult, doubt, and dread;
    But for all the sleight he used
    There was never squadron loosed,
And the brands he flung flew dying and fell dead.

Yet to Dives came Atlantis and the Captains of the West —
And their hates were nothing weakened nor their anger nor
        unrest —
    And they pawned their utmost trade
    For the dry, decreeing blade;
And Dives lent and took of them their best.

Then Satan said to Dives: — " Declare thou by The Name,
" The secret of thy subtlety that turneth mine to shame.
    " It is known through all the Hells
    " How my peoples mocked my spells,
" And my faithless Kings denied me ere I came."

Then answered cunning Dives: " Do not gold and hate abide
" At the heart of every Magic, yea, and senseless fear beside?
    " With gold and fear and hate
    " I have harnessed state to state,
" And with hate and fear and gold their hates are tied.

" For hate men seek a weapon, for fear they seek a shield —
" Keener blades and broader targes than their frantic neigh-
        bours wield —

" For gold I arm their hands,
" And for gold I buy their lands,
" And for gold I sell their enemies the yield.

" Their nearest foes may purchase, or their furthest friends
　　may lease,
" One by one from Ancient Accad to the Islands of the Seas.
　" And their covenants they make
　" For the naked iron's sake,
" But I — I trap them armoured into peace.

" The flocks that Egypt pledged me to Assyria I drave,
" And Pharaoh hath the increase of the herds that Sargon
　　gave.
　" Not for Ashdod overthrown
　" Will the Kings destroy their own,
" Or their peoples wake the strife they feign to brave.

" Is not Calno like Carchemish?　For the steeds of their
　　desire
" They have sold me seven harvests that I sell to Crowning
　　Tyre;
　" And the Tyrian sweeps the plains
　" With a thousand hired wains,
" And the Cities keep the peace and — share the hire.

" Hast thou seen the pride of Moab?　For the swords about his
　　path,
" His bond is to Philistia, in half of all he hath.
　" And he dare not draw the sword
　" Till Gaza give the word,
" And he show release from Askalon and Gath.

" Wilt thou call again thy peoples, wilt thou craze anew thy
　　Kings?
" Lo! my lightnings pass before thee, and their whistling
　　servant brings,

" Ere the drowsy street hath stirred —
" Every masked and midnight word,
" And the nations break their fast upon these things.

" So I make a jest of Wonder, and a mock of Time and Space,
" The roofless Seas an hostel, and the Earth a market-place,
  " Where the anxious traders know
  " Each is surety for his foe,
" And none may thrive without his fellows' grace.

" Now this is all my subtlety and this is all my wit,
" God give thee good enlightenment, My Master in the Pit.
  " But behold all Earth is laid
  " In the Peace which I have made,
" And behold I wait on thee to trouble it!"

AN IMPERIAL RESCRIPT

1890

Now this is the tale of the Council the German Kaiser
    decreed,
To ease the strong of their burden, to help the weak in their
    need,
He sent a word to the peoples, who struggle, and pant, and
    sweat,
That the straw might be counted fairly and the tally of bricks
    be set.

The Lords of Their Hands assembled; from the East and the
    West they drew —
Baltimore, Lille, and Essen, Brummagem, Clyde, and Crewe.
And some were black from the furnace, and some were brown
    from the soil,
And some were blue from the dye-vat; but all were wearied of
    toil.

And the young King said: — " I have found it, the road to
    the rest ye seek:
" The strong shall wait for the weary, the hale shall halt for
    the weak;
" With the even tramp of an army where no man breaks from
    the line,
" Ye shall march to peace and plenty in the bond of brother-
    hood — sign!"

The paper lay on the table, the strong heads bowed thereby,
And a wail went up from the peoples: — " Ay, sign — give
    rest, for we die!"
A hand was stretched to the goose-quill, a fist was cramped to
    scrawl,
When — the laugh of a blue-eyed maiden ran clear through
    the council-hall.

And each one heard Her laughing as each one saw Her
    plain —
Saidie, Mimi, or Olga, Gretchen, or Mary Jane.
And the Spirit of Man That is in Him to the light of the
    vision woke;
And the men drew back from the paper, as a Yankee delegate
    spoke: —

" There's a girl in Jersey City who works on the telephone;
" We're going to hitch our horses and dig for a house of our
    own,
" With gas and water connections, and steam heat through to
    the top;
" And, W. Hohenzollern, I guess I shall work till I drop."

And an English delegate thundered: — " The weak an' the
    lame be blowed!
" I've a berth in the Sou'-West workshops, a home in the
    Wandsworth Road;
" And till the 'sociation has footed my buryin' bill,
" I work for the kids an' the missus. Pull up! I'll be damned
    if I will!"

And over the German benches the bearded whisper ran: —
" Lager, der girls und der dollars, dey makes or dey breaks
    a man.
" If Schmitt haf collared der dollars, he collars der girl
    deremit;
" But if Schmitt bust in der pizness, we collars der girl from
    Schmitt."

They passed one resolution: — " Your sub-committee believe
" You can lighten the curse of Adam when you 've lifted
    the curse of Eve.
" But till we are built like angels, with hammer and chisel
    and pen,
" We will work for ourself and a woman, for ever and ever,
    amen."

Now this is the tale of the Council the German Kaiser held —
The day that they razored the Grindstone, the day that the
    Cat was belled,
The day of the Figs from Thistles, the day of the Twisted
    Sands,
The day that the laugh of a maiden made light of the Lords of
    Their Hands.

ET DONA FERENTES

1896

IN extended observation of the ways and works of man,
From the Four-mile Radius roughly to the plains of Hin-
    dustan:
I have drunk with mixed assemblies, seen the racial ruction
    rise,
And the men of half creation damning half creation's eyes.

I have watched them in their tantrums, all that pentecostal
    crew,
French, Italian, Arab, Spaniard, Dutch and Greek, and Russ
    and Jew,
Celt and savage, buff and ochre, cream and yellow, mauve and
    white.
But it never really mattered till the English grew polite;

Till the men with polished toppers, till the men in long frock-
    coats,
Till the men that do not duel, till the men who war with votes,
Till the breed that take their pleasures as Saint Lawrence took
    his grid,
Began to " beg your pardon " and — the knowing croupier
    hid.

Then the bandsmen with their fiddles, and the girls that bring
    the beer,
Felt the psychologic moment, left the lit casino clear;
But the uninstructed alien, from the Teuton to the Gaul,
Was entrapped, once more, my country, by that suave, decep-
    tive drawl.

    .   .   .   .   .   .

As it was in ancient Suez or 'neath wilder, milder skies,
I " observe with apprehension " when the racial ructions rise;
And with keener apprehension, if I read the times aright,
Hear the old casino order: " Watch your man, but be polite.

" Keep your temper. Never answer (*that* was why they spat
    and swore).
Don't hit first, but move together (there 's no hurry) to the
    door.
Back to back, and facing outward while the linguist tells 'em
    how —
' *Nous sommes allong à notre batteau, nous ne voulong pas
    un row.*' "

So the hard, pent rage ate inward, till some idiot went too
    far . . .
"Let 'em have it!" and they had it, and the same was merry
    war.
Fist, umbrella, cane, decanter, lamp and beer-mug, chair and
    boot —
Till behind the fleeing legions rose the long, hoarse yell for
    loot.

Then the oil-cloth with its numbers, like a banner fluttered
    free;
Then the grand piano cantered, on three castors, down the
    quay;
White, and breathing through their nostrils, silent, systematic,
    swift —
They removed, effaced, abolished all that man could heave or
    lift.

Oh, my country, bless the training that from cot to castle
    runs —
The pitfall of the stranger but the bulwark of thy sons —
Measured speech and ordered action, sluggish soul and
    unperturbed,
Till we wake our Island-Devil — nowise cool for being curbed!

When the heir of all the ages " has the honour to remain,"
When he will not hear an insult, though men make it ne'er so
    plain,
When his lips are schooled to meekness, when his back is bowed
    to blows —
Well the keen *aas-vogels* know it — well the waiting jackal
    knows.

Build on the flanks of Etna where the sullen smoke-puffs float—
Or bathe in tropic waters where the lean fin dogs the boat —
Cock the gun that is not loaded, cook the frozen dynamite —
But oh, beware my country, when my country grows polite!

SERVICE SONGS

SOUTH AFRICAN WAR

1900-1902

BEFORE A MIDNIGHT BREAKS
IN STORM

1903

BEFORE a midnight breaks in storm,
  Or herded sea in wrath,
Ye know what wavering gusts inform
  The greater tempest's path ?
    Till the loosed wind
    Drive all from mind,
Except Distress, which, so will prophets cry,
O'ercame them, houseless, from the unhinting sky.

Ere rivers league against the land
  In piratry of flood,
Ye know what waters slip and stand
  Where seldom water stood.
    Yet who will note,
    Till fields afloat,
And washen carcass and the returning well,
Trumpet what these poor heralds strove to tell ?

Ye know who use the Crystal Ball
  (To peer by stealth on Doom),
The Shade that, shaping first of all,
  Prepares an empty room.
    Then doth It pass
    Like breath from glass,
But, on the extorted vision bowed intent,
. *No man considers why It came or went.*
13

Before the years reborn behold
  Themselves with stranger eye,
And the sport-making Gods of old,
  Like Samson slaying, die,
    Many shall hear
    The all-pregnant sphere,
Bow to the birth and sweat, but — speech denied —
Sit dumb or — dealt in part — fall weak and wide.

Yet instant to fore-shadowed need
  The eternal balance swings;
That winged men the Fates may breed
  So soon as Fate hath wings.
    These shall possess
    Our littleness,
And in the imperial task (as worthy) lay
Up our lives' all to piece one giant day.

THE BELL BUOY

1896

THEY christened my brother of old —
  And a saintly name he bears —
They gave him his place to hold
  At the head of the belfry-stairs,
  Where the minster-towers stand
And the breeding kestrels cry.
  Would I change with my brother a league inland?
(*Shoal! 'Ware shoal!*) Not I!

In the flush of the hot June prime,
  O'er smooth flood-tides afire,
I hear him hurry the chime
  To the bidding of checked Desire;

Till the sweated ringers tire
And the wild bob-majors die.
   Could I wait for my turn in the godly choir?
(*Shoal! 'Ware shoal!*) Not I!

When the smoking scud is blown,
   When the greasy wind-rack lowers,
Apart and at peace and alone,
   He counts the changeless hours.
   He wars with darkling Powers
(I war with a darkling sea);
   Would he stoop to my work in the gusty mirk?
(*Shoal! 'Ware shoal!*) Not he!

There was never a priest to pray,
   There was never a hand to toll,
When they made me guard of the bay,
   And moored me over the shoal.
   I rock, I reel, and I roll —
My four great hammers ply —
   Could I speak or be still at the Church's will?
(*Shoal! 'Ware shoal!*) Not I!

The landward marks have failed,
   The fog-bank glides unguessed,
The seaward lights are veiled,
   The spent deep feigns her rest:
   But my ear is laid to her breast,
I lift to the swell — I cry!
   Could I wait in sloth on the Church's oath?
(*Shoal! 'Ware shoal!*) Not I!

At the careless end of night
   I thrill to the nearing screw;
I turn in the clearing light
   And I call to the drowsy crew;

And the mud boils foul and blue
As the blind bow backs away.
  Will they give me their thanks if they clear the banks?
(*Shoal! 'Ware shoal!*) Not they!

The beach-pools cake and skim,
  The bursting spray-heads freeze,
I gather on crown and rim
  The grey, grained ice of the seas,
  Where, sheathed from bitt to trees,
The plunging colliers lie.
  Would I barter my place for the Church's grace?
(*Shoal! 'Ware shoal!*) Not I!

Through the blur of the whirling snow,
  Or the black of the inky sleet,
The lanterns gather and grow,
  And I look for the homeward fleet.
  Rattle of block and sheet —
" Ready about — stand by! "
  Shall I ask them a fee ere they fetch the quay?
(*Shoal! 'Ware shoal!*) Not I!

I dip and I surge and I swing
  In the rip of the racing tide,
By the gates of doom I sing,
  On the horns of death I ride.
  A ship-length overside,
Between the course and the sand,
  Fretted and bound I bide
      Peril whereof I cry.
  Would I change with my brother a league inland?
(*Shoal! 'Ware shoal!*) Not I!

THE OLD ISSUE

October 9, 1899

"*Here is nothing new nor aught unproven,*" *say the*
  Trumpets,
  "*Many feet have worn it and the road is old indeed.*
"*It is the King — the King we schooled aforetime!*"
  (*Trumpets in the marshes — in the eyot at Runnymede!*)

"*Here is neither haste, nor hate, nor anger,*" *peal the*
  Trumpets,
  "*Pardon for his penitence or pity for his fall.*
"*It is the King!*" — *inexorable Trumpets* —
  (*Trumpets round the scaffold at the dawning by White-*
  hall!)
  .   .   .   .

"*He hath veiled the crown and hid the sceptre,*" *warn the*
  Trumpets,
  "*He hath changed the fashion of the lies that cloak his*
  will.
"*Hard die the Kings — ah hard — dooms hard!*" *declare*
  the Trumpets,
  Trumpets at the gang-plank where the brawling troop-
  decks fill!

Ancient and Unteachable, abide — abide the trumpets!
  Once again the Trumpets, for the shuddering ground-swell
  brings
Clamour over ocean of the harsh pursuing Trumpets —
  Trumpets of the Vanguard that have sworn no truce with
  Kings!

All we have of freedom, all we use or know —
This our fathers bought for us long and long ago.

Ancient Right unnoticed as the breath we draw —
Leave to live by no man's leave, underneath the Law.

Lance and torch and tumult, steel and grey-goose wing
Wrenched it, inch and ell and all, slowly from the King.

Till our fathers 'stablished, after bloody years,
How our King is one with us, first among his peers.

So they bought us freedom — not at little cost —
Wherefore must we watch the King, lest our gain be lost.

Over all things certain, this is sure indeed,
Suffer not the old King: for we know the breed.

Give no ear to bondsmen bidding us endure,
Whining " He is weak and far "; crying " Time shall cure."

(Time himself is witness, till the battle joins,
Deeper strikes the rottenness in the people's loins.)

Give no heed to bondsmen masking war with peace.
Suffer not the old King here or overseas.

They that beg us barter — wait his yielding mood —
Pledge the years we hold in trust — pawn our brother's
        blood —

Howso' great their clamour, whatsoe'er their claim,
Suffer not the old King under any name!

Here is naught unproven — here is naught to learn.
It is written what shall fall if the King return.

He shall mark our goings, question whence we came,
Set his guards about us, as in Freedom's name.

He shall take a tribute, toll of all our ware;
He shall change our gold for arms — arms we may not bear.

He shall break his Judges if they cross his word;
He shall rule above the Law calling on the Lord.

He shall peep and mutter; and the night shall bring
Watchers 'neath our window, lest we mock the King —

Hate and all division; hosts of hurrying spies;
Money poured in secret, carrion breeding flies.

Strangers of his counsel, hirelings of his pay,
These shall deal our Justice: sell — deny — delay.

We shall drink dishonour, we shall eat abuse
For the Land we look to — for the Tongue we use.

We shall take our station, dirt beneath his feet,
While his hired captains jeer us in the street.

Cruel in the shadow, crafty in the sun,
Far beyond his borders shall his teachings run.

Sloven, sullen, savage, secret, uncontrolled —
Laying on a new land evil of the old;

Long-forgotten bondage, dwarfing heart and brain —
All our fathers died to loose he shall bind again.

Here is naught at venture, random nor untrue —
Swings the wheel full-circle, brims the cup anew.

Here is naught unproven, here is nothing hid:
Step for step and word for word — so the old Kings did!

Step by step, and word by word: who is ruled may read.
Suffer not the old Kings — for we know the breed —

All the right they promise — all the wrong they bring.
Stewards of the Judgment, suffer not this King!

THE LESSON

(1899 – 1902)

LET us admit it fairly, as a business people should,
We have had no end of a lesson: it will do us no end of good.

Not on a single issue, or in one direction or twain,
But conclusively, comprehensively, and several times and
　　again,
Were all our most holy illusions knocked higher than Gilde-
　　roy's kite.
We have had a jolly good lesson, and it serves us jolly well
　　right!

This was not bestowèd us under the trees, nor yet in the shade
　　of a tent,
But swingingly, over eleven degrees of a bare brown conti-
　　nent.
From Lamberts to Delagoa Bay, and from Pietersburg to
　　Sutherland,
Fell the phenomenal lesson we learned — with a fulness ac-
　　corded no other land.

It was our fault, and our very great fault, and *not* the
　　judgment of Heaven.
We made an Army in our own image, on an island nine by
　　seven,
Which faithfully mirrored its makers' ideals, equipment, and
　　mental attitude —
And so we got our lesson: and we ought to accept it with
　　gratitude.

We have spent two hundred million pounds to prove the fact
　　once more,
That horses are quicker than men afoot, since two and two
　　make four:

And horses have four legs, and men have two legs, and two
into four goes twice,
And nothing over except our lesson — and very cheap at the
price.

For remember (this our children shall know: we are too near
for that knowledge)
Not our mere astonied camps, but Council and Creed and
College —
All the obese, unchallenged old things that stifle and overlie
us —
Have felt the effects of the lesson we got — an advantage no
money could buy us!

Then let us develop this marvellous asset which we alone
command,
And which, it may subsequently transpire, will be worth as
much as the Rand:
Let us approach this pivotal fact in a humble yet hopeful
mood —
We have had no end of a lesson: it will do us no end of good!

It was our fault, and our very great fault — and now we
must turn it to use;
We have forty million reasons for failure, but not a single
excuse!
So the more we work and the less we talk the better results
we shall get —
We have had an Imperial lesson; it may make us an Empire
yet!

THE ISLANDERS

1902

No doubt but ye are the People — your throne is above th[e]
    King's.
Whoso speaks in your presence must say acceptable things[,]
Bowing the head in worship, bending the knee in fear —
Bringing the word well smoothen — such as a King shoul[d]
    hear.

Fenced by your careful fathers, ringed by your leaden sea[s,]
Long did ye wake in quiet and long lie down at ease;
Till ye said of Strife, " What is it? " of the Sword, " It is fa[r]
    from our ken ";
Till ye made a sport of your shrunken hosts and a toy of you[r]
    armed men.
Ye stopped your ears to the warning — ye would neith[er]
    look nor heed —
Ye set your leisure before their toil and your lusts above the[ir]
    need.
Because of your witless learning and your beasts of warre[n]
    and chase,
Ye grudged your sons to their service and your fields for the[ir]
    camping-place.
Ye forced them glean in the highways the straw for the bric[k]
    they brought;
Ye forced them follow in byways the craft that ye neve[r]
    taught.
Ye hindered and hampered and crippled; ye thrust out o[f]
    sight and away
Those that would serve you for honour and those that serve[d]
    you for pay:
Then were the judgments loosened; then was your sham[e]
    revealed,
At the hands of a little people, few but apt in the field.

Yet ye were saved by a remnant (and your land's long-
suffering star),
When your strong men cheered in their millions while your
striplings went to the war.
Sons of the sheltered city — unmade, unhandled, unmeet —
Ye pushed them raw to the battle as ye picked them raw from
the street.
And what did ye look they should compass? Warcraft
learned in a breath,
Knowledge unto occasion at the first far view of Death?
So! And ye train your horses and the dogs ye feed and
prize?
How are the beasts more worthy than the souls your sacrifice?
But ye said, " Their valour shall show them "; but ye said,
" The end is close."
And ye sent them comfits and pictures to help them harry
your foes,
And ye vaunted your fathomless power, and ye flaunted your
iron pride,
Ere — ye fawned on the Younger Nations for the men who
could shoot and ride!
Then ye returned to your trinkets; then ye contented your
souls
With the flannelled fools at the wicket or the muddied oafs at
the goals.
Given to strong delusion, wholly believing a lie,
Ye saw that the land lay fenceless, and ye let the months go
by
Waiting some easy wonder: hoping some saving sign —
Idle — openly idle — in the lee of the forespent Line.
Idle — except for your boasting — and what is your boast-
ing worth
If ye grudge a year of service to the lordliest life on earth?
Ancient, effortless, ordered, cycle on cycle set,
Life so long untroubled, that ye who inherit forget
It was not made with the mountains, it is not one with the
deep.

Men, not gods, devised it.   Men, not gods, must keep.
Men, not children, servants, or kinsfolk called from afar,
But each man born in the Island broke to the matter of wa
Soberly and by custom taken and trained for the same;
Each man born in the Island entered at youth to the game —
As it were almost cricket, not to be mastered in haste,
But after trial and labour, by temperance, living chaste.
As it were almost cricket — as it were even your play,
Weighed and pondered and worshipped, and practised da
    and day.
So ye shall bide sure-guarded when the restless lightning
    wake
In the womb of the blotting war-cloud, and the pallid natior
    quake.
So, at the haggard trumpets, instant your soul shall leap
Forthright, accoutred, accepting — alert from the wells c
    sleep.
So at the threat ye shall summon — so at the need ye sha
    send
Men, not children or servants, tempered and taught to th
    end;
Cleansed of servile panic, slow to dread or despise,
Humble because of knowledge, mighty by sacrifice. . . .
But ye say, " It will mar our comfort."   Ye say, " It wi
    minish our trade."
Do ye wait for the spattered shrapnel ere ye learn how a gu
    is laid?
For the low, red glare to southward when the raided coast
    towns burn?
(Light ye shall have on that lesson, but little time to learn.
Will ye pitch some white pavilion, and lustily even the odd
With nets and hoops and mallets, with rackets and bats an
    rods?
Will the rabbit war with your foemen — the red deer hor
    them for hire?
Your kept cock-pheasant keep you? — he is master of man
    a shire.

Arid, aloof, incurious, unthinking, unthanking, gelt,
Will ye loose your schools to flout them till their brow-beat
columns melt?
Will ye pray them or preach them, or print them, or ballot
them back from your shore?
Will your workmen issue a mandate to bid them strike no
more?
Will ye rise and dethrone your rulers? (Because ye were idle
both?
Pride by Insolence chastened? Indolence purged by Sloth?)
No doubt but ye are the People; who shall make you afraid?
Also your gods are many; no doubt but your gods shall aid.
Idols of greasy altars built for the body's ease;
Proud little brazen Baals and talking fetishes;
Teraphs of sept and party and wise wood-pavement gods —
These shall come down to the battle and snatch you from
under the rods?
From the gusty, flickering gun-roll with viewless salvoes
rent,
And the pitted hail of the bullets that tell not whence they
were sent.
When ye are ringed as with iron, when ye are scourged as
with whips,
When the meat is yet in your belly, and the boast is yet on
your lips;
When ye go forth at morning and the noon beholds you
broke,
Ere ye lie down at even, your remnant, under the yoke?

No doubt but ye are the People — absolute, strong, and wise;
Whatever your heart has desired ye have not withheld from
your eyes.
On your own heads, in your own hands, the sin and the saving
lies!

THE DYKES

1902

We have no heart for the fishing, we have no hand for the
    oar —
All that our fathers taught us of old pleases us now no more;
All that our own hearts bid us believe we doubt where we do
    not deny —
There is no proof in the bread we eat or rest in the toil we
    ply.

Look you, our foreshore stretches far through sea-gate,
    dyke, and groin —
Made land all, that our fathers made, where the flats and the
    fairway join.
They forced the sea a sea-league back. They died, and their
    work stood fast.
We were born to peace in the lee of the dykes, but the time
    of our peace is past.

Far off, the full tide clambers and slips, mouthing and testing
    all,
Nipping the flanks of the water-gates, baying along the wall;
Turning the shingle, returning the shingle, changing the set
    of the sand . . .
We are too far from the beach, men say, to know how the out-
    works stand.

So we come down, uneasy, to look, uneasily pacing the beach.
These are the dykes our fathers made: we have never known
    a breach.
Time and again has the gale blown by and we were not afraid;
Now we come only to look at the dykes — at the dykes our
    fathers made.

O'er the marsh where the homesteads cower apart the har-
ried sunlight flies,
Shifts and considers, wanes and recovers, scatters and sickens
and dies —
An evil ember bedded in ash — a spark blown west by the
wind . . .
We are surrendered to night and the sea — the gale and the
tide behind!

At the bridge of the lower saltings the cattle gather and blare,
Roused by the feet of running men, dazed by the lantern
glare.
Unbar and let them away for their lives — the levels drown
as they stand,
Where the flood-wash forces the sluices aback and the ditches
deliver inland.

Ninefold deep to the top of the dykes the galloping breakers
stride,
And their overcarried spray is a sea — a sea on the landward
side.
Coming, like stallions they paw with their hooves, going they
snatch with their teeth,
Till the bents and the furze and the sand are dragged out,
and the old-time hurdles beneath!

Bid men gather fuel for fire, the tar, the oil and the tow —
Flame we shall need, not smoke, in the dark if the riddled
sea-banks go.
Bid the ringers watch in the tower (who knows what the
dawn shall prove?)
Each with his rope between his feet and the trembling bells
above.

Now we can only wait till the day, wait and apportion our
shame.
These are the dykes our fathers left, but we would not look
to the same.

Time and again were we warned of the dykes, time and again
    we delayed:
Now, it may fall, we have slain our sons as our fathers we
    have betrayed.

.   .   .   .

Walking along the wreck of the dykes, watching the work of
    the seas,
These were the dykes our fathers made to our great profit
    and ease;
But the peace is gone and the profit is gone, and the old sure
    day withdrawn . . .
That our own houses show as strange when we come back in
    the dawn!

THE WAGE–SLAVES

1902

OH glorious are the guarded heights
    Where guardian souls abide —
Self-exiled from our gross delights —
    Above, beyond, outside:
An ampler arc their spirit swings —
    Commands a juster view —
We have their word for all these things,
    Nor doubt their words are true.

Yet we the bondslaves of our day,
    Whom dirt and danger press —
Co-heirs of insolence, delay,
    And leagued unfaithfulness —
Such is our need must seek indeed
    And, having found, engage
The men who merely do the work
    For which they draw the wage.

From forge and farm and mine and bench,
   Deck, altar, outpost lone —
Mill, school, battalion, counter, trench,
   Rail, senate, sheepfold, throne —
Creation's cry goes up on high
   From age to cheated age:
" Send us the men who do the work
   " For which they draw the wage."

Words cannot help nor wit achieve,
   Nor e'en the all-gifted fool,
Too weak to enter, bide, or leave
   The lists he cannot rule.
Beneath the sun we count on none
   Our evil to assuage,
Except the men that do the work
   For which they draw the wage.

When through the Gates of Stress and Strain
   Comes forth the vast Event —
The simple, sheer, sufficing, sane
   Result of labour spent —
They that have wrought the end unthought
   Be neither saint nor sage,
But only men who did the work
   For which they drew the wage.

Wherefore to these the Fates shall bend
   (And all old idle things —)
Wherefore on these shall Power attend
   Beyond the grip of kings:
Each in his place, by right, not grace,
   Shall rule his heritage —
The men who simply do the work
   For which they draw the wage.
14

Not such as scorn the loitering street,
    Or waste to earn its praise,
Their noontide's unreturning heat
    About their morning ways:
But such as dower each mortgaged hour
    Alike with clean couràge —
Even the men who do the work
    For which they draw the wage —
Men like to Gods that do the work
    For which they draw the wage —
Begin — continue — close that work
    For which they draw the wage!

RIMMON

1903

DULY with knees that feign to quake —
    Bent head and shaded brow, —
Yet once again, for my father's sake,
    In Rimmon's House I bow.

The curtains part, the trumpet blares,
    And the eunuchs howl aloud;
And the gilt, swag-bellied idol glares
    Insolent over the crowd.

" *This is Rimmon, Lord of the Earth —*
    " *Fear Him and bow the knee!* "
And I watch my comrades hide their mirth
    That rode to the wars with me.

For we remember the sun and the sand
    And the rocks whereon we trod,
Ere we came to a scorched and a scornful land
    That did not know our God;

As we remember the sacrifice
  Dead men an hundred laid —
Slain while they served His mysteries
  And that He would not aid.

Not though we gashed ourselves and wept,
  For the high-priest bade us wait;
Saying He went on a journey or slept,
  Or was drunk or had taken a mate.

(*Praise ye Rimmon, King of Kings,*
  Who ruleth Earth and Sky!
And again I bow as the censer swings
  And the God Enthroned goes by.)

Ay, we remember His sacred ark
  And the virtuous men that knelt
To the dark and the hush behind the dark
  Wherein we dreamed He dwelt;

Until we entered to hale Him out,
  And found no more than an old
Uncleanly image girded about
  The loins with scarlet and gold.

Him we o'erset with the butts of our spears —
  Him and his vast designs —
To be the scorn of our muleteers
  And the jest of our halted lines.

By the picket-pins that the dogs defile,
  In the dung and the dust He lay,
Till the priests ran and chattered awhile
  And wiped Him and took Him away.

Hushing the matter before it was known,
  They returned to our fathers afar,
And hastily set Him afresh on His throne
  Because He had won us the war.

Wherefore with knees that feign to quake —
  Bent head and shaded brow —   .
To this dead dog, for my father's sake,
  In Rimmon's House I bow.

THE REFORMERS

1 9 0 1

NOT in the camp his victory lies
  Or triumph in the market-place,
Who is his Nation's sacrifice
  To turn the judgment from his race.

Happy is he who, bred and taught
  By sleek, sufficing Circumstance —
Whose Gospel was the apparelled thought,
  Whose Gods were Luxury and Chance —

Sees, on the threshold of his days,
  The old life shrivel like a scroll,
And to unheralded dismays
  Submits his body and his soul;

The fatted shows wherein he stood
  Foregoing, and the idiot pride,
That he may prove with his own blood
  All that his easy sires denied —

Ultimate issues, primal springs,
  Demands, abasements, penalties —
The imperishable plinth of things
  Seen and unseen, that touch our peace.

For, though ensnaring ritual dim
   His vision through the after-years,
Yet virtue shall go out of him:
   Example profiting his peers.

With great things charged he shall not hold
   Aloof till great occasion rise,
But serve, full-harnessed, as of old,
   The Days that are the Destinies.

He shall forswear and put away
   The idols of his sheltered house;
And to Necessity shall pay
   Unflinching tribute of his vows.

He shall not plead another's act,
   Nor bind him in another's oath
To weigh the Word above the Fact,
   Or make or take excuse for sloth.

The yoke he bore shall press him still,
   And long-ingrained effort goad
To find, to fashion, and fulfil
   The cleaner life, the sterner code.

Not in the camp his victory lies —
   The world (unheeding his return)
Shall see it in his children's eyes
   And from his grandson's lips shall learn!

THE OLD MEN

1902

THIS is our lot if we live so long and labour unto the end —
That we outlive the impatient years and the much too patient
friend :
And because we know we have breath in our mouth and think
we have thought in our head,
We shall assume that we are alive, whereas we are really dead.

We shall not acknowledge that old stars fade or alien planets
arise
(That the sere bush buds or the desert blooms or the ancient
well-head dries),
Or any new compass wherewith new men adventure 'neath
new skies.

We shall lift up the ropes that constrained our youth, to bind
on our children's hands ;
We shall call to the water below the bridges to return and
replenish our lands ;
We shall harness horses (Death's own pale horses) and
scholarly plough the sands.

We shall lie down in the eye of the sun for lack of a light on
our way —
We shall rise up when the day is done and chirrup, " Behold,
it is day ! "
We shall abide till the battle is won ere we amble into the
fray.

We shall peck out and discuss and dissect, and evert and ex-
trude to our mind,
The flaccid tissues of long-dead issues offensive to God and
mankind —
(Precisely like vultures over an ox that the Army has left
behind).

We shall make walk preposterous ghosts of the glories we once
    created —
(Immodestly smearing from muddled palettes amazing pig-
    ments mismated)
And our friends will weep when we ask them with boasts if
    our natural force be abated.

The Lamp of our Youth will be utterly out: but we shall
    subsist on the smell of it,
And whatever we do, we shall fold our hands and suck our
    gums and think well of it.
Yes, we shall be perfectly pleased with our work, and that
    is the Perfectest Hell of it!

This is our lot if we live so long and listen to those who love
    us —
That we are shunned by the people about and shamed by the
    Powers above us.
Wherefore be free of your harness betimes; but being free be
    assured,
That he who hath not endured to the death, from his birth he
    hath never endured!

THE WHITE MAN'S BURDEN

1899

TAKE up the White Man's burden —
    Send forth the best ye breed —
Go bind your sons to exile
    To serve your captives' need;
To wait in heavy harness,
    On fluttered folk and wild —
Your new-caught, sullen peoples,
    Half-devil and half-child.

Take up the White Man's burden —
  In patience to abide,
To veil the threat of terror
  And check the show of pride;
By open speech and simple,
  An hundred times made plain,
To seek another's profit,
  And work another's gain.

Take up the White Man's burden —
  The savage wars of peace —
Fill full the mouth of Famine
  And bid the sickness cease;
And when your goal is nearest
  The end for others sought,
Watch Sloth and heathen Folly
  Bring all your hope to nought.

Take up the White Man's burden —
  No tawdry rule of kings,
But toil of serf and sweeper —
  The tale of common things.
The ports ye shall not enter,
  The roads ye shall not tread,
Go make them with your living,
  And mark them with your dead.

Take up the White Man's burden —
  And reap his old reward:
The blame of those ye better,
  The hate of those ye guard —
The cry of hosts ye humour
  (Ah, slowly!) toward the light: —
" Why brought ye us from bondage,
  " Our loved Egyptian night? "

Take up the White Man's burden —
  Ye dare not stoop to less —
Nor call too loud on Freedom
  To cloak your weariness;

By all ye cry or whisper,
  By all ye leave or do,
The silent, sullen peoples
  Shall weigh your Gods and you.

Take up the White Man's burden —
  Have done with childish days —
The lightly proffered laurel,
  The easy, ungrudged praise.
Comes now, to search your manhood
  Through all the thankless years,
Cold, edged with dear-bought wisdom,
  The judgment of your peers! '

HYMN BEFORE ACTION

1 8 9 6

THE earth is full of anger,
  The seas are dark with wrath,
The Nations in their harness
  Go up against our path:
Ere yet we loose the legions —
  Ere yet we draw the blade,
Jehovah of the Thunders,
  Lord God of Battles, aid!

High lust and froward bearing,
  Proud heart, rebellious brow —
Deaf ear and soul uncaring,
  We seek Thy mercy now!
The sinner that forswore Thee,
  The fool that passed Thee by,
Our times are known before Thee —
  Lord, grant us strength to die!

For those who kneel beside us
    At altars not Thine own,
Who lack the lights that guide us,
    Lord, let their faith atone!
If wrong we did to call them,
    By honour bound they came;
Let not Thy Wrath befall them,
    But deal to us the blame.

From panic, pride, and terror,
    Revenge that knows no rein,
Light haste and lawless error,
    Protect us yet again.
Cloke Thou our undeserving,
    Make firm the shuddering breath,
In silence and unswerving
    To taste Thy lesser death!

Ah, Mary pierced with sorrow,
    Remember, reach and save
The soul that comes to-morrow
    Before the God that gave!
Since each was born of woman,
    For each at utter need —
True comrade and true foeman —
    Madonna, intercede!

E'en now their vanguard gathers,
    E'en now we face the fray —
As Thou didst help our fathers,
    Help Thou our host to-day!
Fulfilled of signs and wonders,
    In life, in death made clear —
Jehovah of the Thunders,
    Lord God of Battles, hear!

RECESSIONAL

1897

GOD of our fathers, known of old,
  Lord of our far-flung battle-line,
Beneath whose awful Hand we hold
  Dominion over palm and pine —
Lord God of Hosts, be with us yet,
Lest we forget — lest we forget!

The tumult and the shouting dies;
  The captains and the kings depart:
Still stands Thine ancient sacrifice,
  An humble and a contrite heart.
Lord God of Hosts, be with us yet,
Lest we forget — lest we forget!

Far-called, our navies melt away;
  On dune and headland sinks the fire:
Lo, all our pomp of yesterday,
  Is one with Nineveh and Tyre!
Judge of the Nations, spare us yet,
Lest we forget — lest we forget!

If, drunk with sight of power, we loose
  Wild tongues that have not Thee in awe,
Such boastings as the Gentiles use,
  Or lesser breeds without the Law —
Lord God of Hosts, be with us yet,
Lest we forget — lest we forget!

For heathen heart that puts her trust
  In reeking tube and iron shard,
All valiant dust that builds on dust,
  And guarding, calls not Thee to guard,
For frantic boast and foolish word —
Thy Mercy on Thy People, Lord!

THE THREE–DECKER

1894

" The three-volume novel is extinct."

FULL thirty foot she towered from waterline to rail.
It cost a watch to steer her, and a week to shorten sail;
But, spite all modern notions, I 've found her first and best —
The only certain packet for the Islands of the Blest.

Fair held the breeze behind us — 't was warm with lovers' prayers.
We 'd stolen wills for ballast and a crew of missing heirs.
They shipped as Able Bastards till the Wicked Nurse confessed,
And they worked the old three-decker to the Islands of the Blest.

By ways no gaze could follow, a course unspoiled of cook,
Per Fancy, fleetest in man, our titled berths we took
With maids of matchless beauty and parentage unguessed,
And a Church of England parson for the Islands of the Blest.

We asked no social questions — we pumped no hidden shame —
We never talked obstetrics when the Little Stranger came:
We left the Lord in Heaven, we left the fiends in Hell.
We were n't exactly Yussufs, but — Zuleika did n't tell.

No moral doubt assailed us, so when the port we neared,
The villain had his flogging at the gangway, and we cheered.
'T was fiddle in the forc's'le — 't was garlands on the mast,
For every one got married, and I went ashore at last.

I left 'em all in couples akissing on the decks.
I left the lovers loving and the parents signing cheques.
In endless English comfort, by county-folk caressed,
I left the old three-decker at the Islands of the Blest!

That route is barred to steamers: you 'll never lift again
Our purple-painted headlands or the lordly keeps of Spain.
They 're just beyond your skyline, howe'er so far you cruise
In a ram-you-damn-you liner with a brace of bucking screws.

Swing round your aching search-light — 't will show no
    haven's peace.
Ay, blow your shrieking sirens at the deaf, grey-bearded seas!
Boom out the dripping oil-bags to skin the deep's unrest —
And you are n't one knot the nearer to the Islands of the Blest!

But when you 're threshing, crippled, with broken bridge and
    rail,
At a drogue of dead convictions to hold you head to gale,
Calm as the Flying Dutchman, from truck to taffrail dressed,
You 'll see the old three-decker for the Islands of the Blest.

You 'll see her tiering canvas in sheeted silver spread;
You 'll hear the long-drawn thunder 'neath her leaping figure-
    head;
While far, so far above you, her tall poop-lanterns shine
Unvexed by wind or weather like the candles round a shrine!

Hull down — hull down and under — she dwindles to a speck,
With noise of pleasant music and dancing on her deck.
All 's well — all 's well aboard her — she 's left you far
    behind,
With a scent of old-world roses through the fog that ties you
    blind.

Her crew are babes or madmen? Her port is all to make?
You 're manned by Truth and Science, and you steam for
    steaming's sake?
Well, tinker up your engines — you know your business
    best —
She 's taking tired people to the Islands of the Blest!

THE RHYME OF THE THREE CAPTAINS

1890

[*This ballad appears to refer to one of the exploits of the notorious Paul Jones, an American pirate. It is founded on fact.*]

. . . AT the close of a winter day,
Their anchors down, by London town, the Three Great Captains lay;
And one was Admiral of the North from Solway Firth to Skye,
And one was Lord of the Wessex coast and all the lands thereby,
And one was Master of the Thames from Limehouse to Blackwall,
And he was Captain of the Fleet — the bravest of them all.
Their good guns guarded the great grey sides that were thirty foot in the sheer,
When there came a certain trading brig with news of a privateer.
Her rigging was rough with the clotted drift that drives in a Northern breeze,
Her sides were clogged with the lazy weed that spawns in the Eastern seas.
Light she rode in the rude tide-rip, to left and right she rolled,
And the skipper sat on the scuttle-butt and stared at an empty hold.
" I ha' paid Port dues for your Law," quoth he, " and where is the Law ye boast
" If I sail unscathed from a heathen port to be robbed on a Christian coast?
" Ye have smoked the hives of the Laccadives as we burn the lice in a bunk,

" We tack not now to a Gallang prow or a plunging Pei-ho
    junk;
" I had no fear but the seas were clear as far as a sail might
    fare
" Till I met with a lime-washed Yankee brig that rode off
    Finisterre.
" There were canvas blinds to his bow-gun ports to screen the
    weight he bore,
" And the signals ran for a merchantman from Sandy Hook
    to the Nore.
" He would not fly the Rovers' flag — the bloody or the black,
" But now he floated the Gridiron and now he flaunted the
    Jack.
" He spoke of the Law as he crimped my crew — he swore
    it was only a loan;
" But when I would ask for my own again, he swore it was
    none of my own.
" He has taken my little parrakeets that nest beneath the Line,
" He has stripped my rails of the shaddock-frails and the
    green unripened pine;
" He has taken my bale of dammer and spice I won beyond
    the seas,
" He has taken my grinning heathen gods — and what should
    he want o' these?
" My foremast would not mend his boom, my deck-house
    patch his boats;
" He has whittled the two, this Yank Yahoo, to peddle for
    shoe-peg oats.
" I could not fight for the failing light and a rough beam-sea
    beside,
" But I hulled him once for a clumsy crimp and twice because
    he lied.
" Had I had guns (as I had goods) to work my Christian
    harm,
" I had run him up from his quarter-deck to trade with his
    own yard-arm;
" I had nailed his ears to my capstan-head, and ripped them
    off with a saw,

" And soused them in the bilgewater, and served them to him
    raw;
" I had flung him blind in a rudderless boat to rot in the rock-
    ing dark,
" I had towed him aft of his own craft, a bait for his brother
    shark;
" I had lapped him round with cocoa husk, and drenched him
    with the oil,
" And lashed him fast to his own mast to blaze above my
    spoil;
" I had stripped his hide for my hammock-side, and tasselled
    his beard i' the mesh,
" And spitted his crew on the live bamboo that grows through
    the gangrened flesh;
" I had hove him down by the mangroves brown, where the
    mud-reef sucks and draws,
" Moored by the heel to his own keel to wait for the land-crab's
    claws!
" He is lazar within and lime without, ye can nose him far
    enow,
" For he carries the taint of a musky ship — the reek of the
    slaver's dhow!"
The skipper looked at the tiering guns and the bulwarks tall
    and cold,   .
And the Captains Three full courteously peered down at the
    gutted hold,
And the Captains Three called courteously from deck to
    scuttle-butt: —
" Good Sir, we ha' dealt with that merchantman or ever your
    teeth were cut.
" Your words be words of a lawless race, and the Law it
    standeth thus:
" He comes of a race that have never a Law, and he never has
    boarded us.
" We ha' sold him canvas and rope and spar — we know that
    his price is fair,
" And we know that he weeps for the lack of a Law as he rides
    off Finisterre.

" And since he is damned for a gallows-thief by you and better
    than you,
" We hold it meet that the English fleet should know that we
    hold him true."
The skipper called to the tall taffrail: — " And what is that
    to me?
" Did ever you hear of a Yankee brig that rifled a Seventy-
    three?
" Do I loom so large from your quarter-deck that I lift like a
    ship o' the Line?
" He has learned to run from a shotted gun and harry such
    craft as mine.
" There is never a Law on the Cocos Keys to hold a white
    man in,
" But we do not steal the niggers' meal, for that is a nigger's
    sin.
" Must he have his Law as a quid to chaw, or laid in brass on
    his wheel?
" Does he steal with tears when he buccaneers?   'Fore Gad,
    then, why does he steal? "
The skipper bit on a deep-sea word, and the word it was not
    sweet,
For he could see the Captains Three had signalled to the Fleet.
But three and two, in white and blue, the whimpering flags
    began: —
" We have heard a tale of a — foreign sail, but he is a mer-
    chantman."
The skipper peered beneath his palm and swore by the Great
    Horn Spoon: —
" 'Fore Gad, the Chaplain of the Fleet would bless my pica-
    roon ! "
By two and three the flags blew free to lash the laughing
    air: —
" We have sold our spars to the merchantman — we know that
    his price is fair."
The skipper winked his Western eye, and swore by a China
    storm: —

15

" They ha' rigged him a Joseph's jury-coat to keep hi
    honour warm."
The halliards twanged against the tops, the bunting bellie
    broad,
The skipper spat in the empty hold and mourned for a waste
    cord.
Masthead — masthead, the signal sped by the line o' the Brit
    ish craft:
The skipper called to his Lascar crew, and put her about an
    laughed: —
" It 's mainsail haul, my bully boys all — we 'll out to the sea
    again —
" Ere they set us to paint their pirate saint, or scrub at hi
    grapnel-chain.
" It 's fore-sheet free, with her head to the sea, and the swing
    of the unbought brine —
" We 'll make no sport in an English court till we come as
    ship o' the Line:
" Till we come as a ship o' the Line, my lads, of thirty foot i
    the sheer,
" Lifting again from the outer main with news of a privateer
" Flying his pluck at our mizzen-truck for weft of Admiralty
" Heaving his head for our dipsy-lead in sign that we kee
    the sea.
" Then fore-sheet home as she lifts to the foam — we stand o
    the outward tack,
" We are paid in the coin of the white man's trade — th
    bezant is hard, ay, and black.
" The frigate-bird shall carry my word to the Kling and th
    Orang-Laut
" How a man may sail from a heathen coast to be robbed in
    Christian port;
" How a man may be robbed in Christian port while Thre
    Great Captains there
" Shall dip their flag to a slaver's rag — to show that hi
    trade is fair! "

THE CONUNDRUM OF THE WORKSHOPS

1890

WHEN the flush of a new-born sun fell first on Eden's
     green and gold,   ·
Our father Adam sat under the Tree and scratched with a stick
     in the mould;
And the first rude sketch that the world had seen was joy to his
     mighty heart,
Till the Devil whispered behind the leaves, "It's pretty, but is
     it Art?"

Wherefore he called to his wife, and fled to fashion his work
     anew —
The first of his race who cared a fig for the first, most dread
     review;
And he left his lore to the use of his sons — and that was a
     glorious gain
When the Devil chuckled "Is it Art?" in the ear of the branded
     Cain.

They builded a tower to shiver the sky and wrench the stars
     apart,
Till the Devil grunted behind the bricks: "It's striking, but is
     it Art?"
The stone was dropped at the quarry-side and the idle derrick
     swung,
While each man talked of the aims of Art, and each in an alien
     tongue.

They fought and they talked in the North and the South; they
     talked and they fought in the West,
Till the waters rose on the pitiful land, and the poor Red Clay
     had rest —

Had rest till the dank blank-canvas dawn when the dove was
    preened to start,
And the Devil bubbled below the keel: "It's human, but is it
    Art?"

The tale is as old as the Eden Tree — and new as the new-cut
    tooth —
For each man knows ere his lip-thatch grows he is master of Art
    and Truth;
And each man hears as the twilight nears, to the beat of his dying
    heart,
The Devil drum on the darkened pane: "You did it, but was
    it Art?"

We have learned to whittle the Eden Tree to the shape of a
    surplice-peg,
We have learned to bottle our parents twain in the yelk of an
    addled egg,
We know that the tail must wag the dog, for the horse is drawn
    by the cart;
But the Devil whoops, as he whooped of old: "It's clever, but
    is it Art?"

When the flicker of London sun falls faint on the Club-room's
    green and gold,
The sons of Adam sit them down and scratch with their pens in
    the mould —
They scratch with their pens in the mould of their graves, and
    the ink and the anguish start,
For the Devil mutters behind the leaves: "It's pretty, but is it
    Art?"

Now, if we could win to the Eden Tree where the Four Great
    Rivers flow,
And the Wreath of Eve is red on the turf as she left it long ago,
And if we could come when the sentry slept and softly scurry
    through,
By the favour of God we might know as much — as our father
    Adam knew.

EVARRA AND HIS GODS

1890

*R*EAD *here:*
This is the story of Evarra — man —
Maker of Gods in lands beyond the sea.
    Because the city gave him of her gold,
    Because the caravans brought turquoises,
    Because his life was sheltered by the King,
    So that no man should maim him, none should steal,
    Or break his rest with babble in the streets
    When he was weary after toil, he made
    An image of his God in gold and pearl,
    With turquoise diadem and human eyes,
    A wonder in the sunshine, known afar,
    And worshipped by the King; but, drunk with pride,
    Because the city bowed to him for God,
    He wrote above the shrine: "*Thus Gods are made,*
    "*And whoso makes them otherwise shall die.*"
    And all the city praised him. . . . Then he died.

Read here the story of Evarra — man —
Maker of Gods in lands beyond the sea.
    Because the city had no wealth to give,
    Because the caravans were spoiled afar,
    Because his life was threatened by the King,
    So that all men despised him in the streets,
    He hewed the living rock, with sweat and tears,
    And reared a God against the morning-gold,
    A terror in the sunshine, seen afar,
    And worshipped by the King; but, drunk with pride,
    Because the city fawned to bring him back,
    He carved upon the plinth: "*Thus Gods are made,*
    "*And whoso makes them otherwise shall die.*"
    And all the people praised him. . . . Then he died.

Read here the story of Evarra — man —
Maker of Gods in lands beyond the sea.
   Because he lived among a simple folk,
   Because his village was between the hills,
   Because he smeared his cheeks with blood of ewes,
   He cut an idol from a fallen pine,
   Smeared blood upon its cheeks, and wedged a shell
   Above its brows for eyes, and gave it hair
   Of trailing moss, and plaited straw for crown.
   And all the village praised him for this craft,
   And brought him butter, honey, milk, and curds.
   Wherefore, because the shoutings drove him mad,
   He scratched upon that log: " *Thus Gods are made,*
   "*And whoso makes them otherwise shall die.*"
   And all the people praised him. . . . Then he died.

Read here the story of Evarra — man —
Maker of Gods in lands beyond the sea.
   Because his God decreed one clot of blood
   Should swerve one hair's-breadth from the pulse's path,
   And chafe his brain, Evarra mowed alone,
   Rag-wrapped, among the cattle in the fields,
   Counting his fingers, jesting with the trees,
   And mocking at the mist, until his God
   Drove him to labour.   Out of dung and horns
   Dropped in the mire he made a monstrous God,
   Uncleanly, shapeless, crowned with plantain tufts,
   And when the cattle lowed at twilight-time,
   He dreamed it was the clamour of lost crowds,
   And howled among the beasts: " *Thus Gods are made,*
   "*And whoso makes them otherwise shall die.*"
   Thereat the cattle bellowed. . . . Then he died.

   Yet at the last he came to Paradise,
   And found his own four Gods, and that he wrote;
   And marvelled, being very near to God,
   What oaf on earth had made his toil God's law,

Till God said mocking: "Mock not.   These be thine."
Then cried Evarra: "I have sinned!" — "Not so.
"If thou hadst written otherwise, thy Gods
"Had rested in the mountain and the mine,
"And I were poorer by four wondrous Gods,
"And thy more wondrous law, Evarra.   Thine,
"Servant of shouting crowds and lowing kine!"

Thereat, with laughing mouth, but tear-wet eyes,
Evarra cast his Gods from Paradise.

This is the story of Evarra — man —
Maker of Gods in lands beyond the sea.

IN THE NEOLITHIC AGE

1895

IN the Neolithic Age savage warfare did I wage
  For food and fame and woolly horses' pelt;
I was singer to my clan in that dim, red Dawn of Man,
  And I sang of all we fought and feared and felt.

Yea, I sang as now I sing, when the Prehistoric spring
  Made the piled Biscayan ice-pack split and shove;
And the troll and gnome and dwerg, and the Gods of Cliff and
    Berg
  Were about me and beneath me and above.

But a rival, of Solutré, told the tribe my style was *outré* —
  'Neath a tomahawk, of diorite, he fell.
And I left my views on Art, barbed and tanged, below the
    heart
  Of a mammothistic etcher at Grenelle

Then I stripped them, scalp from skull, and my hunting dogs
      fed full,
   And their teeth I threaded neatly on a thong;
And I wiped my mouth and said, "It is well that they are
      dead,
   " For I know my work is right and theirs was wrong."

But my Totem saw the shame; from his ridgepole shrine he
      came,
   And he told me in a vision of the night: —
"There are nine and sixty ways of constructing tribal lays,
   "And every single one of them is right!"

       .   .   .   .

Then the silence closed upon me till They put new clothing
      on me
   Of whiter, weaker flesh and bone more frail;
And I stepped beneath Time's finger, once again a tribal singer,
   [And a minor poet certified by Trraill].

Still they skirmish to and fro, men my messmates on the snow,
   When we headed off the aurochs turn for turn;
When the rich Allobrogenses never kept amanuenses,
   And our only plots were piled in lakes at Berne.

Still a cultured Christian age sees us scuffle, squeak, and rage,
   Still we pinch and slap and jabber, scratch and dirk;
Still we let our business slide — as we dropped the half-dressed
      hide —
   To show a fellow-savage how to work.

Still the world is wondrous large, — seven seas from marge to
      marge, —
   And it holds a vast of various kinds of man;
And the wildest dreams of Kew are the facts of Khatmandhu,
   And the crimes of Clapham chaste in Martaban.

Here's my wisdom for your use, as I learned it when the moose
  And the reindeer roared where Paris roars to-night: —
" There are nine and sixty ways of constructing tribal lays,
  " And — every — single — one — of — them — is — right ! "

THE STORY OF UNG

1 8 9 4

ONCE, on a glittering ice-field, ages and ages ago,
Ung, a maker of pictures, fashioned an image of snow.
Fashioned the form of a tribesman — gaily he whistled and
    sung,
Working the snow with his fingers. *Read ye the Story of Ung!*

Pleased was his tribe with that image — came in their hundreds
    to scan —
Handled it, smelt it, and grunted: "Verily, this is a man !
" Thus do we carry our lances — thus is a war-belt slung.
" Lo ! it is even as we are.   Glory and honour to Ung ! "

Later he pictured an aurochs — later he pictured a bear —
Pictured the sabre-tooth tiger dragging a man to his lair —
Pictured the mountainous mammoth, hairy, abhorrent, alone —
Out of the love that he bore them, scriving them clearly on bone.

Swift came his tribe to behold them, peering and pushing and
    still —
Men of the berg-battered beaches, men of the boulder-hatched
    hill —
Hunters and fishers and trappers, presently whispering low:
"Yea, they are like — and it may be — But how does the
    Picture-man know ?

"Ung — hath he slept with the Aurochs — watched where the Mastodon roam?

" Spoke on the ice with the Bow-head — followed the Sabre-tooth home?

" Nay! These are toys of his fancy! If he have cheated us so,

" How is there truth in his image — the man that he fashioned of snow?"

Wroth was that maker of pictures — hotly he answered the call:

"Hunters and fishers and trappers, children and fools are ye all!

" Look at the beasts when ye hunt them!" Swift from the tumult he broke,

Ran to the cave of his father and told him the shame that they spoke.

And the father of Ung gave answer, that was old and wise in the craft,

Maker of pictures aforetime, he leaned on his lance and laughed:

"If they could see as thou seest they would do what thou hast done,

" And each man would make him a picture, and — what would become of my son?

"There would be no pelts of the reindeer, flung down at thy cave for a gift,

"Nor dole of the oily timber that comes on the Baltic drift;

"No store of well-drilled needles, nor ouches of amber pale;

"No new-cut tongues of the bison, nor meat of the stranded whale.

" *Thou* hast not toiled at the fishing when the sodden trammels freeze,

"Nor worked the war-boats outward through the rush of the rock-staked seas,

"Yet they bring thee fish and plunder — full meal and an easy bed —

"And all for the sake of thy pictures." And Ung held down his head.

"*Thou* hast not stood to the Aurochs when the red snow reeks
   of the fight;
"Men have no time at the houghing to count his curls aright
"And the heart of the hairy Mammoth, thou sayest, they do
   not see,
"Yet they save it whole from the beaches and broil the best
   for thee.

"And now do they press to thy pictures, with opened mouth
   and eye,
"And a little gift in the doorway, and the praise no gift can
   buy:
"But — sure they have doubted thy pictures, and that is a griev-
   ous stain —
"Son that can see so clearly, return them their gifts again!"

And Ung looked down at his deerskins — their broad shell-
   tasselled bands —
And Ung drew downward his mitten and looked at his naked
   hands;
And he gloved himself and departed, and he heard his father,
   behind:
"Son that can see so clearly, rejoice that thy tribe is blind!"

Straight on the glittering ice-field, by the caves of the lost
   Dordogne,
Ung, a maker of pictures, fell to his scriving on bone
Even to mammoth editions.   Gaily he whistled and sung,
Blessing his tribe for their blindness. *Heed ye the Story of Ung!*

THE FILES

1903

(The Sub-editor Speaks)

Files —
The Files —
Office Files !
Oblige me by referring to the files.
Every question man can raise,
Every phrase of every phase
Of that question is on record in the files —
(Threshed out threadbare — fought and finished in the files).
Ere the Universe at large
Was our new-tipped arrows' targe —
Ere we rediscovered Mammon and his wiles —
Faenza, gentle reader, spent her — five-and-twentieth leader
(You will find him, and some others, in the files).
Warn all future Robert Brownings and Carlyles,
It will interest them to hunt among the files,
Where unvisited, a-cold,
Lie the crowded years of old
In that Kensall-Green of greatness called the files
(In our newspaPère-la-Chaise the office files),
Where the dead men lay them down
Meekly sure of long renown,
And above them, sere and swift,
Packs the daily deepening drift
Of the all-recording, all-effacing files —
The obliterating, automatic files.
Count the mighty men who slung
Ink, Evangel, Sword, or Tongue
When Reform and you were young —
Made their boasts and spake according in the files —
(Hear the ghosts that wake applauding in the files !)

Trace each all-forgot career
From long primer through brevier
Unto Death, a para minion in the files
(Para minion — solid — bottom of the files). . . .
Some successful Kings and Queens adorn the files,
They were great, their views were leaded,
And their deaths were triple-headed,
So they catch the eye in running through the files
(Show as blazes in the mazes of the files);
For their "paramours and priests,"
And their gross, jack-booted feasts,
And their "epoch-marking actions" see the files.
Was it Bomba fled the blue Sicilian isles?
Was it Saffi, a professor
Once of Oxford, brought redress or
Garibaldi? Who remembers
Forty-odd-year old Septembers? —
Only sextons paid to dig among the files
(Such as I am, born and bred among the files).
You must hack through much deposit
Ere you know for sure who was it
Came to burial with such honour in the files
(Only seven seasons back beneath the files).
"Very great our loss and grievous —
"So our best and brightest leave us,
"And it ends the Age of Giants," say the files;
All the '60 — '70 — '80 — '90 files
(The open-minded, opportunist files —
The easy "O King, live for ever" files).
It is good to read a little in the files;
'T is a sure and sovereign balm
Unto philosophic calm,
Yea, and philosophic doubt when Life beguiles.
When you know Success is Greatness,
When you marvel at your lateness
In apprehending facts so plain to Smiles
(Self-helpful, wholly strenuous Samuel Smiles).

When your Imp of Blind Desire
Bids you set the Thames afire,
You 'll remember men have done so — in the files.
You 'll have seen those flames transpire — in the files
(More than once that flood has run so — in the files).
When the Conchimarian horns
Of the reboantic Norns
Usher gentlemen and ladies
With new lights on Heaven and Hades,
Guaranteeing to Eternity
All yesterday's modernity;
When Brocken-spectres made by
Some one's breath on ink parade by,
Very earnest and tremendous,
Let not shows of shows offend us.
When of everything we like we
Shout ecstatic: — " *Quod ubique*,
" *Quod ab omnibus* means *semper!* "
Oh, my brother, keep your temper!
Light your pipe and take a look along the files!
You 've a better chance to guess
At the meaning of Success
(Which is Greatness — *vide* press)
When you 've seen it in perspective in the files.

THE LEGENDS OF EVIL

1890

I

THIS is the sorrowful story
   Told as the twilight fails
And the monkeys walk together
   Holding their neighbour's tails: —

"Our fathers lived in the forest,
  "Foolish people were they,
''They went down to the cornland
  "To teach the farmers to play.

"Our fathers frisked in the millet,
  "Our fathers skipped in the wheat,
"Our fathers hung from the branches
  "Our fathers danced in the street.

"Then came the terrible farmers,
  "Nothing of play they knew,
"Only . . . they caught our fathers
  "And set them to labour too !

"Set them to work in the cornland
  "With ploughs and sickles and flails,
"Put them in mud-walled prisons
  "And — cut off their beautiful tails !

"Now, we can watch our fathers,
  "Sullen and bowed and old,
"Stooping over the millet,
  "Sharing the silly mould,

"Driving a foolish furrow,
  "Mending a muddy yoke,
"Sleeping in mud-walled prisons,
  "Steeping their food in smoke.

"We may not speak with our fathers,
  "For if the farmers knew
"They would come up to the forest
  "And set us to labour too. "

This is the horrible story
  Told as the twilight fails
And the monkeys walk together
  Holding their neighbour's tails.

II

'T was when the rain fell steady an' the Ark was pitched an'
    ready,
  That Noah got his orders for to take the bastes below;
He dragged them all together by the horn an' hide an' feather,
  An' all excipt the Donkey was agreeable to go.

Thin Noah spoke him fairly, thin talked to him severely,
  An' thin he cursed him squarely to the glory av the Lord: —
"Divil take the ass that bred you, and the greater ass that
    fed you —
  "Divil go wid you, ye spalpeen!" an' the Donkey wint
    aboard.

But the wind was always failin', an' 't was most onaisy sailin',
  An' the ladies in the cabin could n't stand the stable air;
An' the bastes betwuxt the hatches, they tuk an' died in batches,
  Till Noah said: — "'There's wan av us that has n't paid his
    fare!'"

For he heard a flusteration 'mid the bastes av all creation —
  The trumpetin' av elephints an' bellowin' av whales;
An' he saw forninst the windy whin he wint to stop the shindy
  The Divil wid a stable-fork bedivillin' their tails.

The Divil cursed outrageous, but Noah said umbrageous: —
  "'To what am I indebted for this tenant-right invasion?"
An' the Divil gave for answer: — "Evict me if you can, sir,
  " For I came in wid the Donkey — on Your Honour's
    invitation."

TOMLINSON

1891

Now Tomlinson gave up the ghost in his house in Berkeley
Square,
And a Spirit came to his bedside and gripped him by the hair —
A Spirit gripped him by the hair and carried him far away,
Till he heard as the roar of a rain-fed ford the roar of the Milky
Way:
Till he heard the roar of the Milky Way die down and drone and
cease,
And they came to the Gate within the Wall where Peter holds
the keys.
"Stand up, stand up now, Tomlinson, and answer loud and
high
"The good that ye did for the sake of men or ever ye came to
die —
"The good that ye did for the sake of men in little earth so lone!"
And the naked soul of Tomlinson grew white as a rain-washed
bone.
"O I have a friend on earth," he said, "that was my priest and
guide,
"And well would he answer all for me if he were by my side."
— "For that ye strove in neighbour-love it shall be written fair,
"But now ye wait at Heaven's Gate and not in Berkeley Square:
"Though we called your friend from his bed this night, he could
not speak for you,
"For the race is run by one and one and never by two and two."
Then Tomlinson looked up and down, and little gain was there,
For the naked stars grinned overhead, and he saw that his soul
was bare:
The Wind that blows between the Worlds, it cut him like a knife,
And Tomlinson took up the tale and spoke of his good in life.
"O this I have read in a book," he said, "and that was told to me,
16

"And this I have thought that another man thought of a Princ
  in Muscovy."
The good souls flocked like homing doves and bade him clea
  the path,
And Peter twirled the jangling keys in weariness and wrath.
"Ye have read, ye have heard, ye have thought," he said, "an
  the tale is yet to run:
"By the worth of the body that once ye had, give answer —
  what ha' ye done?"
Then Tomlinson looked back and forth, and little good it bore
For the darkness stayed at his shoulder-blade and Heaven'
  Gate before: —
"O this I have felt, and this I have guessed, and this I have hear
  men say,
"And this they wrote that another man wrote of a carl i
  Norroway."
"Ye have read, ye have felt, ye have guessed, good lack! Y
  have hampered Heaven's Gate;
"There's little room between the stars in idleness to prate!
"O none may reach by hired speech of neighbour, priest, and ki
"Through borrowed deed to God's good meed that lies so fai
  within;
"Get hence, get hence to the Lord of Wrong, for doom has ye
  to run,
"And . . . the faith that ye share with Berkeley Square up
  hold you, Tomlinson!"

  .   .   .   .

The Spirit gripped him by the hair, and sun by sun they fell
Till they came to the belt of Naughty Stars that rim the mout
  of Hell:
The first are red with pride and wrath, the next are white wit
  pain,
But the third are black with clinkered sin that cannot bur
  again:
They may hold their path, they may leave their path, wit
  never a soul to mark,
They may burn or freeze, but they must not cease in the Scor
  of the Outer Dark.

The Wind that blows between the Worlds, it nipped him to
    the bone,
And he yearned to the flare of Hell-gate there as the light of
    his own hearth-stone.
The Devil he sat behind the bars, where the desperate legions
    drew,
But he caught the hasting Tomlinson and would not let him
    through.
"Wot ye the price of good pit-coal that I must pay?" said he,
"That ye rank yoursel' so fit for Hell and ask no leave of me?
"I am all o'er-sib to Adam's breed that ye should give me
    scorn,
"For I strove with God for your First Father the day that he
    was born.
"Sit down, sit down upon the slag, and answer loud and high
"The harm that ye did to the Sons of Men or ever you came
    to die."
And Tomlinson looked up and up, and saw against the night
The belly of a tortured star blood-red in Hell-Mouth light;
And Tomlinson looked down and down, and saw beneath his
    feet
The frontlet of a tortured star milk-white in Hell-Mouth heat.
"O I had a love on earth," said he, "that kissed me to my
    fall,
"And if ye would call my love to me I know she would answer
    all."
— "All that ye did in love forbid it shall be written fair,
"But now ye wait at Hell-Mouth Gate and not in Berkeley
    Square:
"Though we whistled your love from her bed to-night, I trow
    she would not run,
"For the sin ye do by two and two ye must pay for one by
    one!"
The Wind that blows between the Worlds, it cut him like a
    knife,
And Tomlinson took up the tale and spoke of his sin in life: —
"Once I ha' laughed at the power of Love and twice at the grip
    of the Grave,

"And thrice I ha' patted my God on the head that men might
  call me brave."
The Devil he blew on a brandered soul and set it aside to
  cool: —
"Do ye think I would waste my good pit-coal on the hide of
  a brain-sick fool?
"I see no worth in the hobnailed mirth or the jolthead jest ye did
"That I should waken my gentlemen that are sleeping three
  on a grid."
Then Tomlinson looked back and forth, and there was little
  grace,
For Hell-Gate filled the houseless Soul with the Fear of Naked
  Space.
"Nay, this I ha' heard," quo' Tomlinson, "and this was noised
  abroad,
"And this I ha' got from a Belgian book on the word of a dead
  French lord."
— "Ye ha' heard, ye ha' read, ye ha' got, good lack! and the
  tale begins afresh —
"Have ye sinned one sin for the pride o' the eye or the sinful
  lust of the flesh?"
Then Tomlinson he gripped the bars and yammered, "Let
  me in —
"For I mind that I borrowed my neighbour's wife to sin the
  deadly sin."
The Devil he grinned behind the bars, and banked the fires
  high:
"Did ye read of that sin in a book?" said he; and Tomlinson
  said, "Ay!"
The Devil he blew upon his nails, and the little devils ran,
And he said: "Go husk this whimpering thief that comes in
  the guise of a man:
"Winnow him out 'twixt star and star, and sieve his proper
  worth:
"There's sore decline in Adam's line if this be spawn of earth."
Empusa's crew, so naked-new they may not face the fire,
But weep that they bin too small to sin to the height of their
  desire,

Over the coal they chased the Soul, and racked it all abroad,
As children rifle a caddis-case or the raven's foolish hoard.
And back they came with the tattered Thing, as children after
  play,
And they said: "The soul that he got from God he has bar-
  tered clean away.
"We have threshed a stook of print and book, and winnowed
  a chattering wind
"And many a soul wherefrom he stole, but his we cannot find:
"We have handled him, we have dandled him, we have seared
  him to the bone,
"And sure if tooth and nail show truth he has no soul of his own."
The Devil he bowed his head on his breast and rumbled deep
  and low: —
"I 'm all o'er-sib to Adam's breed that I should bid him go.
"Yet close we lie, and deep we lie, and if I gave him place,
"My gentlemen that are so proud would flout me to my face;
"They 'd call my house a common stews and me a careless host,
"And — I would not anger my gentlemen for the sake of a
  shiftless ghost."
The Devil he looked at the mangled Soul that prayed to feel the
  flame,
And he thought of Holy Charity, but he thought of his own
  good name: —
"Now ye could haste my coal to waste, and sit ye down to fry:
"Did ye think of that theft for yourself?" said he; and Tom-
  linson said, "Ay!"
The Devil he blew an outward breath, for his heart was free
  from care: —
"Ye have scarce the soul of a louse," he said, "but the roots of
  sin are there,
"And for that sin should ye come in were I the lord alone.
"But sinful pride has rule inside — and mightier than my own.
"Honour and Wit, fore-damned they sit, to each his Priest and
  Whore:
"Nay, scarce I dare myself go there, and you they 'd torture sore.
"Ye are neither spirit nor spirk," he said; "ye are neither book
  nor brute —

"Go, get ye back to the flesh again for the sake of Man's repute.
"I'm all o'er-sib to Adam's breed that I should mock your pain,
"But look that ye win to worthier sin ere ye come back again.
"Get hence, the hearse is at your door — the grim black stallions wait —
"They bear your clay to place to-day.   Speed, lest ye come too late!
"Go back to Earth with a lip unsealed — go back with an open eye,
"And carry my word to the Sons of Men or ever ye come to die:
"That the sin they do by two and two they must pay for one by one —
"And . . . the God that you took from a printed book be with you, Tomlinson!"

THE EXPLANATION

1890

LOVE and Death once ceased their strife
At the Tavern of Man's Life.
Called for wine, and threw — alas! —
Each his quiver on the grass.
When the bout was o'er they found
Mingled arrows strewed the ground.
Hastily they gathered then
Each the loves and lives of men.
Ah, the fateful dawn deceived!
Mingled arrows each one sheaved;
Death's dread armoury was stored
With the shafts he most abhorred;
Love's light quiver groaned beneath
Venom-headed darts of Death.

Thus it was they wrought our woe
At the Tavern long ago.
Tell me, do our masters know,
Loosing blindly as they fly,
Old men love while young men die?

THE ANSWER

1892

A ROSE, in tatters on the garden path,
Cried out to God and murmured 'gainst His Wrath,
Because a sudden wind at twilight's hush
Had snapped her stem alone of all the bush.
And God, Who hears both sun-dried dust and sun,
Had pity, whispering to that luckless one.
"Sister, in that thou sayest We did not well —
What voices heardst thou when thy petals fell?"
And the Rose answered, "In that evil hour
"A voice said, 'Father, wherefore falls the flower?
"'For lo, the very gossamers are still.'
"And a voice answered, 'Son, by Allah's will!'"

Then softly as a rain-mist on the sward,
Came to the Rose the Answer of the Lord:
"Sister, before We smote the Dark in twain,
"Ere yet the stars saw one another plain,
"Time, Tide, and Space, We bound unto the task
"That thou shouldst fall, and such an one should ask."
Whereat the withered flower, all content,
Died as they die whose days are innocent;
While he who questioned why the flower fell
Caught hold of God and saved his soul from Hell.

THE GIFT OF THE SEA

1890

THE dead child lay in the shroud,
  And the widow watched beside;
And her mother slept, and the Channel swept
  The gale in the teeth of the tide.

But the mother laughed at all.
  "I have lost my man in the sea,
"And the child is dead. Be still," she said,
  "What more can ye do to me?"

The widow watched the dead,
  And the candle guttered low,
And she tried to sing the Passing Song
  That bids the poor soul go.

And "Mary take you now," she sang,
  "That lay against my heart."
And "Mary smooth your crib to-night,"
  But she could not say "Depart."

Then came a cry from the sea,
  But the sea-rime blinded the glass,
And "Heard ye nothing, mother?" she said,
  "'T is the child that waits to pass."

And the nodding mother sighed.
  "'T is a lambing ewe in the whin,
"For why should the christened soul cry out
  "That never knew of sin?"

"O feet I have held in my hand,
  "O hands at my heart to catch,
"How should they know the road to go,
  "And how should they lift the latch?"

They laid a sheet to the door,
    With the little quilt atop,
That it might not hurt from the cold or the dirt,
    But the crying would not stop.

The widow lifted the latch
    And strained her eyes to see,
And opened the door on the bitter shore
    To let the soul go free.

There was neither glimmer nor ghost,
    There was neither spirit nor spark,
And "Heard ye nothing, mother?" she said,
    "'T is crying for me in the dark."

And the nodding mother sighed:
    "'T is sorrow makes ye dull;
"Have ye yet to learn the cry of the tern,
    "Or the wail of the wind-blown gull?"

"The terns are blown inland,
    "The grey gull follows the plough.
"'T was never a bird, the voice I heard,
    "O mother, I hear it now!"

"Lie still, dear lamb, lie still;
    "The child is passed from harm,
"'T is the ache in your breast that broke your rest,
    "And the feel of an empty arm."

She put her mother aside,
    "In Mary's name let be!
"For the peace of my soul I must go," she said,
    And she went to the calling sea.

In the heel of the wind-bit pier,
    Where the twisted weed was piled,
She came to the life she had missed by an hour
    For she came to a little child.

She laid it into her breast,
  And back to her mother she came,
But it would not feed and it would not heed,
  Though she gave it her own child's name.

And the dead child dripped on her breast,
  And her own in the shroud lay stark;
And "God forgive us, mother," she said,
  "We let it die in the dark!"

THE KING

1894

"FAREWELL, Romance!" the Cave-men said;
  "With bone well carved he went away,
" Flint arms the ignoble arrowhead,
  " And jasper tips the spear to-day.
" Changed are the Gods of Hunt and Dance,
" And he with these.   Farewell, Romance! "

"Farewell, Romance!" the Lake-folk sighed;
  "We lift the weight of flatling years;
" The caverns of the mountain-side
  " Hold him who scorns our hutted piers.
" Lost hills whereby we dare not dwell,
" Guard ye his rest.   Romance, Farewell!"

"Farewell, Romance!" the Soldier spoke;
  "By sleight of sword we may not win,
" But scuffle 'mid uncleanly smoke
  " Of arquebus and culverin.
"Honour is lost, and none may tell
"Who paid good blows.   Romance, farewell!"

"Farewell, Romance!" the Traders cried;
   "Our keels have lain with every sea;
"The dull-returning wind and tide
   "Heave up the wharf where we would be;
"The known and noted breezes swell
"Our trudging sail. Romance, farewell!"

"Good-bye, Romance!" the Skipper said;
   "He vanished with the coal we burn;
"Our dial marks full steam ahead,
   "Our speed is timed to half a turn.
"Sure as the ferried barge we ply
"'Twixt port and port. Romance, good-bye!"

"Romance!" the season-tickets mourn,
   "*He* never ran to catch his train,
"But passed with coach and guard and horn —
   "And left the local — late again!"
Confound Romance! . . . And all unseen
Romance brought up the nine-fifteen.

His hand was on the lever laid,
   His oil-can soothed the worrying cranks,
His whistle waked the snowbound grade,
   His fog-horn cut the reeking Banks;
By dock and deep and mine and mill
The Boy-god reckless laboured still!

Robed, crowned and throned, he wove his spell,
   Where heart-blood beat or hearth-smoke curled,
With unconsidered miracle,
   Hedged in a backward-gazing world:
Then taught his chosen bard to say:
"Our King was with us — yesterday!"

THE LAST RHYME OF TRUE
THOMAS

1893

THE King has called for priest and cup,
  The King has taken spur and blade
To dub True Thomas a belted knight,
  And all for the sake o' the songs he made.   .

They have sought him high, they have sought him low,
  They have sought him over down and lea;
They have found him by the milk-white thorn
  That guards the gates o' Faerie.

'T was bent beneath and blue above,
  Their eyes were held that they might not see
The kine that grazed beneath the knowes,
  Oh, they were the Queens o' Faerie!

"Now cease your song," the King he said,
  "Oh, cease your song and get you dight
"To vow your vow and watch your arms,
  "For I will dub you a belted knight.

"For I will give you a horse o' pride,
  " Wi' blazon and spur and page and squire;
"Wi' keep and tail and seizin and law,
  "And land to hold at your desire."

True Thomas smiled above his harp,
  And turned his face to the naked sky,
Where, blown before the wastrel wind
  The thistle-down she floated by.

"I ha' vowed my vow in another place,
  "And bitter oath it was on me,
"I ha' watched my arms the lee-long night,
  "Where five-score fighting men would flee.

"My lance is tipped o' the hammered flame,
  "My shield is beat o' the moonlight cold;
"And I won my spurs in the Middle World,
  "A thousand fathom beneath the mould.

"And what should I make wi' a horse o' pride,
  "And what should I make wi' a sword so brown,
"But spill the rings o' the Gentle Folk
  "And flyte my kin in the Fairy Town?

"And what should I make wi' blazon and belt,
  "Wi' keep and tail and seizin and fee,
"And what should I do wi' page and squire
  "That am a king in my own countrie?

"For I send east and I send west,
  "And I send far as my will may flee,
"By dawn and dusk and the drinking rain,
  "And syne my Sendings return to me.

"They come wi' news of the groanin' earth,
  "They come wi' news o' the roarin' sea,
"Wi' word of Spirit and Ghost and Flesh,
  "And man, that's mazed among the three."

The King he bit his nether lip,
  And smote his hand upon his knee:
"By the faith o' my soul, True Thomas," he said,
  "Ye waste no wit in courtesie!

"As I desire, unto my pride,
  "Can I make Earls by three and three,
"To run before and ride behind
  "And serve the sons o' my body."

"And what care I for your row-foot earls,
    "Or all the sons o' your body?
"Before they win to the Pride o' Name,
    "I trow they all ask leave o' me.

"For I make Honour wi' muckle mouth,
    "As I make Shame wi' mincin' feet,
"To sing wi' the priests at the market-cross,
    "Or run wi' the dogs in the naked street.

"And some they give me the good red gold,
    "And some they give me the white money,
"And some they give me a clout o' meal,
    "For they be people of low degree.

"And the song I sing for the counted gold
    "The same I sing for the white money,
"But best I sing for the clout o' meal
    "That simple people given me."

The King cast down a silver groat,
    A silver groat o' Scots money,
"If I come wi' a poor man's dole," he said,
    "True Thomas, will ye harp to me?"

"Whenas I harp to the children small,
    "They press me close on either hand.
"And who are you," True Thomas said,
    "That you should ride while they must stand?

"Light down, light down from your horse o' pride,
    "I trow ye talk too loud and hie,
"And I will make you a triple word,
    "And syne, if ye dare, ye shall 'noble me."

He has lighted down from his horse o' pride,
    And set his back against the stone.
"Now guard you well," True Thomas said,
    "Ere I rax your heart from your breast-bone!"

True Thomas played upon his harp,
  The fairy harp that couldna lee,
And the first least word the proud King heard,
  It harpit the salt tear out o' his e'e.

"Oh, I see the love that I lost long syne,
  "I touch the hope that I may not see,
"And all that I did o' hidden shame,
  "Like little snakes they hiss at me.

"The sun is lost at noon — at noon !
  "The dread o' doom has grippit me.
"True Thomas, hide me under your cloak,
  "God wot, I'm little fit to dee !"

'T was bent beneath and blue above —
  'T was open field and running flood —
Where, hot on heath and dyke and wall,
  The high sun warmed the adder's brood.

"Lie down, lie down," True Thomas said.
  "The God shall judge when all is done
"But I will bring you a better word
  "And lift the cloud that I laid on."

True Thomas played upon his harp,
  That birled and brattled to his hand,
And the next least word True Thomas made,
  It garred the King take horse and brand.

"Oh, I hear the tread o' the fighting-men,
  "I see the sun on splent and spear.
"I mark the arrow outen the fern
  "That flies so low and sings so clear !

"Advance my standards to that war,
  "And bid my good knights prick and ride ;
"The gled shall watch as fierce a fight
  "As e'er was fought on the Border side !"

'T was bent beneath and blue above,
'T was nodding grass and naked sky,
Where, ringing up the wastrel mind,
The eyass stooped upon the pye.

True Thomas sighed above his harp,
And turned the song on the midmost string;
And the last least word True Thomas made,
He harpit his dead youth back to the King.

"Now I am prince, and I do well
"To love my love withouten fear;
"To walk wi' man in fellowship,
"And breathe my horse behind the deer.

"My hounds they bay unto the death,
"The buck has couched beyond the burn,
"My love she waits at her window
"To wash my hands when I return.

"For that I live am I content
" (Oh! I have seen my true love's eyes)
"To stand wi' Adam in Eden-glade,
"And run in the woods o' Paradise!"

'T was naked sky and nodding grass,
'T was running flood and wastrel wind,
Where, checked against the open pass,
The red deer turned to wait the hind.

True Thomas laid his harp away,
And louted low at the saddle-side;
He has taken stirrup and hauden rein,
And set the King on his horse o' pride.

"Sleep ye or wake," True Thomas said,
"That sit so still, that muse so long;
"Sleep ye or wake? — till the Latter Sleep
"I trow ye'll not forget my song.

"I ha' harpit a shadow out o' the sun
  "To stand before your face and cry;
"I ha' armed the earth beneath your heel,
  "And over your head I ha' dusked the sky.

"I ha' harpit ye up to the throne o' God,
  "I ha' harpit your midmost soul in three;
"I ha' harpit ye down to the Hinges o' Hell,
  "And — ye — would — make — a Knight o' me !"

THE PALACE

1 9 0 2

WHEN I was a King and a Mason — a Master proven and
    skilled —
I cleared me ground for a Palace such as a King should build.
I decreed and dug down to my levels.   Presently, under the silt,
I came on the wreck of a Palace such as a King had built.

There was no worth in the fashion — there was no wit in the
    plan —
Hither and thither, aimless, the ruined footings ran —
Masonry, brute, mishandled, but carven on every stone:
"*After me cometh a Builder.   Tell him, I too have known.*"

Swift to my use in my trenches, where my well-planned ground-
    works grew,
I tumbled his quoins and his ashlars, and cut and reset them
    anew.
Lime I milled of his marbles; burned it, slacked it, and spread:
Taking and leaving at pleasure the gifts of the humble dead.

17

Yet I despised not nor gloried; yet, as we wrenched them apart,
I read in the razed foundations the heart of that builder's heart.
As he had risen and pleaded, so did I understand
The form of the dream he had followed in the face of the thing
    he had planned.

.   .   .   .   .   .

When I was a King and a Mason — in the open noon of my
    pride,
They sent me a Word from the Darkness — They whispered
    and called me aside.
They said — "The end is forbidden." They said — "Thy use
    is fulfilled.
"Thy Palace shall stand as that other's — the spoil of a King
    who shall build."

I called my men from my trenches, my quarries, my wharves,
    and my sheers.
All I had wrought I abandoned to the faith of the faithless years.
Only I cut on the timber — only I carved on the stone:
After me cometh a Builder. Tell him, I too have known!

BARRACK ROOM BALLADS

I

INDIAN SERVICE

1889–1891

TO THOMAS ATKINS

I HAVE made for you a song,
And it may be right or wrong,
But only you can tell me if it's true;
I have tried for to explain
Both your pleasure and your pain,
And, Thomas, here's my best respects to you!

O there'll surely come a day
When they'll give you all your pay,
And treat you as a Christian ought to do;
So, until that day comes round,
Heaven keep you safe and sound,
And, Thomas, here's my best respects to you!

R. K.

DANNY DEEVER

"WHAT are the bugles blowin' for?" said Files-on-
    Parade.
"To turn you out, to turn you out," the Colour-Sergeant said.
"What makes you look so white, so white?" said Files-on-
    Parade.
"I'm dreadin' what I've got to watch," the Colour-Sergeant
    said.

For they 're hangin' Danny Deever, you can hear the Dead
    March play,
The regiment 's in 'ollow square — they 're hangin' him to-
    day;   .
They 've taken of his buttons off an' cut his stripes away,
An' they 're hangin' Danny Deever in the mornin'.

"What makes the rear-rank breathe so 'ard ?" said Files-on-
    Parade.
"It 's bitter cold, it 's bitter cold," the Colour-Sergeant said.
"What makes that front-rank man fall down ?" says Files-on-
    Parade.
"A touch o' sun, a touch o' sun," the Colour-Sergeant said.
    They are hangin' Danny Deever, they are marchin' of 'im
        round,
    They 'ave 'alted Danny Deever by 'is coffin on the ground;
    An' 'e 'll swing in 'arf a minute for a sneakin' shootin'
        hound —
    O they 're hangin' Danny Deever in the mornin' !

" 'Is cot was right-'and cot to mine," said Files-on-Parade.
" 'E 's sleepin' out an' far to-night," the Colour-Sergeant said.
"I 've drunk 'is beer a score o' times," said Files-on-Parade.
" 'E 's drinkin' bitter beer alone," the Colour-Sergeant said.
    They are hangin' Danny Deever, you must mark 'im to
        'is place,
    For 'e shot a comrade sleepin' — you must look 'im in the
        face;
    Nine 'undred of 'is county an' the regiment's disgrace,
    While they 're hangin' Danny Deever in the mornin'.

"What 's that so black agin the sun ?" said Files-on-Parade.
"It 's Danny fightin' 'ard for life," the Colour-Sergeant said.
"What 's that that whimpers over'ead ?" said Files-on-Parade
"It 's Danny's soul that 's passin' now," the Colour-Sergeant
    said.

For they're done with Danny Deever, you can 'ear the
    quickstep play,
The regiment's in column, an' they're marchin' us away;
Ho! the young recruits are shakin', an' they'll want their
    beer to-day,
After hangin' Danny Deever in the mornin'.

TOMMY

I WENT into a public-'ouse to get a pint o' beer,
The publican 'e up an' sez, "We serve no red-coats here."
The girls be'ind the bar they laughed an' giggled fit to die,
I outs into the street again an' to myself sez I:
    O it's Tommy this, an' Tommy that, an' "Tommy, go
        away";
    But it's "Thank you, Mister Atkins," when the band
        begins to play,
    The band begins to play, my boys, the band begins to
        play,
    O it's "Thank you, Mister Atkins," when the band begins
        to play.

I went into a theatre as sober as could be,
They gave a drunk civilian room, but 'ad n't none for me;
They sent me to the gallery or round the music-'alls,
But when it comes to fightin', Lord! they'll shove me in the
    stalls!
    For it's Tommy this, an' Tommy that, an' "Tommy, wait
        outside";
    But it's "Special train for Atkins" when the trooper's on
        the tide,
    The troopship's on the tide, my boys, the troopship's on
        the tide,
    O it's "Special train for Atkins" when the trooper's on
        the tide.

Yes, makin' mock o' uniforms that guard you while you sleep
Is cheaper than them uniforms, an' they're starvation cheap;
An' hustlin' drunken soldiers when they're goin' large a bit
Is five times better business than paradin' in full kit.
    Then it's Tommy this, an' Tommy that, an' "Tommy,
        'ow's yer soul?"
    But it's "Thin red line of 'eroes" when the drums begin
        to roll,
    The drums begin to roll, my boys, the drums begin to roll,
    O it's "Thin red line of 'eroes" when the drums begin to
        roll.

We aren't no thin red 'eroes, nor we aren't no blackguards
    too,
But single men in barricks, most remarkable like you;
An' if sometimes our conduck isn't all your fancy paints,
Why, single men in barricks don't grow into plaster saints;
    While it's Tommy this, an' Tommy that, an' "Tommy,
        fall be'ind,"
    But it's "Please to walk in front, sir," when there's trouble
        in the wind,
    There's trouble in the wind, my boys, there's trouble in
        the wind,
    O it's "Please to walk in front, sir," when there's trouble
        in the wind.

You talk o' better food for us, an' schools, an' fires, an' all:
We'll wait for extry rations if you treat us rational.
Don't mess about the cook-room slops, but prove it to our face
The Widow's Uniform is not the soldier-man's disgrace.
    For it's Tommy this, an' Tommy that, an' "Chuck him
        out, the brute!"
    But it's "Saviour of 'is country" when the guns begin to
        shoot;
    An' it's Tommy this, an' Tommy that, an' anything you
        please;
    An' Tommy ain't a bloomin' fool — you bet that Tommy
        sees!

" FUZZY–WUZZY "

(Soudan Expeditionary Force)

WE 'VE fought with many men acrost the seas,
  An' some of 'em was brave an' some was not:
The Paythan an' the Zulu an' Burmese;
  But the Fuzzy was the finest o' the lot.
We never got a ha'porth's change of 'im:
  'E squatted in the scrub an' 'ocked our 'orses,
'E cut our sentries up at Sua*kim*,
  An' 'e played the cat an' banjo with our forces.
      So 'ere's *to* you, Fuzzy-Wuzzy, at your 'ome in the
        Soudan;
      You're a pore benighted 'eathen but a first-class fightin'
        man;
      We gives you your certificate, an' if you want it signed
      We'll come an' 'ave a romp with you whenever you're
        inclined.

We took our chanst among the Kyber 'ills,
  The Boers knocked us silly at a mile,
The Burman give us Irriwaddy chills,
  An' a Zulu *impi* dished us up in style:
But all we ever got from such as they
  Was pop to what the Fuzzy made us swaller;
We 'eld our bloomin' own, the papers say,
  But man for man the Fuzzy knocked us 'oller.
      Then 'ere's *to* you, Fuzzy-Wuzzy, an' the missis and the
        kid;
      Our orders was to break you, an' of course we went an'
        did.
      We sloshed you with Martinis, an' it was n't 'ardly fair;
      But for all the odds agin' you, Fuzzy-Wuz, you broke
        the square.

'E 'as n't got no papers of 'is own,
    'E 'as n't got no medals nor rewards,
So we must certify the skill 'e's shown
    In usin' of 'is long two-'anded swords:
When 'e's 'oppin' in an' out among the bush
    With 'is coffin-'eaded shield an' shovel-spear,
An 'appy day with Fuzzy on the rush
    Will last an 'ealthy Tommy for a year.
        So 'ere's *to* you, Fuzzy-Wuzzy, an' your friends which are
            no more,
        If we 'ad n't lost some messmates we would 'elp you to
            deplore;
        But give an' take's the gospel, an' we'll call the bargain
            fair,
        For if you 'ave lost more than us, you crumpled up the
            square!

'E rushes at the smoke when we let drive,
    An', before we know, 'e's 'ackin' at our 'ead;
'E's all 'ot sand an' ginger when alive,
    An' 'e's generally shammin' when 'e's dead.
'E's a daisy, 'e's a ducky, 'e's a lamb!
    'E's a injia-rubber idiot on the spree,
'E's the on'y thing that does n't give a damn
    For a Regiment o' British Infantree!
        So 'ere's *to* you, Fuzzy-Wuzzy, at your 'ome in the
            Soudan;
        You're a pore benighted 'eathen but a first-class fightin'
            man;
        An' 'ere's *to* you, Fuzzy-Wuzzy, with your 'ayrick 'ead
            of 'air —
        You big black boundin' beggar — for you broke a British
            square!

SOLDIER, SOLDIER

"Soldier, soldier come from the wars,
"Why don't you march with my true love?"
"We're fresh from off the ship an' 'e's, maybe, give the slip,
"An' you'd best go look for a new love."

> New love!   True love!
> Best go look for a new love,
> The dead they cannot rise, an' you'd better dry your eyes,
> An' you'd best go look for a new love.

"Soldier, soldier come from the wars,
"What did you see o' my true love?"
"I seen 'im serve the Queen in a suit o' rifle-green,
"An' you'd best go look for a new love."

"Soldier, soldier come from the wars,
"Did ye see no more o' my true love?"
"I seen 'im runnin' by when the shots begun to fly —
"But you'd best go look for a new love."

"Soldier, soldier come from the wars,
"Did aught take 'arm to my true love?"
"I could n't see the fight, for the smoke it lay so white —
"An' you'd best go look for a new love."

"Soldier, soldier come from the wars,
"I'll up an' tend to my true love!"
"'E's lying on the dead with a bullet through 'is 'ead,
"An' you'd best go look for a new love."

"Soldier, soldier come from the wars,
"I'll down an' die with my true love!"
"The pit we dug 'll 'ide 'im an' the twenty men beside 'im —
"An' you'd best go look for a new love."

"Soldier, soldier come from the wars,
"Do you bring no sign from my true love?"
"I bring a lock of 'air that 'e allus used to wear,
"An' you'd best go look for a new love."

"Soldier, soldier come from the wars,
"O then I know it's true I've lost my true love!"
"An' I tell you truth again — when you've lost the feel o' pain
"You'd best take me for your new love."

   True love! New love!
   Best take 'im for a new love,
   The dead they cannot rise, an' you'd better dry your eyes,
   An' you'd best take 'im for your new love.

SCREW-GUNS

SMOKIN' my pipe on the mountings, sniffin' the mornin'-
  cool,
I walks in my old brown gaiters along o' my old brown mule,
With seventy gunners be'ind me, an' never a beggar forgets
It's only the pick of the Army that handles the dear little pets
  — 'Tss! 'Tss!
  For you all love the screw-guns — the screw-guns they all
   love you!
  So when we call round with a few guns, o' course you
   will know what to do — hoo! hoo!
  Jest send in your Chief an' surrender — it's worse if you
   fights or you runs:
  You can go where you please, you can skid up the trees,
   but you don't get away from the guns!

They sends us along where the roads are, but mostly we goes
        where they ain't:
We 'd climb up the side of a sign-board an' trust to the stick
        o' the paint:
We 've chivied the Naga an' Looshai, we 've give the Afreedee-
        man fits,
For we fancies ourselves at two thousand, we guns that are built
        in two bits — 'Tss! 'Tss!
        For you all love the screw-guns . . .

If a man does n't work, why, we drills 'im an' teaches 'im 'ow
        to behave;
If a beggar can't march, why, we kills 'im an' rattles 'im into
        'is grave.
You 've got to stand up to our business an' spring without
        snatchin' or fuss.
D' you say that you sweat with the field-guns? By God, you
        must lather with us — 'Tss! 'Tss!
        For you all love the screw-guns . . .

The eagles is screamin' around us, the river 's a-moanin' below,
We 're clear o' the pine an' the oak-scrub, we 're out on the
        rocks an' the snow,
An' the wind is as thin as a whip-lash what carries away to
        the plains
The rattle an' stamp o' the lead-mules — the jinglety jink o'
        the chains — 'Tss! 'Tss!
        For you all love the screw-guns . . .

There 's a wheel on the Horns o' the Mornin', an' a wheel on
        the edge o' the Pit,
An' a drop into nothin' beneath you as straight as a beggar
        can spit:
With the sweat runnin' out o' your shirt-sleeves, an' the sun off
        the snow in your face,
An' 'arf o' the men on the drag-ropes to hold the old gun in 'er
        place — 'Tss! 'Tss!
        For you all love the screw-guns . . .

Smokin' my pipe on the mountings, sniffin' the mornin'-cool,
I climbs in my old brown gaiters along o' my old brown mule.
The monkey can say what our road was — the wild-goat 'e
  knows where we passed.
Stand easy, you long-eared old darlin's! Out drag-ropes! With
  shrapnel! Hold fast — 'Tss! 'Tss!
  For you all love the screw-guns — the screw-guns they all
    love you!
  So when we take tea with a few guns, o' course you will
    know what to do — hoo! hoo!
  Jest send in your Chief an' surrender — it 's worse if you
    fights or you runs:
  You may hide in the caves, they 'll be only your graves,
    but you can't get away from the guns!

CELLS

I 'VE a head like a concertina: I 've a tongue like a button-
  stick:
I 've a mouth like an old potato, and I 'm more than a little
  sick,
But I 've had my fun o' the Corp'ral's Guard: I 've made the
  cinders fly,
And I 'm here in the Clink for a thundering drink and blacking
  the Corporal's eye.

        With a second-hand overcoat under my head,
          And a beautiful view of the yard,
      O it 's pack-drill for me and a fortnight's C.B.
          For "drunk and resisting the Guard!"
          Mad drunk and resisting the Guard —
          'Strewth, but I socked it them hard!
      So it 's pack-drill for me and a fortnight's C.B.
          For "drunk and resisting the Guard."

I started o' canteen porter, I finished o' canteen beer,
But a dose o' gin that a mate slipped in, it was that that brought
 me here.
'T was that and an extry double Guard that rubbed my nose in
 the dirt;
But I fell away with the Corp'ral's stock and the best of the
 Corp'ral's shirt.

I left my cap in a public-house, my boots in the public road,
And Lord knows where, and I don't care, my belt and my tunic
 goed;
They'll stop my pay, they'll cut away the stripes I used to wear,
But I left my mark on the Corp'ral's face, and I think he'll keep
 it there!

My wife she cries on the barrack-gate, my kid in the barrack-
 yard,
It ain't that I mind the Ord'ly room — it's *that* that cuts so hard.
I'll take my oath before them both that I will sure abstain,
But as soon as I'm in with a mate and gin, I know I'll do it
 again!

> With a second-hand overcoat under my head,
> And a beautiful view of the yard,
> Yes, it's pack-drill for me and a fortnight's C. B.
> For "drunk and resisting the Guard!"
> Mad drunk and resisting the Guard —
> 'Strewth, but I socked it them hard!
> So it's pack-drill for me and a fortnight's C. B.
> For "drunk and resisting the Guard."

GUNGA DIN

YOU may talk o' gin and beer
When you're quartered safe out 'ere,
An' you're sent to penny-fights an' Aldershot it;
But when it comes to slaughter

You will do your work on water,
An' you 'll lick the bloomin' boots of 'im that 's got it.
Now in Injia's sunny clime,
Where I used to spend my time
A-servin' of 'Er Majesty the Queen,
Of all them blackfaced crew
The finest man I knew
Was our regimental bhisti, Gunga Din.
           He was "Din! Din! Din!
   "You limpin' lump o' brick-dust, Gunga Din!
        "Hi! slippery *hitherao!*
        "Water, get it!   *Panee lao!* [1]
   "You squidgy-nosed old idol, Gunga Din."

The uniform 'e wore
Was nothin' much before,
An' rather less than 'arf o' that be'ind,
For a piece o' twisty rag
An' a goatskin water-bag
Was all the field-equipment 'e could find.
When the sweatin' troop-train lay
In a sidin' through the day,
Where the 'eat would make your bloomin' eyebrows crawl,
We shouted "Harry By!" [2]
Till our throats were bricky-dry,
Then we wopped 'im 'cause 'e could n't serve us all.
           It was "Din! Din! Din!
   "You 'eathen, where the mischief 'ave you been?
        "You put some *juldee* [3] in it
        "Or I 'll *marrow* [4] you this minute
   "If you don't fill up my helmet, Gunga Din!"

'E would dot an' carry one
Till the longest day was done;
An' 'e did n't seem to know the use o' fear.
If we charged or broke or cut,

---

[1] Bring water swiftly.   [2] Mr. Atkins's equivalent for "O Brother."
[3] Be quick.   [4] Hit you.

You could bet your bloomin' nut,
'E'd be waitin' fifty paces right flank rear.
With 'is mussick [1] on 'is back,
'E would skip with our attack,
An' watch us till the bugles made "Retire "
An' for all 'is dirty 'ide
'E was white, clear white, inside
When 'e went to tend the wounded under fire!
      It was "Din! Din! Din!"
  With the bullets kickin' dust-spots on the green
      When the cartridges ran out,
      You could hear the front-ranks shout,
  "Hi! ammunition-mules an' Gunga Din!"

I sha'n't forgit the night
When I dropped be'ind the fight
With a bullet where my belt-plate should 'a' been.
I was chokin' mad with thirst,
An' the man that spied me first
Was our good old grinnin', gruntin' Gunga Din.
'E lifted up my 'ead,
An' he plugged me where I bled,
An' 'e guv me 'arf-a-pint o' water-green:
It was crawlin' and it stunk,
But of all the drinks I've drunk,
I'm gratefullest to one from Gunga Din.
      It was "Din! Din! Din!
  "'Ere's a beggar with a bullet through 'is spleen;
      "'E's chawin' up the ground,
      "An' 'e's kickin' all around:
  "For Gawd's sake git the water, Gunga Din!"

'E carried me away
To where a dooli lay,
An' a bullet come an' drilled the beggar clean.
'E put me safe inside,

---

[1] Water-skin.

An' just before 'e died,
"I 'ope you liked your drink," sez Gunga Din.
So I'll meet 'im later on
At the place where 'e is gone —
Where it's always double drill and no canteen;
'E'll be squattin' on the coals
Givin' drink to poor damned souls,
An' I'll get a swig in hell from Gunga Din!
        Yes, Din! Din! Din!
   You Lazarushian-leather Gunga Din!
       Though I've belted you and flayed you,
       By the livin' Gawd that made you,
You're a better man than I am, Gunga Din!

OONTS

(*Northern India Transport Train*)

WOT makes the soldier's 'eart to penk, wot makes 'im to
    perspire?
It isn't standin' up to charge nor lyin' down to fire;
But it's everlastin' waitin' on a everlastin' road
For the commissariat camel an' 'is commissariat load.
   O the oont,[1] O the oont, O the commissariat oont!
     With 'is silly neck a-bobbin' like a basket full o' snakes;
   We packs 'im like an idol, an' you ought to 'ear 'im grunt,
     An' when we gets 'im loaded up 'is blessed girth-rope
      breaks.

Wot makes the rear-guard swear so 'ard when night is drorin' in,
An' every native follower is shiverin' for 'is skin?
It ain't the chanst o' being rushed by Paythans from the 'ills,
It's the commissariat camel puttin' on 'is bloomin' frills!

[1] Camel: — *oo* is pronounced like *u* in "bull," but by Mr. Atkins to rhyme
with "front."

O the oont, O the oont, O the hairy scary oont!
    A-trippin' over tent-ropes when we've got the night
      alarm!
We socks 'im with a stretcher-pole an' 'eads 'im off in front,
    An' when we've saved 'is bloomin' life 'e chaws our
      bloomin' arm.

The 'orse 'e knows above a bit, the bullock's but a fool,
The elephant's a gentleman, the battery-mule's a mule;
But the commissariat cam-u-el, when all is said an' done,
'E's a devil an' a ostrich an' a orphan-child in one.
    O the oont, O the oont, O the Gawd-forsaken oont!
      The lumpy-'umpy 'ummin'-bird a-singin' where 'e lies,
    'E's blocked the whole division from the rear-guard to the
      front,
      An' when we get him up again — the beggar goes an' dies!

'E'll gall an' chafe an' lame an' fight — 'e smells most awful
    vile;
'E'll lose 'isself for ever if you let 'im stray a mile;
'E's game to graze the 'ole day long an' 'owl the 'ole night
    through,
An' when 'e comes to greasy ground 'e splits 'isself in two.
    O the oont, O the oont, O the floppin', droppin' oont!
      When 'is long legs give from under an' 'is meltin' eye is
      dim,
    The tribes is up be'ind us, and the tribes is out in front —
      It ain't no jam for Tommy, but it's kites an' crows for 'im.

So when the cruel march is done, an' when the roads is blind,
An' when we sees the camp in front an' 'ears the shots be'ind,
Ho! then we strips 'is saddle off, and all 'is woes is past:
'E thinks on us that used 'im so, and gets revenge at last.
    O the oont, O the oont, O the floatin', bloatin' oont!
      The late lamented camel in the water-cut 'e lies;
    We keeps a mile be'ind 'im an' we keeps a mile in front,
      But 'e gets into the drinkin'-casks, and then o' course we
      dies.

LOOT

IF you 've ever stole a pheasant-egg be'ind the keeper's back,
　If you 've ever snigged the washin' from the line,
If you 've ever crammed a gander in your bloomin' 'aversack,
　You will understand this little song o' mine.
But the service rules are 'ard, an' from such we are debarred,
　For the same with English morals does not suit.
　　　　(*Cornet:* Toot! toot!)
W'y, they call a man a robber if 'e stuffs 'is marchin' clobber
　With the —
(*Chorus*) Loo! loo!　Lulu! lulu!　Loo! loo!　Loot! loot!
　　loot!
　　　　　Ow the loot!
　　　　　Bloomin' loot!
　　　　That 's the thing to make the boys git up an' shoot!
　　　　　It 's the same with dogs an' men,
　　　　　If you 'd make 'em come again
　　　　Clap 'em forward with a Loo! loo!　Lulu!　Loot!
　(*ff*)　Whoopee!　Tear 'im, puppy!　Loo! loo!　Lulu!
　　Loot! loot! loot!

If you 've knocked a nigger edgeways when 'e 's thrustin' for
　　your life,
　You must leave 'im very careful where 'e fell;
An' may thank your stars an' gaiters if you did n't feel 'is
　　knife
　That you ain't told off to bury 'im as well.
Then the sweatin' Tommies wonder as they spade the beggars
　　under
　Why lootin' should be entered as a crime;
So if my song you 'll 'ear, I will learn you plain an' clear
　'Ow to pay yourself for fightin' overtime.
　　　　(*Chorus*)　With the loot, . . .

Now remember when you're 'acking round a gilded Burma
    god
  That 'is eyes is very often precious stones;
An' if you treat a nigger to a dose o' cleanin'-rod
  'E's like to show you everything 'e owns.
When 'e won't prodooce no more, pour some water on the
    floor
  Where you 'ear it answer 'ollow to the boot
        (*Cornet:* Toot! toot!) —
When the ground begins to sink, shove your baynick down the
    chink,
  An' you're sure to touch the —
(*Chorus*) Loo! loo! Lulu! Loot! loot! loot!
    Ow the loot! . . .

When from 'ouse to 'ouse you're 'unting, you must always
    work in pairs —
  It 'alves the gain, but safer you will find —
For a single man gets bottled on them twisty-wisty stairs,
  An' a woman comes and clobs 'im from be'ind.
When you've turned 'em inside out, an' it seems beyond a
    doubt
  As if there were n't enough to dust a flute
        (*Cornet:* Toot! toot!) —
Before you sling your 'ook, at the 'ousetops take a look,
  For it's underneath the tiles they 'ide the loot.
        (*Chorus*)   Ow the loot! . . .

You can mostly square a Sergint an' a Quartermaster too,
  If you only take the proper way to go;
I could never keep my pickin's, but I've learned you all I
    knew —
  An' don't you never say I told you so.
An' now I'll bid good-bye, for I'm gettin' rather dry,
  An' I see another tunin' up to toot
        (*Cornet:* Toot! toot!) —

So 'ere's good-luck to those that wears the Widow's clo'es,
  An' the Devil send 'em all they want o' loot!
        (*Chorus*)   Yes, the loot,
                    Bloomin' loot!
      In the tunic an' the mess-tin an' the boot!
        It's the same with dogs an' men,
        If you'd make 'em come again.
(*fff*) Whoop 'em forward with a Loo! loo! Lulu! Loot!
        loot! loot!
      Heeya!   Sick 'im, puppy! Loo! loo! Lulu!
        Loot! loot! loot!

"SNARLEYOW"

T HIS 'appened in a battle to a batt'ry of the corps
Which is first among the women an' amazin' first in war;
An' what the bloomin' battle was I don't remember now,
But Two's off-lead 'e answered to the name o' *Snarleyow*.
        Down in the Infantry, nobody cares;
        Down in the Cavalry, Colonel 'e swears;
        But down in the lead with the wheel at the flog
        Turns the bold Bombardier to a little whipped dog!

They was movin' into action, they was needed very sore,
To learn a little schoolin' to a native army corps,
They 'ad nipped against an uphill, they was tuckin' down the
      brow,
When a tricky, trundlin' roundshot give the knock to *Snarleyow*.

They cut 'im loose an' left 'im — 'e was almost tore in two —
But he tried to follow after as a well-trained 'orse should do;
'E went an' fouled the limber, an' the Driver's Brother squeals:
"Pull up, pull up for *Snarleyow* — 'is head's between 'is 'eels!"

The Driver 'umped 'is shoulder, for the wheels was goin' round,
An' there ain't no "Stop, conductor!" when a batt'ry 's changin'
    ground;
Sez 'e: "I broke the beggar in, an' very sad I feels,
"But I could n't pull up, not for *you* — your 'ead between your
    'eels!"

'E 'ad n't 'ardly spoke the word, before a droppin' shell
A little right the batt'ry an' between the sections fell;
An' when the smoke 'ad cleared away, before the limber wheels,
There lay the Driver's Brother with 'is 'ead between 'is 'eels.

Then sez the Driver's Brother, an' 'is words was very plain,
"For Gawd's own sake get over me, an' put me out o' pain."
They saw 'is wounds was mortial, an' they judged that it was
    best,
So they took an' drove the limber straight across 'is back an'
    chest.

The Driver 'e give nothin' 'cept a little coughin' grunt,
But 'e swung 'is 'orses 'andsome when it came to "Action
    Front!"
An' if one wheel was juicy, you may lay your Monday head
'T was juicier for the niggers when the case begun to spread.

The moril of this story, it is plainly to be seen:
You 'av n't got no families when servin' of the Queen —
You 'av n't got no brothers, fathers, sisters, wives, or sons —
If you want to win your battles take an' work your bloomin'
    guns!
        Down in the Infantry, nobody cares;
        Down in the Cavalry, Colonel 'e swears;
        But down in the lead with the wheel at the flog
        Turns the bold Bombardier to a little whipped dog!

THE WIDOW AT WINDSOR

'AVE you 'eard o' the Widow at Windsor
  With a hairy gold crown on 'er 'ead?
She 'as ships on the foam — she 'as millions at 'ome,
  An' she pays us poor beggars in red.
      (Ow, poor beggars in red!)
There 's 'er nick on the cavalry 'orses,
  There 's 'er mark on the medical stores —
An' 'er troopers you 'll find with a fair wind be'ind
  That takes us to various wars.
      (Poor beggars! — barbarious wars!)
        Then 'ere 's to the Widow at Windsor,
          An' 'ere 's to the stores an' the guns,
        The men an' the 'orses what makes up the forces
          O' Missis Victorier's sons.
        (Poor beggars! Victorier's sons!)

Walk wide o' the Widow at Windsor,
  For 'alf o' Creation she owns:
We 'ave bought 'er the same with the sword an' the flame,
  An' we 've salted it down with our bones.
      (Poor beggars! — it 's blue with our bones!)
Hands off o' the sons o' the Widow,
  Hands off o' the goods in 'er shop,
For the Kings must come down an' the Emperors frown
  When the Widow at Windsor says " Stop! "
      (Poor beggars! — we 're sent to say " Stop! ")
        Then 'ere 's to the Lodge o' the Widow,
          From the Pole to the Tropics it runs —
        To the Lodge that we tile with the rank an' the
            file,
          An' open in form with the guns.
        (Poor beggars! — it 's always they guns!)

We 'ave 'eard o' the Widow at Windsor,
 It 's safest to let 'er alone:
For 'er sentries we stand by the sea an' the land
 Wherever the bugles are blown.
   (Poor beggars! — an' don't we get blown!)
Take 'old o' the Wings o' the Mornin',
 An' flop round the earth till you 're dead;
But you won't get away from the tune that they play
 To the bloomin' old rag over'ead.
   (Poor beggars! — it 's 'ot over'ead!)
   Then 'ere 's to the sons o' the Widow,
    Wherever, 'owever they roam.
   'Ere 's all they desire, an' if they require
    A speedy return to their 'ome.
   (Poor beggars! — they 'll never see 'ome!)

BELTS

THERE was a row in Silver Street that 's near to Dublin
 Quay,
Between an Irish regiment an' English cavalree;
It started at Revelly an' it lasted on till dark:
The first man dropped at Harrison's, the last forninst the
 Park.
   For it was: — " Belts, belts, belts, an' that 's one for
    you! "
   An' it was " Belts, belts, belts, an' that 's done for
    you! "
   O buckle an' tongue
   Was the song that we sung
   From Harrison's down to the Park!

There was a row in Silver Street — the regiments was out,
They called us " Delhi Rebels," an' we answered " Threes
 about! "

That drew them like a hornet's nest — we met them good an'
    large,
The English at the double an' the Irish at the charge.
    Then it was: — " Belts . . .

There was a row in Silver Street — an' I was in it too;
We passed the time o' day, an' then the belts went whirraru!
I misremember what occurred, but subsequint the storm
A *Freeman's Journal Supplemint* was all my uniform.
    O it was: — " Belts . . .

There was a row in Silver Street — they sent the Polis there,
The English were too drunk to know, the Irish did n't care;
But when they grew impertinint we simultaneous rose,
Till half o' them was Liffey mud an' half was tatthered clo'es.
    For it was: — " Belts . . .

There was a row in Silver Street — it might ha' raged till
    now,
But some one drew his side-arm clear, an' nobody knew how;
'T was Hogan took the point an' dropped; we saw the red
    blood run:
An' so we all was murderers that started out in fun.
    While it was: " Belts . . .

There was a row in Silver Street — but that put down the
    shine,
Wid each man whisperin' to his next: — " 'T was never work
    o' mine! "
We went away like beaten dogs, an' down the street we bore
    him,
The poor dumb corpse that could n't tell the bhoys were sorry
    for him.
    When it was: — " Belts . . .

There was a row in Silver Street — it is n't over yet,
For half of us are under guard wid punishments to get;
'T is all a merricle to me as in the Clink I lie:
There was a row in Silver Street — begod, I wonder why!
But it was: — " Belts, belts, belts, an' that 's one for
you! "
An' it was " Belts, belts, belts, an' that 's done for
you! "
O buckle an' tongue
Was the song that we sung
From Harrison's down to the Park!

THE YOUNG BRITISH SOLDIER

WHEN the 'arf-made recruity goes out to the East
'E acts like a babe an' 'e drinks like a beast,
An' 'e wonders because 'e is frequent deceased
Ere 'e 's fit for to serve as a soldier.
Serve, serve, serve as a soldier,
Serve, serve, serve as a soldier,
Serve, serve, serve, as a soldier,
So-oldier *of* the Queen!

Now all you recruities what 's drafted to-day,
You shut up your rag-box an' 'ark to my lay,
An' I 'll sing you a soldier as far as I may:
A soldier what 's fit for a soldier.
Fit, fit, fit for a soldier . . .

First mind you steer clear o' the grog-sellers' huts,
For they sell you Fixed Bay'nets that rots out your guts—
Ay, drink that 'ud eat the live steel from your butts —
An' it 's bad for the young British Soldier.
Bad, bad, bad for the soldier . . .

When the cholera comes — as it will past a doubt —
Keep out of the wet and don't go on the shout,
For the sickness gets in as the liquor dies out,
    An' it crumples the young British soldier.
        Crum-, crum-, crumples the soldier . . .

But the worst o' your foes is the sun over'ead:
You *must* wear your 'elmet for all that is said:
If 'e finds you uncovered 'e 'll knock you down dead,
    An' you 'll die like a fool of a soldier.
        Fool, fool, fool of a soldier . . .

If you 're cast for fatigue by a sergeant unkind,
Don't grouse like a woman nor crack on nor blind;
Be handy and civil, and then you will find
    That it 's beer for the young British soldier.
        Beer, beer, beer for the soldier . . .

Now, if you must marry, take care she is old —
A troop-sergeant's widow 's the nicest, I 'm told,
For beauty won't help if your rations is cold,
    Nor love ain't enough for a soldier.
        'Nough, 'nough, 'nough for a soldier . . .

If the wife should go wrong with a comrade, be loth
To shoot when you catch 'em — you 'll swing, on my
    oath! —
Make 'im take 'er and keep 'er: that 's Hell for them both,
    An' you 're shut o' the curse of a soldier.
        Curse, curse, curse of a soldier . . .

When first under fire an' you 're wishful to duck,
Don't look nor take 'eed at the man that is struck,
Be thankful you 're livin', and trust to your luck
    And march to your front like a soldier.
        Front, front, front like a soldier . . .

When 'arf of your bullets fly wide in the ditch,
Don't call your Martini a cross-eyed old bitch;
She's human as you are — you treat her as sich,
    An' she 'll fight for the young British soldier.
       Fight, fight, fight for the soldier . . .

When shakin' their bustles like ladies so fine,
The guns o' the enemy wheel into line,
Shoot low at the limbers an' don't mind the shine,
    For noise never startles the soldier.
       Start-, start-, startles the soldier . . .

If your officer 's dead and the sergeants look white,
Remember it 's ruin to run from a fight:
So take open order, lie down, and sit tight,
    And wait for supports like a soldier.
       Wait, wait, wait like a soldier . . .

When you 're wounded and left on Afghanistan's plains,
And the women come out to cut up what remains,
Jest roll to your rifle and blow out your brains
    An' go to your Gawd like a soldier.
       Go, go, go like a soldier,
       Go, go, go like a soldier,
       Go, go, go like a soldier,
         So-oldier *of* the Queen!

MANDALAY

By the old Moulmein Pagoda, lookin' eastward to the sea,
There 's a Burma girl a-settin', and I know she thinks o' me;
For the wind is in the palm-trees, and the temple-bells they
    say:
" Come you back, you British soldier; come you back to
    Mandalay!"

Come you back to Mandalay,
Where the old Flotilla lay:
Can't you 'ear their paddles chunkin' from Rangoon to
    Mandalay?
On the road to Mandalay,
Where the flyin'-fishes play,
An' the dawn comes up like thunder outer China 'crost
    the Bay!

'Er petticoat was yaller an' 'er little cap was green,
An' 'er name was Supi-yaw-lat — jes' the same as Theebaw's
    Queen,
An' I seed her first a-smokin' of a whackin' white cheroot,
An' a-wastin' Christian kisses on an 'eathen idol's foot:
        Bloomin' idol made o' mud —
        Wot they called the Great Gawd Budd —
        Plucky lot she cared for idols when I kissed 'er where
            she stud!
        On the road to Mandalay . . .

When the mist was on the rice-fields an' the sun was droppin'
    slow,
She 'd git 'er little banjo an' she 'd sing "*Kulla-lo-lo!*"
With 'er arm upon my shoulder an' 'er cheek agin my cheek
We useter watch the steamers an' the *hathis* pilin' teak.
        Elephints a-pilin' teak
        In the sludgy, squdgy creek,
        Where the silence 'ung that 'eavy you was 'arf afraid
            to speak!
        On the road to Mandalay . . .

But that 's all shove be'ind me — long ago an' fur away,
An' there ain't no 'busses runnin' from the Bank to Man-
    dalay;
An' I 'm learnin' 'ere in London what the ten-year soldier tells:
" If you 've 'eard the East a-callin', you won't never 'eed
    naught else."

No! you won't 'eed nothin' else
But them spicy garlic smells,'
An' the sunshine an' the palm-trees an' the tinkly
temple-bells;
On the road to Mandalay . . .

I am sick o' wastin' leather on these gritty pavin'-stones,
An' the blasted Henglish drizzle wakes the fever in my bones;
Tho' I walks with fifty 'ousemaids outer Chelsea to the Strand,
An' they talks a lot o' lovin', but wot do they understand?
Beefy face an' grubby 'and —
Law! wot do they understand?
I 've a neater, sweeter maiden in a cleaner, greener
land!
On the road to Mandalay . . .

Ship me somewheres east of Suez, where the best is like the
worst,
Where there are n't no Ten Commandments an' a man can
raise a thirst;
For the temple-bells are callin', an' it 's there that I would
be —
By the old Moulmein Pagoda, looking lazy at the sea;
On the road to Mandalay,
Where the old Flotilla lay,
With our sick beneath the awnings when we went to
Mandalay!
O the road to Mandalay,
Where the flyin'-fishes play,
An' the dawn comes up like thunder outer China 'crost
the Bay!

TROOPIN'

(*English Army in the East*)

Troopin', troopin', troopin' to the sea:
'Ere's September come again — the six-year men are free.
O leave the dead be'ind us, for they cannot come away
To where the ship's a-coalin' up that takes us 'ome to-day.
    We're goin' 'ome, we're goin' 'ome,
      Our ship is at the shore,
    An' you must pack your 'aversack,
      For we won't come back no more.
    Ho, don't you grieve for me,
      My lovely Mary-Ann,
    For I'll marry you yit on a fourp'ny bit
      As a time-expired man.

The Malabar's in 'arbour with the Jumner at 'er tail,
An' the time-expired's waitin' of 'is orders for to sail.
Ho! the weary waitin' when on Khyber 'ills we lay,
But the time-expired's waitin' of 'is orders 'ome to-day.

They'll turn us out at Portsmouth wharf in cold an' wet an'
    rain,
All wearin' Injian cotton kit, but we will not complain;
They'll kill us of pneumonia — for that's their little way —
But damn the chills and fever, men, we're goin' 'ome to-day!

Troopin', troopin', winter's round again!
See the new draf's pourin' in for the old campaign;
Ho, you poor recruities, but you've got to earn your pay —
What's the last from Lunnon, lads? We're goin' there
    to-day.

Troopin', troopin', give another cheer —
'Ere 's to English women an' a quart of English beer.
The Colonel an' the regiment an' all who 've got to stay,
Gawd's mercy strike 'em gentle — Whoop! we 're goin'
    'ome to-day.
        We 're goin' 'ome, we 're goin' 'ome,
          Our ship is at the shore,
        An' you must pack your 'aversack,
          For we won't come back no more.
        Ho, don't you grieve for me,
          My lovely Mary-Ann,
        For I 'll marry you yit on a fourp'ny bit
          As a time-expired man.

THE WIDOW'S PARTY

"Where have you been this while away,
        Johnnie, Johnnie?"
Out with the rest on a picnic lay.
        Johnnie, my Johnnie, aha!
They called us out of the barrack-yard
To Gawd knows where from Gosport Hard,
And you can't refuse when you get the card,
        And the Widow gives the party.
          (*Bugle:* Ta—rara—ra-ra-rara!)

"What did you get to eat and drink,
        Johnnie, Johnnie?"
Standing water as thick as ink,
        Johnnie, my Johnnie, aha!
A bit o' beef that were three year stored,
A bit o' mutton as tough as a board,
And a fowl we killed with a sergeant's sword,
        When the Widow give the party.
        19

"What did you do for knives and forks,
          Johnnie, Johnnie?"
We carries 'em with us wherever we walks,
          Johnnie, my Johnnie, aha!
And some was sliced and some was halved,
And some was crimped and some was carved,
And some was gutted and some was starved,
          When the Widow give the party.

"What ha' you done with half your mess,
          Johnnie, Johnnie?"
They could n't do more and they would n't do less,
          Johnnie, my Johnnie, aha!
They ate their whack and they drank their fill,
And I think the rations has made them ill,
For half my comp'ny 's lying still
          Where the Widow give the party.

"How did you get away — away,
          Johnnie, Johnnie?"
On the broad o' my back at the end o' the day,
          Johnnie, my Johnnie, aha!
I comed away like a bleedin' toff,
For I got four niggers to carry me off,
As I lay in the bight of a canvas trough,
          When the Widow give the party.

"What was the end of all the show,
          Johnnie, Johnnie?"
Ask my Colonel, for I don't know,
          Johnnie, my Johnnie, aha!
We broke a King and we built a road —
A court-house stands where the reg'ment goed.
And the river 's clean where the raw blood flowed
          When the Widow give the party.
               (*Bugle:* Ta—rara—ra-ra-rara!)

FORD O' KABUL RIVER

Cabul town 's by Kabul river —
  Blow the bugle, draw the sword —
There I lef' my mate for ever,
  Wet an' drippin' by the ford.
    Ford, ford, ford o' Kabul river,
      Ford o' Kabul river in the dark!
    There 's the river up and brimmin', an' there 's 'arf a
        squadron swimmin'
      'Cross the ford o' Kabul river in the dark.

Kabul town 's a blasted place —
  Blow the bugle, draw the sword —
'Strewth I sha'n't forget 'is face
  Wet an' drippin' by the ford!
    Ford, ford, ford o' Kabul river,
      Ford o' Kabul river in the dark!
    Keep the crossing-stakes beside you, an' they will surely
        guide you
      'Cross the ford o' Kabul river in the dark.

Kabul town is sun and dust —
  Blow the bugle, draw the sword —
I 'd ha' sooner drownded fust
  'Stead of 'im beside the ford.
    Ford, ford, ford o' Kabul river,
      Ford o' Kabul river in the dark!
    You can 'ear the 'orses threshin', you can 'ear the men
        a-splashin',
      'Cross the ford o' Kabul river in the dark.

Kabul town was ours to take —
  Blow the bugle, draw the sword —
I 'd ha' left it for 'is sake —
  'Im that left me by the ford.

Ford, ford, ford o' Kabul river,
　　Ford o' Kabul river in the dark!
It 's none so bloomin' dry there; ain't you never comin'
　　　nigh there,
　　'Cross the ford o' Kabul river in the dark?

Kabul town 'll go to hell —
　Blow the bugle, draw the sword —
'Fore I see him 'live an' well —
　　'Im the best beside the ford.
　　　Ford, ford, ford o' Kabul river,
　　　　Ford o' Kabul river in the dark!
　　　Gawd 'elp 'em if they blunder, for their boots 'll pull 'em
　　　　under,
　　　　By the ford o' Kabul river in the dark.

Turn your 'orse from Kabul town —
　Blow the bugle, draw the sword —
'Im an' 'arf my troop is down,
　　Down and drownded by the ford.
　　　Ford, ford, ford o' Kabul river,
　　　　Ford o' Kabul river in the dark!
　　　There 's the river low an' fallin', but it ain't no use o'
　　　　callin'
　　　　'Cross the ford o' Kabul river in the dark.

GENTLEMEN-RANKERS

To the legion of the lost ones, to the cohort of the damned,
　To my brethren in their sorrow overseas,
Sings a gentleman of England cleanly bred, machinely
　　crammed,
　And a trooper of the Empress, if you please.

Yea, a trooper of the forces who has run his own six horses,
    And faith he went the pace and went it blind,
And the world was more than kin while he held the ready tin,
    But to-day the Sergeant's something less than kind.
        We 're poor little lambs who 've lost our way,
           Baa! Baa! Baa!
        We 're little black sheep who 've gone astray,
           Baa — aa — aa!
        Gentlemen-rankers out on the spree,
        Damned from here to Eternity,
        God ha' mercy on such as we,
           Baa! Yah! Bah!

Oh, it 's sweet to sweat through stables, sweet to empty kitchen
    slops,
    And it 's sweet to hear the tales the troopers tell,
To dance with blowzy housemaids at the regimental hops
    And thrash the cad who says you waltz too well.
Yes, it makes you cock-a-hoop to be " Rider " to your troop,
    And branded with a blasted worsted spur,
When you envy, O how keenly, one poor Tommy being cleanly
    Who blacks your boots and sometimes calls you " Sir."

If the home we never write to, and the oaths we never keep,
    And all we know most distant and most dear,
Across the snoring barrack-room return to break our sleep,
    Can you blame us if we soak ourselves in beer?
When the drunken comrade mutters and the great guard-
    lantern gutters
    And the horror of our fall is written plain,
Every secret, self-revealing on the aching whitewashed ceiling,
    Do you wonder that we drug ourselves from pain?

We have done with Hope and Honour, we are lost to Love and
    Truth,
    We are dropping down the ladder rung by rung,
And the measure of our torment is the measure of our youth.
    God help us, for we knew the worst too young!

Our shame is clean repentance for the crime that brought the
    sentence,
  Our pride it is to know no spur of pride,
And the Curse of Reuben holds us till an alien turf enfolds us
  And we die, and none can tell Them where we died.
      We 're poor little lambs who 've lost our way,
        Baa! Baa! Baa!
      We 're little black sheep who 've gone astray,
        Baa — aa — aa!
      Gentlemen-rankers out on the spree,
      Damned from here to Eternity,
      God ha' mercy on such as we,
        Baa! Yah! Bah!

ROUTE MARCHIN'

WE 'RE marchin' on relief over Injia's sunny plains,
A little front o' Christmas-time an' just be'ind the Rains;
Ho! get away you bullock-man, you 've 'eard the bugle
    blowed,
There 's a regiment a-comin' down the Grand Trunk Road;
    With its best foot first
    And the road a-sliding past,
    An' every blooming campin'-ground exactly like the
      last;
    While the Big Drum says,
    With 'is " *rowdy-dowdy-dow!* " —
    " *Kiko kissywarsti* don't you *hamsher argy jow?* " [1]

Oh, there 's them Injian temples to admire when you see,
There 's the peacock round the corner an' the monkey up the
    tree,
An' there 's that rummy silver-grass a-wavin' in the wind,
An' the old Grand Trunk a-trailin' like a rifle-sling be'ind.
    While it 's best foot first, . . .

[1] Why don't you get on?

At half-past five 's Revelly, an' our tents they down must
    come,
Like a lot of button mushrooms when you pick 'em up at
    'ome.
But it 's over in a minute, an' at six the column starts,
While the women and the kiddies sit an' shiver in the carts.
    An' it 's best foot first, . . .

Oh, then it 's open order, an' we lights our pipes an' sings,
An' we talks about our rations an' a lot of other things,
An' we thinks o' friends in England, an' we wonders what
    they 're at,
An' 'ow they would admire for to hear us sling the *bat*.[1]
    An' it 's best foot first, . . .

It 's none so bad o' Sunday, when you 're lyin' at your
    ease,
To watch the kites a-wheelin' round them feather-'eaded
    trees,
For although there ain't no women, yet there ain't no barrick-
    yards,
So the orficers goes shootin' an' the men they plays at cards.
    Till it 's best foot first, . . .

So 'ark an' 'eed, you rookies, which is always grumblin' sore,
There 's worser things than marchin' from Umballa to Cawn-
    pore;
An' if your 'eels are blistered an' they feels to 'urt like 'ell,
You drop some tallow in your socks an' that will make 'em
    well.
    For it 's best foot first, . . .

We 're marchin' on relief over Injia's coral strand,
Eight 'undred fightin' Englishmen, the Colonel, and the Band;

[1] Language. Thomas's first and firmest conviction is that he is a profound
Orientalist and a fluent speaker of Hindustani. As a matter of fact, he de-
pends largely on the sign-language.

Ho! get away you bullock-man, you 've 'eard the bugle blowed,
There 's a regiment a-comin' down the Grand Trunk Road;
    With its best foot first
    And the road a-sliding past,
    An' every bloomin' campin'-ground exactly like the last;
    While the Big Drum says,
    With 'is " *rowdy-dowdy-dow!* "—
    " *Kiko kissywarsti* don't you *hamsher argy jow?* "

SHILLIN' A DAY

MY name is O'Kelly, I 've heard the Revelly
From Birr to Bareilly, from Leeds to Lahore,
Hong-Kong and Peshawur,
Lucknow and Etawah,
And fifty-five more all endin' in " pore."
Black Death and his quickness, the depth and the thickness,
Of sorrow and sickness I 've known on my way,
But I 'm old and I 'm nervis,
I 'm cast from the Service,
And all I deserve is a shillin' a day.

    (*Chorus*) Shillin' a day,
              Bloomin' good pay —
              Lucky to touch it, a shillin' a day!

Oh, it drives me half crazy to think of the days I
Went slap for the Ghazi, my sword at my side,
When we rode Hell-for-leather
Both squadrons together,
That did n't care whether we lived or we died.
But it 's no use despairin', my wife must go charin'

An' me commissairin' the pay-bills to better,
So if me you be'old
In the wet and the cold,
By the Grand Metropold won't you give me a letter?

(*Full chorus*)   Give 'im a letter —
          'Can't do no better,
          Late Troop-Sergeant-Major an' — runs with
            a letter!
          Think what 'e 's been,
          Think what 'e 's seen.
          Think of his pension an' ——

              GAWD SAVE THE QUEEN!

BARRACK ROOM BALLADS

II

GENERAL

1892–1896

When 'Omer smote 'is bloomin' lyre,
  He 'd 'eard men sing by land an' sea;
An' what he thought 'e might require,
  'E went an' took — the same as me!

The market-girls an' fishermen,
  The shepherds an' the sailors, too,
They 'eard old songs turn up again,
  But kep' it quiet — same as you!

They knew 'e stole; 'e knew they knowed.
  They didn't tell, nor make a fuss,
But winked at 'Omer down the road,
  An' 'e winked back — the same as us!

"BACK TO THE ARMY AGAIN"

I 'M 'ere in a ticky ulster an' a broken billycock 'at,
A-layin' on to the sergeant I don't know a gun from a bat;
My shirt 's doin' duty for jacket, my sock 's stickin' out o'
    my boots,
An' I 'm learnin' the damned old goose-step along o' the new
    recruits!

> Back to the Army again, sergeant,
>   Back to the Army again.
> Don't look so 'ard, for I 'ave n't no card,
>   I 'm back to the Army again!

I done my six years' service. 'Er Majesty sez: " Good day —
You 'll please to come when you 're rung for, an' 'ere 's your
    'ole back-pay;
An' four-pence a day for baccy — an' bloomin' gen'rous, too;
An' now you can make your fortune — the same as your
    orf'cers do."

> Back to the Army again, sergeant,
>   Back to the Army again;
> 'Ow did I learn to do right-about turn?
>   I 'm back to the Army again!

A man o' four-an'-twenty that 'as n't learned of a trade —
Beside " Reserve " agin' him — 'e 'd better be never made.
I tried my luck for a quarter, an' that was enough for me,
An' I thought of 'Er Majesty's barricks, an' I thought I 'd
    go an' see.

Back to the Army again, sergeant,
    Back to the Army again;
'T is n't my fault if I dress when I 'alt —
    I 'm back to the Army again!

The sergeant arst no questions, but 'e winked the other eye,
'E sez to me, " 'Shun!" an' I shunted, the same as in days
    gone by;
For 'e saw the set o' my shoulders, an' I could n't 'elp 'oldin'
    straight
When me an' the other rookies come under the barrick gate.

    Back to the Army again, sergeant,
        Back to the Army again;
    'Oo would ha' thought I could carry an' port?
        I 'm back to the Army again!

I took my bath, an' I wallered — for, Gawd, I needed it so!
I smelt the smell o' the barricks, I 'eard the bugles go.
I 'eard the feet on the gravel — the feet o' the men what
    drill —
An' I sez to my flutterin' 'eart-strings, I sez to 'em, "Peace,
    be still!"

    Back to the Army again, sergeant,
        Back to the Army again;
    'Oo said I knew when the troopship was due?
        I 'm back to the Army again!

I carried my slops to the tailor; I sez to 'im, " None o' your
    lip!
You tight 'em over the shoulders, an' loose 'em over the 'ip,
For the set o' the tunic 's 'orrid." An' 'e sez to me, " Strike
    me dead,
But I thought you was used to the business!" an' so 'e done
    what I said.

Back to the Army again, sergeant,
　　Back to the Army again.
Rather too free with my fancies? Wot — me?
　　I 'm back to the Army again!

Next week I 'll 'ave 'em fitted; I 'll buy me a swagger-cane;
They 'll let me free o' the barricks to walk on the Hoe again
In the name o' William Parsons, that used to be Edward Clay,
An' — any pore beggar that wants it can draw my fourpence
　　a day!

　　Back to the Army again, sergeant,
　　　Back to the Army again:
　　Out o' the cold an' the rain, sergeant,
　　　Out o' the cold an' the rain.

　　　　　'Oo 's there?
A man that 's too good to be lost you,
　　A man that is 'andled an' made —
A man that will pay what 'e cost you
　　In learnin' the others their trade — parade!
You 're droppin' the pick o' the Army
　　Because you don't 'elp 'em remain,
But drives 'em to cheat to get out o' the street
　　An' back to the Army again!

"BIRDS OF PREY" MARCH

(*Troops for Foreign Service*)

MARCH! The mud is cakin' good about our trousies.
　　Front! — eyes front, an' watch the Colour-casin's drip.
Front! The faces of the women in the 'ouses
　　Ain't the kind o' things to take aboard the ship.

Cheer!   An' we 'll never march to victory.
Cheer!   An' we 'll never live to 'ear the cannon roar!
*   The Large Birds o' Prey*
*   They will carry us away,*
An' you 'll never see your soldiers any more!

Wheel!   Oh, keep your touch; we 're goin' round a corner.
    Time! — mark time, an' let the men be'ind us close.
Lord!   The transport 's full, an' 'alf our lot not on 'er —
    Cheer, O cheer!   We 're going off where no one knows.

March!   The Devil 's none so black as 'e is painted!
    Cheer!   We 'll 'ave some fun before we 're put away.
'Alt an' 'and 'er out — a woman 's gone and fainted!
    Cheer!   Get on! — Gawd 'elp the married men to-day!

Hoi!   Come up, you 'ungry beggars, to yer sorrow.
    ('Ear them say they want their tea, an' want it quick!)
You won't have no mind for slingers, not to-morrow —
    No; you 'll put the 'tween-decks stove out, bein' sick!

'Alt!   The married kit 'as all to go before us!
    'Course it 's blocked the bloomin' gangway up again!
Cheer, O cheer the 'Orse Guards watchin' tender o'er us,
    Keepin' us since eight this mornin' in the rain!

Stuck in 'eavy marchin'-order, sopped and wringin' —
    Sick, before our time to watch 'er 'eave an' fall,
'Ere 's your 'appy 'ome at last, an' stop your singin'.
    'Alt!   Fall in along the troop-deck!   Silence all!

Cheer!   For we 'll never live to see no bloomin' victory!
Cheer!   An' we 'll never live to 'ear the cannon roar!
*   (One cheer more!)*
*   The jackal an' the kite*
*   'Ave an 'ealthy appetite,*
An' you 'll never see your soldiers any more!   ('Ip! Urroar!)
*   The eagle an' the crow*
*   They are waitin' ever so,*

An' you 'll never see your soldiers any more!   ('Ip! Urroar!)
    Yes, the Large Birds o' Prey
       They will carry us away,
An' you 'll never see your soldiers any more!

"SOLDIER AN' SAILOR TOO"

(*Royal Regiment of Marines*)

As I was spittin' into the Ditch aboard o' the *Crocodile*,
I seed a man on a man-o'-war got up in the Reg'lars' style.
'E was scrapin' the paint from off of 'er plates, an' I sez to
   'im, "'Oo are you?"
Sez 'e, " I 'm a Jolly — 'Er Majesty's Jolly — soldier an'
   sailor too!"
Now 'is work begins by Gawd knows when, and 'is work is
   never through;
'E is n't one o' the reg'lar Line, nor 'e is n't one of the crew.
'E 's a kind of a giddy harumfrodite — soldier an' sailor too!

An' after I met 'im all over the world, a-doin' all kinds of
   things,
Like landin' 'isself with a Gatlin' gun to talk to them 'eathen
   kings;
'E sleeps in an 'ammick instead of a cot, an' 'e drills with the
   deck on a slew,
An' 'e sweats like a Jolly — 'Er Majesty's Jolly — soldier
   an' sailor too!
For there is n't a job on the top o' the earth the beggar don't
   know, nor do —
You can leave 'im at night on a bald man's 'ead, to paddle 'is
   own canoe —
'E 's a sort of a bloomin' cosmopolouse — soldier an' sailor
   too.

We 've fought 'em in trooper, we 've fought 'em in dock, and
    drunk with 'em in betweens,
When they called us the seasick scull'ry-maids, an' we called
    'em the Ass-Marines;
But, when we was down for a double fatigue, from Woolwich
    to Bernardmyo,
We sent for the Jollies — 'Er Majesty's Jollies — soldier
    an' sailor too!
They think for 'emselves, an' they steal for 'emselves, and
    they never ask what 's to do,
But they 're camped an' fed an' they 're up an' fed before our
    bugle 's blew.
Ho! they ain't no limpin' procrastitutes — soldier an' sailor
    too.

You may say we are fond of an 'arness-cut, or 'ootin' in
    barrick-yards,
Or startin' a Board School mutiny along o' the Onion
    Guards;
But once in 'a while we can finish in style for the ends of the
    earth to view,
The same as the Jollies — 'Er Majesty's Jollies — soldier
    an' sailor too!
They come of our lot, they was brothers to us; they was
    beggars we 'd met an' knew;
Yes, barrin' an inch in the chest an' the arm, they was doubles
    o' me an' you;
Eor they were n't no special chrysanthemums — soldier an'
    sailor too!

To take your chance in the thick of a rush, with firing all about,
Is nothing so bad when you 've cover to 'and, an' leave an'
    likin' to shout;
But to stand an' be still to the *Birken'ead* drill is a damn
    tough bullet to chew,
An' they done it, the Jollies — 'Er Majesty's Jollies — sol-
    dier an' sailor too!

Their work was done when it 'ad n't begun; they was younger
    nor me an' you;
Their choice it was plain between drownin' in 'eaps an' bein'
    mopped by the screw,
So they stood an' was still to the *Birken'ead* drill, soldier an'
    sailor too!

We 're most of us liars, we 're 'arf of us thieves, an' the rest
    are as rank as can be,
But once in a while we can finish in style (which I 'ope it won't
    'appen to me).
But it makes you think better o' you an' your friends, an' the
    work you may 'ave to do,
When you think o' the sinkin' *Victorier's* Jollies — soldier an'
    sailor too!
Now there is n't no room for to say ye don't know — they
    'ave proved it plain and true —
That whether it 's Widow, or whether it 's ship, Victorier's
    work is to do,
An' they done it, the Jollies — 'Er Majesty's Jollies — sol-
    dier an' sailor too!

SAPPERS

(*Royal Engineers*)

When the Waters were dried an' the Earth did appear,
    (" It 's all one," says the Sapper),
The Lord He created the Engineer,
    Her Majesty's Royal Engineer,
    With the rank and pay of a Sapper!

When the Flood come along for an extra monsoon,
'T was Noah constructed the first pontoon
    To the plans of Her Majesty's, etc.

But after fatigue in the wet an' the sun,
Old Noah got drunk, which he would n't ha' done
   If he 'd trained with, etc.

When the Tower o' Babel had mixed up men's *bat*,[1]
Some clever civilian was managing that,
   An' none of, etc.

When the Jews had a fight at the foot of a hill,
Young Joshua ordered the sun to stand still,
   For he was a Captain of Engineers, etc.

When the Children of Israel made bricks without straw,
They were learnin' the regular work of our Corps,
   The work of, etc.

For ever since then, if a war they would wage,
Behold us a-shinin' on history's page —
   First page for, etc.

We lay down their sidings an' help 'em entrain,
An' we sweep up their mess through the bloomin' campaign,
   In the style of, etc.

They send us in front with a fuse an' a mine
To blow up the gates that are rushed by the Line,
   But bent by, etc.

They send us behind with a pick an' a spade,
To dig for the guns of a bullock-brigade
   Which has asked for, etc.

We work under escort in trousers and shirt,
An' the heathen they plug us tail-up in the dirt,
   Annoying, etc.

          [1] Talk.

We blast out the rock an' we shovel the mud,
We make 'em good roads an' — they roll down the *khud*,[1]
   Reporting, etc.

We make 'em their bridges, their wells, an' their huts,
An' the telegraph-wire the enemy cuts,
   An' it 's blamed on, etc.

An' when we return, an' from war we would cease,
They grudge us adornin' the billets of peace,
   Which are kept for, etc.

We build 'em nice barracks — they swear they are bad,
That our Colonels are Methodist, married or mad,
   Insultin', etc.

They have n't no manners nor gratitude too,
For the more that we help 'em, the less will they do,
   But mock at, etc.

Now the Line 's but a man with a gun in his hand,
An' Cavalry 's only what horses can stand,
   When helped by, etc.

Artillery moves by the leave o' the ground,
But *we* are the men that do something all round,
   For *we* are, etc.

I have stated it plain, an' my argument 's thus
   ("It 's all one," says the Sapper)
There 's only one Corps which is perfect — that 's us;
   An' they call us Her Majesty's Engineers,
   Her Majesty's Royal Engineers,
   With the rank and pay of a Sapper!

           [1] Hillside.

THAT DAY

IT got beyond all orders an' it got beyond all 'ope;
    It got to shammin' wounded an' retirin' from the 'alt.
'Ole companies was lookin' for the nearest road to slope;
    It were just a bloomin' knock-out — an' our fault!

    Now there ain't no chorus 'ere to give,
        Nor there ain't no band to play;
    An' I wish I was dead 'fore I done what I did,
        Or seen what I seed that day!

We was sick o' bein' punished, an' we let 'em know it, too;
    An' a company-commander up an' 'it us with a sword,
An' some one shouted " 'Ook it! " an' it come to *sove-ki-poo*,
    An' we chucked our rifles from us — O my Gawd!

There was thirty dead an' wounded on the ground we
    would n't keep —
No, there was n't more than twenty when the front begun
    to go;
But, Christ! along the line o' flight they cut us up like sheep,
    An' that was all we gained by doin' so!

I 'eard the knives be'ind me, but I dursn't face my man,
    Nor I don't know where I went to, 'cause I did n't 'alt to
    see,
Till I 'eard a beggar squealin' out for quarter as 'e ran,
    An' I thought I knew the voice an' — it was me!

We was 'idin' under bedsteads more than 'arf a march away;
    We was lyin' up like rabbits all about the country side;
An' the major cursed 'is Maker 'cause 'e lived to see that day,
    An' the colonel broke 'is sword acrost, an' cried.

We was rotten 'fore we started — we was never disci*plined;*
  We made it out a favour if an order was obeyed;
Yes, every little drummer 'ad 'is rights an' wrongs to mind,
  So we had to pay for teachin' — an' we paid!

The papers 'id it 'andsome, but you know the Army knows;
  We was put to groomin' camels till the regiments withdrew,
An' they gave us each a medal for subduin' England's foes,
  An' I 'ope you like my song — because it 's true!

> *An' there ain't no chorus 'ere to give,*
>   *Nor there ain't no band to play;*
> *But I wish I was dead 'fore I done what I did,*
>   *Or seen what I seed that day!*

"THE MEN THAT FOUGHT AT MINDEN"

(*In the Lodge of Instruction*)

THE men that fought at Minden, they was rookies in their
      time —
  So was them that fought at Waterloo!
All the 'ole command, yuss, from Minden to Maiwand,
  They was once dam' sweeps like you!

> *Then do not be discouraged, 'Eaven is your 'elper,*
>   *We 'll learn you not to forget;*
> *An' you must n't swear an' curse, or you 'll only catch it*
>   *worse,*
>   *For we 'll make you soldiers yet!*

The men that fought at Minden, they 'ad stocks beneath their
  chins,
    Six inch 'igh an' more;
But fatigue it was their pride, and they *would* not be denied
    To clean the cook-'ouse floor.

The men that fought at Minden, they had anarchistic bombs
    Served to 'em by name of 'and-grenades;
But they got it in the eye (same as you will by an' by)
    When they clubbed their field-parades.

The men that fought at Minden, they 'ad buttons up an'
  down,
    Two-an'-twenty dozen of 'em told;
But they did n't grouse an' shirk at an hour's extry work,
    They kept 'em bright as gold.

The men that fought at Minden, they was armed with mus-
  ketoons,
    Also, they was drilled by 'alberdiers;
I don't know what they were, but the sergeants took good
  care
    They washed be'ind their ears.

The men that fought at Minden, they 'ad ever cash in 'and
    Which they did not bank nor save,
But spent it gay an' free on their betters — such as me —
    For the good advice I gave.

The men that fought at Minden, they was civil — yuss, they
  was —
    Never did n't talk o' rights an' wrongs,
But they got it with the toe (same as you will get it — so!) —
    For interrupting songs.

The men that fought at Minden, they was several other things
    Which I don't remember clear;
But *that 's* the reason why, now the six-year men are dry,
    The rooks will stand the beer!

Then do not be discouraged, 'Eaven is your 'elper,
  We'll learn you not to forget;
An' you must n't swear an' curse, or you'll only catch it
    worse,
And we'll make you soldiers yet!

Soldiers yet, if you've got it in you —
  All for the sake of the Core;
Soldiers yet, if we 'ave to skin you —
  Run an' get the beer, Johnny Raw — Johnny Raw!
  Ho! run an' get the beer, Johnny Raw!

CHOLERA CAMP

(*Infantry in India*)

WE 'VE got the cholerer in camp — it's worse than forty
    fights;
We're dyin' in the wilderness the same as Isrulites;
It's before us, an' be'ind us, an' we cannot get away,
An' the doctor's just reported we've ten more to-day!

  Oh, strike your camp an' go, the bugle's callin',
    The Rains are fallin' —
  The dead are bushed an' stoned to keep 'em safe below;
  The Band's a-doin' all she knows to cheer us;
  The chaplain's gone and prayed to Gawd to 'ear us —
    To 'ear us —
  O Lord, for it's a-killin' of us so!

Since August, when it started, it's been stickin' to our tail,
Though they've 'ad us out by marches an' they've 'ad us
    back by rail;
But it runs as fast as troop-trains, and we can not get away;
An' the sick-list to the Colonel makes ten more to-day.

There ain't no fun in women nor there ain't no bite to drink;
It 's much too wet for shootin'; we can only march and think;
An' at evenin', down the *nullahs,* we can 'ear the jackals say,
" Get up, you rotten beggars, you 've ten more to-day! "

'T would make a monkey cough to see our way o' doin'
    things —
Lieutenants takin' companies an' captains takin' wings,
An' Lances actin' Sergeants — eight file to obey —
For we 've lots o' quick promotion on ten deaths a day!

Our Colonel 's white an' twitterly — 'e gets no sleep nor food,
But mucks about in 'orspital where nothing does no good.
'E sends us 'eaps o' comforts, all bought from 'is pay —
But there are n't much comfort 'andy on ten deaths a day.

Our Chaplain 's got a banjo, an' a skinny mule 'e rides,
An' the stuff 'e says an' sings us, Lord, it makes us split our
    sides!
With 'is black coat-tails a-bobbin' to *Ta-ra-ra Boom-der-ay!*
'E 's the proper kind o' *padre* for ten deaths a day.

An' Father Victor 'elps 'im with our Roman Catholicks —
He knows an 'eap of Irish songs an' rummy conjurin' tricks;
An' the two they works together when it comes to play or
    pray.
So we keep the ball a-rollin' on ten deaths a day.

We 've got the cholerer in camp — we 've got it 'ot an' sweet;
It ain't no Christmas dinner, but it 's 'elped an' we must eat.
We 've gone beyond the funkin', 'cause we 've found it does n't
    pay,
An' we 're rockin' round the Districk on ten deaths a day!

    Then strike your camp an' go, the Rains are fallin',
      The Bugle 's callin'!
    The dead are bushed an' stoned to keep 'em safe below!
    An' them that do not like it they can lump it,

An' them that can not stand it they can jump it;
We 've got to die somewhere — some way — some'ow —
We might as well begin to do it now!
Then, Number One, let down the tent-pole slow,
Knock out the pegs an' 'old the corners — so!
Fold in the flies, furl up the ropes, an' stow!
Oh, strike — oh, strike your camp an' go!
     (Gawd 'elp us!)

THE LADIES

I 'VE taken my fun where I 've found it;
    I 've rogued an' I 've ranged in my time;
I 've 'ad my pickin' o' sweet'earts,
    An' four o' the lot was prime.
One was an 'arf-caste widow,
    One was a woman at Prome,
One was the wife of a *jemadar-sais*,[1]
    An' one is a girl at 'ome.

Now I are n't no 'and with the ladies,
    For, takin' 'em all along,
You never can say till you 've tried 'em,
    An' then you are like to be wrong.
There 's times when you 'll think that you might n't,
    There 's times when you 'll know that you might;
But the things you will learn from the Yellow an' Brown,
    They 'll 'elp you a lot with the White!

I was a young un at 'Oogli,
    Shy as a girl to begin;
Aggie de Castrer she made me,
    An' Aggie was clever as sin;

[1] Head-groom.

Older than me, but my first un —
　More like a mother she were —
Showed me the way to promotion an' pay,
　An' I learned about women from 'er!

Then I was ordered to Burma,
　Actin' in charge o' Bazar,
An' I got me a tiddy live 'eathen
　Through buyin' supplies off 'er pa.
Funny an' yellow an' faithful —
　Doll in a teacup she were,
But we lived on the square, like a true-married pair,
　An' I learned about women from 'er!

Then we was shifted to Neemuch
　(Or I might ha' been keepin' 'er now),
An' I took with a shiny she-devil,
　The wife of a nigger at Mhow;
Taught me the gipsy-folks' *bolee;* [1]
　Kind o' volcano she were,
For she knifed me one night 'cause I wished she was
　　white,
　And I learned about women from 'er!

Then I come 'ome in a trooper,
　'Long of a kid o' sixteen —
Girl from a convent at Meerut,
　The straightest I ever 'ave seen.
Love at first sight was 'er trouble,
　She did n't know what it were;
An' I would n't do such, 'cause I liked 'er too much,
　But — I learned about women from 'er!

I 've taken my fun where I 've found it,
　An' now I must pay for my fun,
For the more you 'ave known o' the others
　· The less will you settle to one;

　　　　　　　[1] Slang.

An' the end of it 's sittin' and thinkin',
  An' dreamin' Hell-fires to see;
So be warned by my lot (which I know you will not),
  An' learn about women from me!

What did the Colonel's Lady think?
  Nobody never knew.
Somebody asked the Sergeant's wife,
  An' she told 'em true!
When you get to a man in the case,
  They 're like as a row of pins —
For the Colonel's Lady an' Judy O'Grady
  Are sisters under their skins!

BILL 'AWKINS

" ' As anybody seen Bill 'Awkins?"
  " Now 'ow in the devil would I know?"
" 'E 's taken my girl out walkin',
  An' I 've got to tell 'im so —
    Gawd — bless — 'im!
  I 've got to tell 'im so."

  " D' yer know what 'e 's like, Bill 'Awkins?"
    " Now what in the devil would I care?"
" 'E 's the livin', breathin' image of an organ-grinder's
      monkey,
  With a pound of grease in 'is 'air —
    Gawd — bless — 'im!
  An' a pound o' grease in 'is 'air."

" An' s'pose you met Bill 'Awkins,
   Now what in the devil 'ud ye do? "
" I 'd open 'is cheek to 'is chin-strap buckle,
   An' bung up 'is both eyes, too —
      Gawd — bless — 'im!
   An' bung up 'is both eyes, too! "

" Look 'ere, where 'e comes, Bill 'Awkins!
   Now what in the devil will you say? "
" It is n't fit an' proper to be fightin' on a Sunday,
   So I 'll pass 'im the time o' day —
      Gawd — bless — 'im!
   I 'll pass 'im the. time o' day! "

———

THE MOTHER–LODGE

THERE was Rundle, Station Master,
   An' Beazeley of the Rail,
An' 'Ackman, Commissariat,
   An' Donkin' o' the Jail;
An' Blake, Conductor-Sargent,
   Our Master twice was 'e,
With 'im that kept the Europe-shop,
   Old Framjee Eduljee.

Outside — " Sergeant! Sir! Salute! Salaam! "
Inside — " Brother," an' it does n't do no 'arm.
We met upon the Level an' we parted on the Square,
An' I was Junior Deacon in my Mother Lodge out there!

We 'd Bola Nath, Accountant,
   An' Saul the Aden Jew,
An' Din Mohammed, draughtsman
   Of the Survey Office too;

There was Babu Chuckerbutty,
  An' Amir Singh the Sikh,
An' Castro from the fittin'-sheds,
  The Roman Catholick!

We 'ad n't good regalia,
  An' our Lodge was old an' bare,
But we knew the Ancient Landmarks,
  An' we kep' 'em to a hair;
An' lookin' on it backwards
  It often strikes me thus,
There ain't such things as infidels,
  Excep', per'aps, it 's us.

For monthly, after Labour,
  We 'd all sit down and smoke
(We durs n't give no banquits,
  Lest a Brother's caste were broke),
An' man on man got talkin'
  Religion an' the rest,
An' every man comparin'
  Of the God 'e knew the best.

So man on man got talkin',
  An' not a Brother stirred
Till mornin' waked the parrots
  An' that dam' brain-fever-bird;
We 'd say 't was 'ighly curious,
  An' we 'd all ride 'ome to bed,
With Mo'ammed, God, an' Shiva
  Changin' pickets in our 'ead.

Full oft on Guv'ment service
  This rovin' foot 'ath pressed,
An' bore fraternal greetin's
  To the Lodges east an' west,

Accordin' as commanded
From Kohat to Singapore,
But I wish that I might see them
In my Mother Lodge once more!

I wish that I might see them,
My Brethren black an' brown,
With the trichies smellin' pleasant
An' the *hog-darn* [1] passin' down ;
An' the old khansamah [2] snorin'
On the bottle-khana [3] floor,
Like a Master in good standing
With my Mother Lodge once more.

Outside — " Sergeant!   Sir!   Salute!   Salaam! "
Inside — " Brother," an' it does n't do no 'arm.
We met upon the Level an' we parted on the Square,
An' I was Junior Deacon in my Mother Lodge out there!

" FOLLOW ME 'OME "

THERE was no one like 'im, 'Orse or Foot,
Nor any o' the Guns I knew ;
An' because it was so, why, o' course 'e went an' died,
Which is just what the best men do.

So it 's knock out your pipes an' follow me!
An' it 's finish up your swipes an' follow me!
Oh, 'ark to the big drum callin',
Follow me — follow me 'ome!

---

[1] Cigar-lighter.   [2] Butler.   [3] Pantry.

'Is mare she neighs the 'ole day long,
    She paws the 'ole night through,
An' she won't take 'er feed 'cause o' waitin' for 'is step,
    Which is just what a beast would do.

    'Is girl she goes with a bombardier
    Before 'er month is through;
An' the banns are up in church, for she's got the beggar
    hooked,
    Which is just what a girl would do.

    We fought 'bout a dog — last week it were —
    No more than a round or two;
But I strook 'im cruel 'ard, an' I wish I 'ad n't now,
    Which is just what a man can't do.

    'E was all that I 'ad in the way of a friend,
    An' I 've 'ad to find one new;
But I 'd give my pay an' stripe for to get the beggar back,
    Which it 's just too late to do.

    So it 's knock out your pipes an' follow me!
    An' it 's finish up your swipes an' follow me!
      Oh, 'ark to the fifes a-crawlin'!
      Follow me — follow me 'ome!

    Take 'im away! 'E 's gone where the best men go.
    Take 'im away! An' the gun-wheels turnin' slow.
    Take 'im away! There 's more from the place 'e come.
    Take 'im away, with the limber an' the drum.

    For it 's " Three rounds blank " an' follow me,
    An' it 's " Thirteen rank " an' follow me;
      Oh, passin' the love o' women,
      Follow me — follow me 'ome!

THE SERGEANT'S WEDDIN'

'E WAS warned agin 'er —
   That 's what made 'im look;
She was warned agin 'im —
   That is why she took.
'Would n't 'ear no reason,
   'Went an' done it blind;
We know all about 'em,
   They 've got all to find!

Cheer for the Sergeant's weddin' —
   Give 'em one cheer more!
Grey gun-'orses in the lando,
   An' a rogue is married to, etc.

What 's the use o' tellin'
   'Arf the lot she 's been?
'E 's a bloomin' robber,
   An' 'e keeps canteen.
'Ow did 'e get 'is buggy?
   Gawd, you need n't ask!
'Made 'is forty gallon
   Out of every cask!

Watch 'im, with 'is 'air cut,
   Count us filin' by —
Won't the Colonel praise 'is
   Pop—u—lar—i—ty!
We 'ave scores to settle —
   Scores for more than beer;
She 's the girl to pay 'em —
   That is why we 're 'ere!

See the chaplain thinkin'?
   See the women smile?
Twig the married winkin'
   As they take the aisle?
Keep your side-arms quiet,
   Dressin' by the Band.
Ho! You 'oly beggars,
   Cough be'ind your 'and!

Now it's done an' over,
   'Ear the organ squeak,
" *'Voice that breathed o'er Eden* " —
   Ain't she got the cheek!
White an' laylock ribbons,
   Think yourself so fine!
I'd pray Gawd to take yer
   'Fore I made yer mine!

Escort to the kerridge,
   Wish 'im luck, the brute!
Chuck the slippers after —
   [Pity 't ain't a boot!]
Bowin' like a lady,
   Blushin' like a lad —
'Oo would say to see 'em
   Both is rotten bad?

Cheer for the Sergeant's weddin' —
   Give 'em one cheer more!
Grey gun-'orses in the lando,
   An' a rogue is married to, etc.

THE JACKET

(*Royal Horse Artillery*)

THROUGH the Plagues of Egyp' we was chasin' Arabi,
　　Gettin' down an' shovin' in the sun;
An' you might 'ave called us dirty, an' you might ha' called us
　　dry,
　　An' you might 'ave 'eard us talkin' at the gun.
But the Captain 'ad 'is jacket, an' the jacket it was new —
　　('Orse Gunners, listen to my song!)
An' the wettin' of the jacket is the proper thing to do,
　　Nor we did n't keep 'im waiting very long.

One day they gave us orders for to shell a sand redoubt,
　　Loadin' down the axle-arms with case;
But the Captain knew 'is dooty, an' he took the crackers out
　　An' he put some proper liquor in its place.
An' the Captain saw the shrapnel, which is six-an'-thirty clear.
　　('Orse Gunners, listen to my song!)
" Will you draw the weight," sez 'e, " or will you draw the
　　beer? "
　　An' we did n't keep 'im waitin' very long.

　　For the Captain, etc.

Then we trotted gentle, not to break the bloomin' glass,
　　Though the Arabites 'ad all their ranges marked;
But we durs n't 'ardly gallop, for the most was bottled Bass,
　　An' we 'd dreamed of it since we was disembarked:
So we fired economic with the shells we 'ad in 'and,
　　('Orse Gunners, listen to my song!)
But the beggars under cover 'ad the impidence to stand,
　　An' we could n't keep 'em waitin' very long.

　　And the Captain, etc.

So we finished 'arf the liquor (an' the Captain took cham-
pagne),
An' the Arabites was shootin' all the while;
An' we left our wounded 'appy with the empties on the plain,
An' we used the bloomin' guns for pro-jectile!
We limbered up an' galloped — there were nothin' else to do —
('Orse Gunners, listen to my song!)
An' the Battery came a-boundin' like a boundin' kangaroo,
But they did n't watch us comin' very long.

    As the Captain, etc.

We was goin' most extended — we was drivin' very fine,
An' the Arabites were loosin' 'igh an' wide,
Till the Captain took the glacis with a rattlin' "right
incline,"
An' we dropped upon their 'eads the other side.
Then we give 'em quarter — such as 'ad n't up and cut
('Orse Gunners, listen to my song!)
An' the Captain stood a limberful of fizzy — somethin' Brutt,
But we did n't leave it fizzing very long.

    For the Captain, etc.

We might ha' been court-martialled, but it all come out all
right
When they signalled us to join the main command.
There was every round expended, there was every gunner
tight,
An' the Captain waved a corkscrew in 'is 'and!

    But the Captain 'ad 'is jacket, etc.

THE 'EATHEN

THE 'eathen in 'is blindness bows down to wood an' stone;
'E don't obey no orders unless they is 'is own;
'E keeps 'is side-arms awful: 'e leaves 'em all about,
An' then comes up the Regiment an' pokes the 'eathen out.

All along o' dirtiness, all along o' mess,
All along o' doin' things rather-more-or-less,
All along of abby-nay,[1] kul,[2] an' hazar-ho,[3]
Mind you keep your rifle an' yourself jus' so!

The young recruit is 'aughty — 'e draf's from Gawd knows
        where;
They bid 'im show 'is stockin's an' lay 'is mattress square;
'E calls it bloomin' nonsense — 'e does n't know, no more —
An' then up comes 'is Company an' kicks 'im round the floor!

The young recruit is 'ammered — 'e takes it very 'ard;
'E 'angs 'is 'ead an' mutters — 'e sulks about the yard;
'E talks o' " cruel tyrants " which 'e 'll swing for by-an'-by,
An' the others 'ears an' mocks 'im, an' the boy goes orf to cry.

The young recruit is silly — 'e thinks o' suicide;
'E 's lost 'is gutter-devil; 'e 'as n't got 'is pride;
But day by day they kicks 'im, which 'elps 'im on a bit,
Till 'e finds 'isself one mornin' with a full an' proper kit.

Gettin' clear o' dirtiness, gettin' done with mess,
Gettin' shut o' doin' things rather-more-or-less;
Not so fond of abby-nay, kul, nor hazar-ho,
Learns to keep 'is rifle an' 'isself jus' so!

[1] Not now.   [2] To-morrow.   [3] Wait a bit.

The young recruit is 'appy — 'e throws a chest to suit;
You see 'im grow mustaches; you 'ear 'im slap 'is boot;
'E learns to drop the " bloodies " from every word 'e slings,
An' 'e shows an 'ealthy brisket when 'e strips for bars an'
    rings.

The cruel-tyrant-sergeants they watch 'im 'arf a year;
They watch 'im with 'is comrades, they watch 'im with 'is beer;
They watch 'im with the women at the regimental dance,
And the cruel-tyrant-sergeants send 'is name along for
    " Lance."

An' now 'e 's 'arf o' nothin', an' all a private yet,
'Is room they up an' rags 'im to see what they will get;
They rags 'im low an' cunnin', each dirty trick they can,
But 'e learns to sweat 'is temper an' 'e learns to sweat 'is man.

An', last, a Colour-Sergeant, as such to be obeyed,
'E schools 'is men at cricket, 'e tells 'em on parade;
They sees 'em quick an' 'andy, uncommon set an' smart,
An' so 'e talks to orficers which 'ave the Core at 'eart.

'E learns to do 'is watchin' without it showin' plain;
'E learns to save a dummy, an' shove 'im straight again;
'E learns to check a ranker that 's buyin' leave to shirk;
An' 'e learns to make men like 'im so they 'll learn to like their
    work.

An' when it comes to marchin' he 'll see their socks are right,
An' when it comes to action 'e shows 'em 'ow to sight;
'E knows their ways of thinkin' and just what 's their mind;
'E knows when they are takin' on an' when they 've fell be'ind.

'E knows each talkin' corpril that leads a squad astray;
'E feels 'is innards 'eavin', 'is bowels givin' way;
'E sees the blue-white faces all tryin' 'ard to grin,
An' 'e stands an' waits an' suffers till it 's time to cap 'em in.

An' now the hugly bullets come peckin' through the dust,
An' no one wants to face 'em, but every beggar must;
So, like a man in irons which is n't glad to go,
They moves 'em off by companies uncommon stiff an' slow.

Of all 'is five years' schoolin' they don't remember much
Excep' the not retreatin', the step an' keepin' touch.
It looks like teachin' wasted when they duck an' spread an' 'op,
But if 'e 'ad n't learned 'em they 'd be all about the shop!

An' now it 's " 'Oo goes backward? " an' now it 's " 'Oo comes
    on? "
And now it 's " Get the doolies," an' now the captain 's gone;
An' now it 's bloody murder, but all the while they 'ear
'Is voice, the same as barrick drill, a-shepherdin' the rear.

'E 's just as sick as they are, 'is 'eart is like to split,
But 'e works 'em, works 'em, works 'em till he feels 'em take the
    bit;
The rest is 'oldin' steady till the watchful bugles play,
An' 'e lifts 'em, lifts 'em, lifts 'em through the charge that wins
    the day!

The 'eathen in 'is blindness bows down to wood an' stone;
'E don't obey no orders unless they is 'is own;
The 'eathen in 'is blindness must end where 'e began,
But the backbone of the Army is the non-commissioned man!

Keep away from dirtiness — keep away from mess,
Don't get into doin' things rather-more-or-less!
Let 's ha' done with abby-nay, kul, an' hazar-ho;
Mind you keep your rifle an' yourself jus' so!

THE SHUT–EYE SENTRY

SEZ the Junior Orderly Sergeant
    To the Senior Orderly Man:
"Our Orderly Orf'cer's *hokee-mut*,[1]
    "You 'elp 'im all you can.
"For the wine was old and the night is cold,
    "An' the best we may go wrong,
"So, 'fore 'e gits to the sentry-box,
    "You pass the word along."

So it was "Rounds! What Rounds?" at two of a frosty night,
  'E 's 'oldin' on by the sergeant's sash, but, sentry, shut your eye.
An' it was "Pass! All's well!" Oh, ain't 'e drippin' tight!
  'E 'll need an affidavit pretty badly by-an'-by.

The moon was white on the barricks,
    The road was white an' wide,
An' the Orderly Orf'cer took it all,
    An' the ten-foot ditch beside.
An' the corporal pulled an' the sergeant pushed,
    An' the three they danced along,
But I 'd shut my eyes in the sentry-box,
    So I did n't see nothin' wrong.

Though it was "Rounds! What Rounds?" O corporal, 'old 'im up!
  'E 's usin' 'is cap as it should n't be used, but, sentry, shut your eye.
An' it was "Pass! All's well!" Ho, shun the foamin' cup!
  'E 'll need, etc.

[1] Very drunk.

'T was after four in the mornin';
    We 'ad to stop the fun,
An' we sent 'im 'ome on a bullock-cart,
    With 'is belt an' stock undone;
But we sluiced 'im down an' we washed 'im out,
    An' a first-class job we made,
When we saved 'im, smart as a bombardier,
    For six o'clock parade.

It 'ad been " Rounds!   What Rounds? "   Oh, shove 'im
    straight again!
  'E 's usin' 'is sword for a bicycle, but, sentry, shut your eye.
An' it was " Pass!   All 's well! "   'E 's called me " Darlin'
    Jane " !
  'E 'll need, etc.

    The drill was long an' 'eavy,
      The sky was 'ot an' blue.
    An' 'is eye was wild an' 'is 'air was wet,
      But 'is sergeant pulled 'im through.
    Our men was good old trusties —
      They 'd done it on their 'ead;
    But you ought to 'ave 'eard 'em markin' time
      To 'ide the things 'e said!

For it was " Right flank — wheel! " for " 'Alt, an' stand at
    ease! "
  An' " Left extend! " for " Centre close! "   O marker, shut
    your eye!
An' it was, " 'Ere, sir, 'ere! before the Colonel sees! "
  So he needed affidavits pretty badly by-an'-by.

    There was two-an'-thirty sergeants,
      There was corp'rals forty-one,
    There was just nine 'undred rank an' file
      To swear to a touch o' sun.

There was me 'e 'd kissed in the sentry-box,
  As I 'ave not told in my song,
But I took my oath, which were Bible truth,
  I 'ad n't seen nothin' wrong.

There 's them that 's 'ot an' 'aughty,
  There 's them that 's cold an' 'ard,
But there comes a night when the best gets tight,
  And then turns out the Guard.
I 've seen them 'ide their liquor
  In every kind o' way,
But most depends on makin' friends
  With Privit Thomas A. !

When it is " Rounds!   What Rounds? "   'E 's breathin'
    through 'is nose.
  'E 's reelin', rollin', roarin' tight, but, sentry, shut your eye.
An' it is " Pass!   All 's well! "   An' that 's the way it goes:
  We 'll 'elp 'im for 'is mother, an' 'e 'll 'elp us by-an'-by!

"MARY, PITY WOMEN !"

YOU call yourself a man,
  For all you used to swear,
An' leave me, as you can,
  My certain shame to bear?
  I 'ear! You do not care —
You done the worst you know.
  I 'ate you, grinnin' there. . . .
Ah, Gawd, I love you so!

Nice while it lasted, an' now it is over —
Tear out your 'eart an' good-bye to your lover!
What 's the use o' grievin', when the mother that bore you
(Mary, pity women!) knew it all before you?

It are n't no false alarm,
   The finish to your fun;
You — you 'ave brung the 'arm,
   An' I 'm the ruined one;
   An' now you 'll off an' run
With some new fool in tow.
   Your 'eart? You 'ave n't none. . . .
Ah, Gawd, I love you so!

When a man is tired there is naught will bind 'im;
'All 'e solemn promised 'e will shove be'ind 'im.
What 's the good o' prayin' for The Wrath to strike 'im
(Mary, pity women!), when the rest are like 'im?

What 'ope for me or — it?
   What 's left for us to do?
I 've walked with men a bit,
   But this — but this is you.
   So 'elp me Christ, it 's true!
Where can I 'ide or go?
   You coward through and through! . . .
Ah, Gawd, I love you so!

All the more you give 'em the less are they for givin' —
Love lies dead, an' you can not kiss 'im livin'.
Down the road 'e led you there is no returnin'
(Mary, pity women!), but you 're late in learnin'!

You 'd like to treat me fair?
   You can't, because we 're pore?
We 'd starve? What do I care!
   We might, but *this* is shore!
   I want the name — no more —
The name, an' lines to show,
   An' not to be an 'ore. . . .
Ah, Gawd, I love you so!

What 's the good o' pleadin', when the mother that bore you
(Mary, pity women!) knew it all before you ?
Sleep on 'is promises an' wake to your sorrow
(Mary, pity women!), for we sail to-morrow!

"FOR TO ADMIRE"

THE Injian Ocean sets an' smiles
    So sof', so bright, so bloomin' blue;
There are n't a wave for miles an' miles
    Excep' the jiggle from the screw.
The ship is swep', the day is done,
    The bugle 's gone for smoke and play;
An' black ag'in the settin' sun
    The Lascar sings, " *Hum deckty hai!* " [1]

For to admire an' for to see,
    For to be'old this world so wide —
It never done no good to me,
    But I can't drop it if I tried!

I see the sergeants pitchin' quoits,
    I 'ear the women laugh an' talk,
I spy upon the quarter-deck
    The orficers an' lydies walk.
I thinks about the things that was,
    An' leans an' looks acrost the sea,
Till, spite of all the crowded ship,
    There 's no one lef' alive but me.

[1] " I 'm looking out."

The things that was which I 'ave seen,
  In barrick, camp, an' action too,
I tells them over by myself,
  An' sometimes wonders if they 're true;
For they was odd — most awful odd —
  But all the same now they are o'er,
There must be 'eaps o' plenty such,
  An' if I wait I 'll see some more.

Oh, I 'ave come upon the books,
  An' frequent broke a barrick rule,
An' stood beside an' watched myself
  Be'avin' like a bloomin' fool.
I paid my price for findin' out,
  Nor never grutched the price I paid,
But sat in Clink without my boots,
  Admirin' 'ow the world was made.

Be'old a cloud upon the beam,
  An' 'umped above the sea appears
Old Aden, like a barrick-stove
  That no one 's lit for years an' years!
I passed by that when I began,
  An' I go 'ome the road I came,
A time-expired soldier-man
  With six years' service to 'is name.

My girl she said, " Oh, stay with me! "
  My mother 'eld me to 'er breast.
They 've never written none, an' so
  They must 'ave gone with all the rest —
With all the rest which I 'ave seen
  An' found an' known an' met along.
I cannot say the things I feel,
  And so I sing my evenin' song:

For to admire an' for to see,
  For to be'old this world so wide —
It never done no good to me,
  But I can't drop it if I tried!

SERVICE SONGS

SOUTH AFRICAN WAR

1900–1902

"Tommy" you was when it began,
But now that it is o'er
You shall be called The Service Man
'Enceforward, evermore.

Batt'ry, brigade, flank, centre, van,
Defaulter, Army corps —
From first to last, The Service Man
'Enceforward, evermore.

From 'Alifax to 'Industan,
From York to Singapore —
'Orse, foot, an' guns, The Service Man
'Enceforward, evermore!

CHANT–PAGAN

(English Irregular discharged)

ME that 'ave been what I 've been,
Me that 'ave gone where I 've gone,
Me that 'ave seen what I 've seen —
   'Ow can I ever take on
With awful old England again,
An' 'ouses both sides of the street,
And 'edges two sides of the lane,
And the parson an' "gentry" between,
An' touchin' my 'at when we meet —
   Me that 'ave been what I 've been ?

Me that 'ave watched 'arf a world
'Eave up all shiny with dew,
Kopje on kop to the sun,
An' as soon as the mist let 'em through
Our 'elios winkin' like fun —
Three sides of a ninety-mile square,
Over valleys as big as a shire —
Are ye there? Are ye there? Are ye there?
An' then the blind drum of our fire . . .
An' I 'm rollin' 'is lawns for the Squire,
                Me!

Me that 'ave rode through the dark
Forty mile, often, on end,
Along the Ma'ollisberg Range,
With only the stars for my mark

An' only the night for my friend,
An' things runnin' off as you pass,
An' things jumpin' up in the grass,
An' the silence, the shine an' the size
Of the 'igh, unexpressible skies. . . .
I am takin' some letters almost
As much as a mile, to the post,
An' "mind you come back with the change!"
                                    Me!

Me that saw Barberton took
When we dropped through the clouds on their 'ead,
An' they 'ove the guns over and fled —
Me that was through Di'mond 'Ill,
An' Pieters an' Springs an' Belfast —
From Dundee to Vereeniging all!
Me that stuck out to the last
(An' five bloomin' bars on my chest) —
I am doin' my Sunday-school best,
By the 'elp of the Squire an' 'is wife
(Not to mention the 'ousemaid an' cook),
To come in an' 'ands up an' be still,
An' honestly work for my bread,
My livin' in that state of life
To which it shall please God to call
                                    Me!

Me that 'ave followed my trade
In the place where the Lightnin's are made,
'Twixt the Rains and the Sun and the Moon;
Me that lay down an' got up
Three years an' the sky for my roof —
That 'ave ridden my 'unger an' thirst
Six thousand raw mile on the hoof,
With the Vaal and the Orange for cup,
An' the Brandwater Basin for dish, —
Oh! it's 'ard to be'ave as they wish,
(Too 'ard, an' a little too soon),
I 'll 'ave to think over it first —
                                    Me!

I will arise an' get 'ence; —
I will trek South and make sure
If it's only my fancy or not
That the sunshine of England is pale,
And the breezes of England are stale,
An' there's somethin' gone small with the lot;
For *I* know of a sun an' a wind,
An' some plains and a mountain be'ind,
An' some graves by a barb-wire fence;
An' a Dutchman I've fought 'oo might give
Me a job were I ever inclined,
To look in an' offsaddle an' live
Where there's neither a road nor a tree —
But only my Maker an' me,
And I think it will kill me or cure,
So I think I will go there an' see.

Me!

M. I.

(*Mounted Infantry of the Line*)

I WISH my mother could see me now, with a fence-post under
my arm,
And a knife and a spoon in my putties that I found on a Boer
farm,
Atop of a sore-backed Argentine, with a thirst that you could n't
buy.
I used to be in the Yorkshires once
(Sussex, Lincolns, and Rifles once),
Hampshires, Glosters, and Scottish once! (*ad lib.*)
But now I am M. I.

That is what we are known as — that is the name you must
call
If you want officers' servants, pickets an' 'orseguards an' all —

Details for buryin'-parties, company-cooks or supply —
Turn out the chronic Ikonas! Roll up the ——— [1] M. I.!

My 'ands are spotty with veldt-sores, my shirt is a button an'
    frill,
An' the things I 've used my bay'nit for would make a tinker
    ill!
An' I don't know whose dam' column I 'm in, nor where we 're
    trekkin' nor why.
    I 've trekked from the Vaal to the Orange once —
    From the Vaal to the greasy Pongolo once —
    (Or else it was called the Zambesi once) —
        For now I am M. I.

That is what we are known as — we are the push you require
For outposts all night under freezin', an' rearguard all day under
    fire.
Anything 'ot or unwholesome?   Anything dusty or dry?
Borrow a bunch of Ikonas! Trot out the ——— M. I.!

Our Sergeant-Major 's a subaltern, our Captain 's a Fusilier —
Our Adjutant 's "late of Somebody's 'Orse," an' a Melbourne
    auctioneer;
But you could n't spot us at 'arf a mile from the crackest
    caval-ry.
    They used to talk about Lancers once,
    Hussars, Dragoons, an' Lancers once,
    'Elmets, pistols, an' carbines once,
        But now we are M. I.!

That is what we are known as — we are the orphans they
    blame
For beggin' the loan of an 'ead-stall an' makin' a mount to the
    same:
'Can't even look at an 'orselines but some one goes bellerin
    "Hi!
"'Ere comes a burglin' Ikona!" Footsack you ——— M. I.!

---

[1] Number according to taste and service of audience.

We're trekkin' our twenty miles a day an' bein' loved by the
Dutch,
But we don't hold on by the mane no more, nor lose our stirrups
— much;
An' we scout with a senior man in charge where the 'oly white
flags fly.
    We used to think they were friendly once,
    Did n't take any precautions once
    (Once, my ducky, an' only once!)
          But now we are M. I.!

That is what we are known as — we are the beggars that got
Three days "to learn equitation," an' six months o' bloomin'
well trot!
Cow-guns, an' cattle, an' convoys — an' Mister De Wet on the
fly —
We are the rollin' Ikonas! We are the —— M. I.!

The new fat regiments come from home, imaginin' vain V. C.'s
(The same as our talky-fighty men which are often Number
Threes[1]),
But our words o' command are "Scatter" an' "Close" an'
"Let your wounded lie."
    We used to rescue 'em noble once, —
    Givin' the range as we raised 'em once,
    Gettin' 'em killed as we saved 'em once —
          But now we are M. I.

That is what we are known as — we are the lanterns you view
After a fight round the kopjes, lookin' for men that we knew;
Whistlin' an' callin' together, 'altin' to catch the reply: —
"'Elp me! O 'elp me, Ikonas! This way, the —— M. I.!"

I wish my mother could see me now, a-gatherin' news on my
own,
When I ride like a General up to the scrub and ride back like
Tod Sloan,

[1] Horse-holders when in action, and therefore generally under cover.

Remarkable close to my 'orse's neck to let the shots go by.
    We used to fancy it risky once
    (Called it a reconnaissance once),
    Under the charge of an orf'cer once,
                    But now we are M. I. !

That is what we are known as — that is the song you must say
When you want men to be Mausered at one and a penny a day;
We are no five-bob Colonials — we are the 'ome made supply,
Ask for the London Ikonas! Ring up the —— M. I. !

I wish myself could talk to myself as I left 'im a year ago;
I could tell 'im a lot that would save 'im a lot on the things that
        'e ought to know!
When I think o' that ignorant barrack-bird, it almost makes
        me cry.
    I used to belong in an Army once
    (Gawd! what a rum little Army once),
    Red little, dead little Army once!
                    But now I am M. I. !

That is what we are known as — we are the men that have
        been
Over a year at the business, smelt it an' felt it an' seen.
We 'ave got 'old of the needful — *you* will be told by and by;
Wait till you 've 'eard the Ikonas, spoke to the old M. I. !

Mount — march, Ikonas!   Stand to your 'orses again!
Mop off the frost on the saddles, mop up the miles on the plain.
Out go the stars in the dawnin', up goes our dust to the sky,
Walk — trot, Ikonas!   Trek jou,[1] the old M. I.!

                    [1] Get ahead.

COLUMNS

(*Mobile Columns of the Later War*)

OUT o' the wilderness, dusty an' dry
  (*Time, an' 'igh time to be trekkin' again!*)
'Oo is it 'eads to the Detail Supply?
  (*A section, a pompom, an' six 'undred men.*)

'Ere comes the clerk with 'is lantern an' keys
  (*Time, an' 'igh time to be trekkin' again!*)
"Surplus of everything — draw what you please
  "*For the section, the pompom, an' six 'undred men.*"

"What are our orders an' where do we lay?"
  (*Time, an' 'igh time to be trekkin' again!*)
"You came after dark — you will leave before day,
  "*You section, you pompom, you six 'undred men!*"

Down the tin street, 'alf awake an' unfed,
'Ark to 'em blessin' the Gen'ral in bed!
Now by the church an' the outspan they wind —
Over the ridge an' it's all lef' be'ind
  For the section, etc.

Soon they will camp as the dawn's growin' grey,
Roll up for coffee an' sleep while they may —
  The section, etc.

Read their 'ome letters, their papers an' such,
For they'll move after dark to astonish the Dutch
  With a section, etc.

'Untin' for shade as the long hours pass,
Blankets on rifles or burrows in grass,
  Lies the section, etc.

Dossin' or beatin' a shirt in the sun,
Watching chameleons or cleanin' a gun,
  Waits the section, etc.

With nothin' but stillness as far as you please,
An' the silly mirage stringin' islands an' seas
  Round the section, etc.

So they strips off their hide an' they grills in their bones,
Till the shadows crawl out from beneath the pore stones
  Towards the section, etc.

An' the Mauser-bird stops an' the jackals begin,
An' the 'orse-guard comes up and the Gunners 'ook in
  As a 'int to the pompom an' six 'undred men. . . .

Off through the dark with the stars to rely on —
(Alpha Centauri an' somethin' Orion)
  Moves the section, etc.

Same bloomin' 'ole which the ant-bear 'as broke,
Same bloomin' stumble an' same bloomin' joke
  Down the section, etc.

Same "which is right?" where the cart-tracks divide,
Same "give it up" from the same clever guide
  To the section, etc.

Same tumble-down on the same 'idden farm,
Same white-eyed Kaffir 'oo gives the alarm
  Of the section, etc.

Same shootin' wild at the end o' the night,
Same flyin' tackle an' same messy fight
  By the section, etc.

Same ugly 'iccup an' same 'orrid squeal,
When it's too dark to see an' it's too late to feel
  In the section, etc.

(Same batch of prisoners, 'airy an' still,
Watchin' their comrades bolt over the 'ill
  From the section, etc.)

Same chilly glare in the eye of the sun
As 'e gets up displeasured to see what was done
  By the section, etc.

Same splash o' pink on the stoep or the kraal,
An' the same quiet face which 'as finished with all
  In the section, the pompom, an' six 'undred men.

*Out o' the wilderness, dusty an' dry
  (Time, an' 'igh time to be trekkin' again!)
'Oo is it 'eads to the Detail Supply?
  (A section, a pompom, an' six 'undred men.)*

THE PARTING OF THE COLUMNS

*". . . On the —th instant a mixed detachment of colonials left
—— for Cape Town, there to rejoin their respective homeward-
bound contingents, after fifteen months' service in the field. They
were escorted to the station by the regular troops in garrison and
the bulk of Colonel ——'s column, which has just come in to refit,
preparatory to further operations. The leave-taking was of the
most cordial character, the men cheering each other continuously."*
          — Any Newspaper, during the South African War.

W E 'VE rode and fought and ate and drunk as rations come
      to hand,
Together for a year and more around this stinkin' land:
Now you are goin' home again, but we must see it through.
We need n't tell we liked you well. Good-bye — good luck to
      you!

You 'ad no special call to come, and so you doubled out,
And learned us how to camp and cook an' steal a horse and
  scout:
Whatever game we fancied most, you joyful played it too,
And rather better on the whole. Good-bye — good luck to you !

There is n't much we 'ave n't shared, since Kruger cut and run,
The same old work, the same old skoff,[1] the same old dust and
  sun ;
The same old chance that laid us out, or winked an' let us
  through ;
The same old Life, the same old Death. Good-bye — good luck
  to you !

Our blood 'as truly mixed with yours — all down the Red Cross
  train,
We 've bit the same thermometer in Bloeming-typhoidtein.
We 've 'ad the same old temp'rature — the same relapses too,
The same old saw-backed fever-chart. Good-bye — good luck
  to you !

But 't was n't merely this an' that (which all the world may
  know),
'T was how you talked an' looked at things which made us like
  you so.
All independent, queer an' odd, but most amazin' new,
My word ! you shook us up to rights. Good-bye — good luck
  to you !

Think o' the stories round the fire, the tales along the trek —
O' Calgary an' Wellin'ton, an' Sydney and Quebec;
Of mine an' farm, an' ranch an' run, an' moose an' cariboo,
An' parrots peckin' lambs to death ! Good-bye — good luck to
  you !

[1] Food.

We've seen your 'ome by word o' mouth, we've watched your
    rivers shine,
We've 'eard your bloomin' forests blow of eucalip' and pine;
Your young, gay countries north an' south, we feel we own 'em
    too,
For they was made by rank an' file. Good-bye — good luck to
    you!

We'll never read the papers now without inquirin' first
For word from all those friendly dorps where you was born an'
    nursed.
Why, Dawson, Galle, an' Montreal — Port Darwin — Timaru,
They're only just across the road! Good-bye — good luck to
    you!

Good-bye! — So-long! Don't lose yourselves — nor us, nor all
    kind friends,
But tell the girls your side the drift we're comin' — when it ends!
Good-bye, you bloomin' Atlases! You've taught us somethin'
    new:
The world's no bigger than a kraal. Good-bye — good luck to
    you!

TWO KOPJES

(Made Yeomanry towards the End of the War)

ONLY two African kopjes,
    Only the cart-tracks that wind
Empty and open between 'em,
    Only the Transvaal behind;
Only an Aldershot column
    Marching to conquer the land . . .
Only a sudden and solemn
    Visit, unarmed, to the Rand.

Then scorn not the African kopje,
  The kopje that smiles in the heat,
The wholly unoccupied kopje,
  The home of Cornelius and Piet.
You can never be sure of your kopje,
  But of this be you blooming well sure,
A kopje is always a kopje,
  And a Boojer is always a Boer!

Only two African kopjes,
  Only the vultures above,
Only baboons — at the bottom,
  Only some buck on the move;
Only a Kensington draper
  Only pretending to scout . . .
Only bad news for the paper,
  Only another knock-out.

  Then mock not the African kopje,
    And rub not your flank on its side,
  The silent and simmering kopje,
    The kopje beloved by the guide.
  You can never be, etc.

Only two African kopjes,
  Only the dust of their wheels,
Only a bolted commando,
  Only our guns at their heels . . .
Only a little barb-wire,
  Only a natural fort,
Only "by sections retire,"
  Only "regret to report!"

  Then mock not the African kopje,
    Especially when it is twins,
  One sharp and one table-topped kopje,
    For that's where the trouble begins.
  You never can be, etc.

Only two African kopjes
  Baited the same as before —
Only we 've had it so often,
  Only we 're taking no more . . .
Only a wave to our troopers,
  Only our flanks swinging past,
Only a dozen voorloopers,
  Only *we*'ve learned it at last!

   Then mock not the African kopje,
     But take off your hat to the same,
   The patient, impartial old kopje,
     The kopje that taught us the game!
   For all that we knew in the Columns,
     And all they 've forgot on the Staff,
   We learned at the Fight o' Two Kopjes,
     Which lasted two years an' a half.

O mock not the African kopje,
  Not even when peace has been signed —
The kopje that is n't a kopje —
  The kopje that copies its kind.
You can never be sure of your kopje,
  But of this be you blooming well sure,
That a kopje is always a kopje,
  And a Boojer is always a Boer!

THE INSTRUCTOR

(*Non-commissioned Officers of the Line*)

AT times when under cover I 've said,
To keep my spirits up an' raise a laugh,
'Earin 'im pass so busy over-'ead —
Old Nickel-Neck, 'oo is n't on the Staff —
"*There 's one above is greater than us all.*"

Before 'im I 'ave seen my Colonel fall,
An' watched 'im write my Captain's epitaph,
So that a long way off it could be read —
He *as* the knack o' makin' men feel small —
Old Whistle Tip, 'oo is n't on the Staff.

There is no sense in fleein' (I 'ave fled),
Better go on an' do the belly-crawl,
An' 'ope 'e 'll 'it some other man instead
Of you 'e seems to 'unt so speshual —
Fitzy van Spitz, 'oo is n't on the Staff.

An' thus in mem'ry's gratis biograph,
Now that the show is over, I recall
The peevish voice an' 'oary mushroom 'ead
Of 'im we owned was greater than us all,
'Oo give instruction to the quick an' the dead —
The Shudderin' Beggar — not upon the Staff!

BOOTS

(Infantry Columns of the Earlier War)

WE'RE foot — slog — slog — slog — sloggin' over Africa!
Foot — foot — foot — foot — sloggin' over Africa —
(Boots — boots — boots — boots — movin' up and down again!
    There's no discharge in the war!

Seven — six — eleven — five — nine-an'-twenty mile to-day —
Four — eleven — seventeen — thirty-two the day before —
(Boots — boots — boots — boots — movin' up and down
    again!)
    There's no discharge in the war!

Don't — don't — don't — don't — look at what's in front of
  you
(Boots — boots — boots — boots — movin' up an' down
  again);
Men — men — men — men —men go mad with watchin' 'em,
    An' there's no discharge in the war!

Try — try — try — try — to think o' something different —
Oh — my — God — keep — me from goin' lunatic!
(Boots — boots — boots — boots — movin' up an' down
  again!)
    There's no discharge in the war!

Count — count — count — count — the bullets in the bando-
  liers;
If — your — eyes — drop — they will get atop o' you
(Boots — boots — boots — boots — movin' up and down
  · again) —
    There's no discharge in the war!

We — can — stick — out — 'unger, thirst, an' weariness,
But — not — not — not — not the chronic sight of 'em —
Boots — boots — boots — boots — movin' up an' down again,
    An' there's no discharge in the war!

'Tain't — so — bad — by — day because o' company,
But — night — brings — long — strings — o' forty thousand
  million
Boots — boots — boots — boots — movin' up an' down again.
    There's no discharge in the war!

I — 'ave — marched — six — weeks in 'Ell an' certify
It — is — not — fire — devils — dark or anything
But boots — boots — boots — boots — movin' up an' down
  again,
    An' there's no discharge in the war!

THE MARRIED MAN

(Reservist of the Line)

THE bachelor 'e fights for one
    As joyful as can be;
But the married man don't call it fun,
    Because 'e fights for three —
For 'Im an' 'Er an' It
    (An' Two an' One makes Three)
'E wants to finish 'is little bit,
    An' 'e wants to go 'ome to 'is tea!

The bachelor pokes up 'is 'ead
    To see if you are gone;
But the married man lies down instead,
    An' waits till the sights come on.
For 'Im an' 'Er an' a hit
    (Direct or ricochee)
'E wants to finish 'is little bit,
    An' 'e wants to go 'ome to 'is tea.

The bachelor will miss you clear
    To fight another day;
But the married man, 'e says "No fear!"
    'E wants you out of the way
Of 'Im an' 'Er an' It
    (An' 'is road to 'is farm or the sea),
'E wants to finish 'is little bit,
    An' 'e wants to go 'ome to 'is tea.

The bachelor 'e fights 'is fight
    An' stretches out an' snores;
But the married man sits up all night —
    For 'e don't like out o' doors:

'E 'll strain an' listen an' peer
   An' give the first alarm —
For the sake o' the breathin' 'e 's used to 'ear
   An' the 'ead on the thick of 'is arm.

The bachelor may risk 'is 'ide
   To 'elp you when you 're downed;
But the married man will wait beside
   Till the ambulance comes round.
'E 'll take your 'ome address
   An' all you 've time to say,
Or if 'e sees there 's 'ope, 'e 'll press
   Your art'ry 'alf the day —

For 'Im an' 'Er an' It
   (An' One from Three leaves Two),
For 'e knows you wanted to finish your bit,
   An' 'e knows 'oo 's wantin' you.
Yes, 'Im an' 'Er an' It
   (Our 'oly One in Three),
We 're all of us anxious to finish our bit,
   An' we want to get 'ome to our tea!

Yes, It an' 'Er an' 'Im,
   Which often makes me think
The married man must sink or swim
   An' — 'e can't afford to sink!
Oh 'Im an' It an' 'Er
   Since Adam an' Eve began!
So I 'd rather fight with the bacheler
   An' be nursed by the married man!

LICHTENBERG

(New South Wales Contingent)

SMELLS are surer than sounds or sights
  To make your heart-strings crack —
They start those awful voices o' nights
  That whisper, "Old man, come back."
That must be why the big things pass
  And the little things remain,
Like the smell of the wattle by Lichtenberg,
  Riding in, in the rain.

There was some silly fire on the flank
  And the small wet drizzling down —
There were the sold-out shops and the bank
  And the wet, wide-open town;
And we were doing escort-duty
  To somebody's baggage-train,
And I smelt wattle by Lichtenberg —
  Riding in, in the rain.

It was all Australia to me —
  All I had found or missed:
Every face I was crazy to see,
  And every woman I'd kissed:
All that I should n't ha' done, God knows!
  (As He knows I'll do it again),
That smell of the wattle round Lichtenberg,
  Riding in, in the rain!

And I saw Sydney the same as ever,
  The picnics and brass-bands;
And my little homestead on Hunter River
  And my new vines joining hands.

It all came over me in one act
    Quick as a shot through the brain —
With the smell of the wattle round Lichtenberg,
    Riding in, in the rain.

I have forgotten a hundred fights,
    But one I shall not forget —
With the raindrops bunging up my sights
    And my eyes bunged up with wet;
And through the crack and the stink of the cordite
    (Ah Christ! My country again!)
The smell of the wattle by Lichtenberg,
    Riding in, in the rain!

STELLENBOSH

(*Composite Columns*)

THE General 'eard the firin' on the flank,
    An' 'e sent a mounted man to bring 'im back
The silly, pushin' person's name an' rank
    'Oo 'd dared to answer Brother Boer's attack.
For there might 'ave been a serious engagement,
    An' 'e might 'ave wasted 'alf a dozen men;
So 'e ordered 'im to stop 'is operations round the kopjes,
    An' 'e told 'im off before the Staff at ten!

    And it all goes into the laundry,
    But it never comes out in the wash,
    'Ow we're sugared about by the old men
    ('Eavy-sterned amateur old men!)
    That 'amper an' 'inder an' scold men
    For fear o' Stellenbosh!

The General 'ad "produced a great effect,"
 The General 'ad the country cleared — almost;
The General "'ad no reason to expect,"
 And the Boers 'ad us bloomin' well on toast!
For we might 'ave crossed the drift before the twilight,
 Instead o' sitting down an' takin' root;
But we was not allowed, so the Boojers scooped the crowd,
 To the last survivin' bandolier an' boot.

The General saw the farm'ouse in 'is rear,
 With its stoep so nicely shaded from the sun;
Sez 'e, "I 'll pitch my tabernacle 'ere,"
 An' 'e kept us muckin' round till 'e 'ad done.
For 'e might 'ave caught the confluent pneumonia
 From sleepin' in his gaiters in the dew;
So 'e took a book an' dozed while the other columns closed,
 And ——'s commando out an' trickled through!

The General saw the mountain-range ahead,
 With their 'elios showin' saucy on the 'eight,
So 'e 'eld us to the level ground instead,
 An' telegraphed the Boojers would n't fight.
For 'e might 'ave gone an' sprayed 'em with pompom,
 Or 'e might 'ave slung a squadron out to see —
But 'e was n't takin' chances in them 'igh an' 'ostile kranzes —
 He was markin' time to earn a K.C.B

The General got 'is decorations thick
 (The men that backed 'is lies could not complain),
The Staff 'ad D.S.O.'s till we was sick,
 An' the soldier — 'ad the work to do again!
For 'e might 'ave known the District was a 'otbed,
 Instead of 'andin' over, upside-down,
To a man 'oo 'ad to fight 'alf a year to put it right,
 While the General went an' slandered 'im in town!

An' it all went into the laundry,
But it never came out in the wash.
We were sugared about by the old men
(Panicky, perishin' old men)
That 'amper an' 'inder an' scold men
For fear o' Stellenbosh !

HALF–BALLAD OF WATERVAL

(Non-commissioned Officers in Charge of Prisoners)

WHEN by the labour of my 'ands
   I 've 'elped to pack a transport tight
With prisoners for foreign lands,
   I ain't transported with delight.
   I know it's only just an' right,
      But yet it somehow sickens me,
   For I 'ave learned at Waterval
      The meanin' of captivity.

Be'ind the pegged barb-wire strands,
   Beneath the tall electric light,
We used to walk in bare-'ead bands,
   Explainin' 'ow we lost our fight.
   An' that is what they 'll do to-night
      Upon the steamer out at sea,
   If I 'ave learned at Waterval
      The meanin' of captivity.

They 'll never know the shame that brands —
   Black shame no livin' down makes white,
The mockin' from the sentry-stands,
   The women's laugh, the gaoler's spite.

We are too bloomin' much polite,
    But that is 'ow I 'd 'ave us be . . .
Since I 'ave learned at Waterval
    The meanin' of captivity.

They 'll get those draggin' days all right,
    Spent as a foreigner commands,
An' 'orrors of the locked-up night,
    With 'Ell's own thinkin' on their 'ands.
I 'd give the gold o' twenty Rands
    (If it was mine) to set 'em free . . .
For I 'ave learned at Waterval
    The meanin' of captivity !

PIET

(*Regular of the Line*)

I DO not love my Empire's foes,
    Nor call 'em angels; still,
What *is* the sense of 'atin' those
    'Oom you are paid to kill ?
So, barrin' all that foreign lot
    Which only joined for spite,
Myself, I 'd just as soon as not
    Respect the man I fight.
      Ah there, Piet ! — 'is trousies to 'is knees,
      'Is coat-tails lyin' level in the bullet-sprinkled breeze;
      'E does not lose 'is rifle an' 'e does not lose 'is seat,
      I 've known a lot o' people ride a dam' sight worse than Piet !

I 've 'eard 'im cryin' from the ground
    Like Abel's blood of old,
An' skirmished out to look, an' found
    The beggar nearly cold;

I 've waited on till 'e was dead ,
  (Which could n't 'elp 'im much),
But many grateful things 'e 's said
  To me for doin' such.
      Ah there, Piet! whose time 'as come to die,
      'Is carcase past rebellion, but 'is eyes inquirin' why.
      Though dressed in stolen uniform with badge o' rank complete,
      I 've known a lot o' fellers go a dam' sight worse than Piet.

An' when there was n't aught to do
  But camp and cattle-guards,
I 've fought with 'im the 'ole day through
  At fifteen 'undred yards;
Long afternoons o' lyin' still,
  An' 'earin' as you lay
The bullets swish from 'ill to 'ill
  Like scythes among the 'ay.
      Ah there, Piet! — be'ind 'is stony kop,
      With 'is Boer bread an' biltong, an' 'is flask of awful Dop;
      'Is Mauser for amusement an' 'is pony for retreat,
      I 've known a lot o' fellers shoot a dam' sight worse than Piet.

He 's shoved 'is rifle 'neath my nose
  Before I 'd time to think,
An' borrowed all my Sunday clo'es
  An' sent me 'ome in pink;
An' I 'ave crept (Lord, 'ow I 've crept!)
  On 'ands an' knees I 've gone,
And spoored and floored and caught and kept
  An' sent him to Ceylon!
      Ah there, Piet! — you 've sold me many a pup,
      When week on week alternate it was you an' me "'ands up!"
      But though I never made *you* walk man-naked in the 'eat,
      I 've known a lot of fellows stalk a dam' sight worse than Piet.

From Plewman's to Marabastad,
  From Ookiep to De Aar,
Me an' my trusty friend 'ave 'ad,
  As you might say, a war;
But seein' what both parties done
  Before 'e owned defeat,
I ain't more proud of 'avin' won,
  Than I am pleased with Piet.
      Ah there, Piet! — picked up be'ind the drive!
      The wonder was n't 'ow 'e fought, but 'ow 'e kep' alive,
      With nothin' in 'is belly, on 'is back, or to 'is feet —
      I've known a lot o' men behave a dam' sight worse than
        Piet.

No more I'll 'ear 'is rifle crack
  Along the block'ouse fence —
The beggar's on the peaceful tack,
  Regardless of expense.
For countin' what 'e eats an' draws,
  An' gifts an' loans as well,
'E's gettin' 'alf the Earth, because
  'E did n't give us 'Ell!
      Ah there, Piet! with your brand-new English plough,
      Your gratis tents an' cattle, an' your most ungrateful frow
      You've made the British taxpayer rebuild your country-
        seat —
      I've known some pet battalions charge a dam' sight less
        than Piet.

"WILFUL–MISSING"

(*Deserters*)

THERE is a world outside the one you know,
  To which for curiousness 'Ell can't compare —
It is the place where "wilful-missings" go,
  As we can testify, for we are there.

You may 'ave read a bullet laid us low,
   That we was gathered in "with reverent care"
And buried proper. But it was not so,
   As we can testify, — for we are there!

They can't be certain — faces alter so
   After the old aasvogel [1] 's 'ad 'is share;
The uniform 's the mark by which they go —
   And — ain't it odd? — the one we best can spare.

We might 'ave seen our chance to cut the show —
   Name, number, record, an' begin elsewhere —
Leavin' some not too late-lamented foe
   One funeral — private — British — for 'is share.

We may 'ave took it yonder in the Low
   Bush-veldt that sends men stragglin' unaware
Among the Kaffirs, till their columns go,
   An' they are left past call or count or care.

We might 'ave been your lovers long ago,
   'Usbands or children — comfort or despair.
Our death (*an'* burial) settles all we owe,
   An' why we done it is our own affair.

Marry again, and we will not say no,
   Nor come to barstardise the kids you bear:
Wait on in 'ope — you 've all your life below
   Before you 'll ever 'ear us on the stair.

There is no need to give our reasons, though
   Gawd knows we all 'ad reasons which were fair;
But other people might not judge 'em so,
   And now it does n't matter what they were.

[1] Vulture.

What man can weigh or size another's woe?
  There are some things too bitter 'ard to bear.
Suffice it we 'ave finished — Domino!
  As we can testify, for we are there,
In the side-world where "wilful-missings" go.

UBIQUE

(*Royal Artillery*)

THERE is a word you often see, pronounce it as you may —
"You bike," "you bykwe," "ubbikwe" — alludin' to R.A.
It serves 'Orse, Field, an' Garrison as motto for a crest,
An' when you 've found out all it means I 'll tell you 'alf the
      rest.

Ubique means the long-range Krupp be'ind the low-range 'ill —
Ubique means you 'll pick it up an' while you do stand still.
Ubique means you 've caught the flash an' timed it by the
      sound.
Ubique means five gunners' 'ash before you 've loosed a round.

Ubique means Blue Fuse,[1] an' make the 'ole to sink the trail.
Ubique means stand up an' take the Mauser's 'alf-mile 'ail.
Ubique means the crazy team not God nor man can 'old.
Ubique means that 'orse's scream which turns your innards cold!

Ubique means "Bank, 'Olborn, Bank — a penny all the
      way" —
The soothin', jingle-bump-an'-clank from day to peaceful day.
Ubique means "They 've caught De Wet, an' now we sha'n't be
      long."
Ubique means "I much regret, the beggar 's goin' strong!"

[1] Extreme range.

Ubique means the tearin' drift where, breech-blocks jammed
    with mud,
The khaki muzzles duck an' lift across the khaki flood.
Ubique means the dancing plain that changes rocks to Boers.
Ubique means the mirage again an' shellin' all outdoors.

Ubique means "Entrain at once for Grootdefeatfontein"!
Ubique means "Off-load your guns" — at midnight in the rain!
Ubique means "More mounted men. Return all guns to store."
Ubique means the R.A.M.R. Infantillery Corps!

Ubique means that warnin' grunt the perished linesman knows,
When o'er 'is strung an' sufferin' front the shrapnel sprays 'is
    foes;
An' as their firin' dies away the 'usky whisper runs
From lips that 'ave n't drunk all day: "The Guns. Thank
    Gawd, the Guns!"

Extreme, depressed, point-blank or short, end-first or any'ow,
From Colesberg Kop to Quagga's Poort — from Ninety-Nine
    till now —
By what I 've 'eard the others tell an' I in spots 'ave seen,
There 's nothin' this side 'Eaven or 'Ell Ubique does n't mean!

THE RETURN

(All Arms)

PEACE is declared, an' I return
    To 'Ackneystadt, but not the same;
Things 'ave transpired which made me learn
    The size and meanin' of the game.
I did no more than others did,
    I don't know where the change began;
I started as a average kid,
    I finished as a thinkin' man.

> *If England was what England seems,*
> *An' not the England of our dreams,*
> *But only putty, brass, an' paint,*
> *'Ow quick we'd drop'er!   But she ain't!*

Before my gappin' mouth could speak
　　I 'eard it in my comrade's tone;
I saw it on my neighbour's cheek
　　Before I felt it flush my own.
An' last it come to me — not pride,
　　Nor yet conceit, but on the 'ole
(If such a term may be applied),
　　The makin's of a bloomin' soul.

Rivers at night that cluck an' jeer,
　　Plains which the moonshine turns to sea,
Mountains which never let you near,
　　An' stars to all eternity;
An' the quick-breathin' dark that fills
　　The 'ollows of the wilderness,
When the wind worries through the 'ills —
　　These may 'ave taught me more or less.

Towns without people, ten times took,
　　An' ten times left an' burned at last;
An' starvin' dogs that come to look
　　For owners when a column passed;
An' quiet, 'omesick talks between
　　Men, met by night, you never knew
Until — 'is face — by shellfire seen —
　　Once — an' struck off.   *They* taught me too.

The day's lay-out — the mornin' sun
　　Beneath your 'at-brim as you sight;
The dinner-'ush from noon till one,
　　An' the full roar that lasts till night;

An' the pore dead that look so old
  An' was so young an hour ago,
An' legs tied down before they 're cold —
  These are the things which make you know.

Also Time runnin' into years —
  A thousand Places left be'ind —
An' Men from both two 'emispheres
  Discussin' things of every kind;
So much more near than I 'ad known,
  So much more great than I 'ad guessed —
An' me, like all the rest, alone —
  But reachin' out to all the rest!

So 'ath it come to me — not pride,
  Nor yet conceit, but on the 'ole
(If such a term may be applied),
  The makin's of a bloomin' soul.
But now, discharged, I fall away
  To do with little things again. . .
Gawd, 'oo knows all I cannot say,
  Look after me in Thamesfontein![1]

    If England was what England seems,
      An' not the England of our dreams,
    But only putty, brass, an' paint,
      'Ow quick we 'd chuck 'er! But she ain't!

    [1] London.

The University Press, Cambridge, U. S. A.

INDEX OF FIRST LINES

INDEX OF SUBJECTS

f

Printed in the United States
121323LV00002B/344/A

9 781406 782059